Room At The Inn
South West England

Series Editor: David Hancock
Senior Editor: Donna Wood
Senior Designer: Kat Mead
Copy Editor: Helen Ridge
Proofreader: Joey Clarke
Cartography provided by the Mapping Services Department of AA Publishing
Image retouching and colour repro: Matt Swann
Production: Rachel Davis
Index: Hilary Bird

Produced by AA Publishing
© Automobile Association Developments Limited 2008

Published by AA Publishing (a trading name of Automobile Association
Developments Limited, whose registered office is Fanum House,
Basing View, Basingstoke RG21 4EA; registered number 1878835).

 This product includes mapping data licensed from
Ordnance Survey ® with the permission of the Controller
of Her Majesty's Stationery Office.
© Crown copyright 2008. All rights reserved. Licence number 100021153.

A03060

ISBN: 978-0-7495-5642-6
A CIP catalogue record for this book is available from the British Library.

The contents of this book are believed correct at the time of printing.
Nevertheless, the publishers cannot be held responsible for any errors
or omissions or for changes in the details given in this book or for the
consequences of any reliance on the information provided by the same.
This does not affect your statutory rights.

We have taken all reasonable steps to ensure that the walks in this book are
safe and achievable by people with a realistic degree of fitness. However,
all outdoor activities involve a degree of risk and the publishers accept no
responsibility for any injuries caused to readers following the walks.
For advice on walking in safety, see page 11.
Some of the walks may appear in other AA books and publications.

Colour reproduction by Keene Group, Andover
Printed and bound in Dubai by Oriental Press

The AA's website address is www.theAA.com/travel

Room At The Inn
South West England

Contents

6   INN LOCATION MAP

8   WELCOME TO... *ROOM AT THE INN*

11   WALKING IN SAFETY

12   THE OLD COASTGUARD HOTEL, Cornwall

16   THE GURNARD'S HEAD, Cornwall

22   THE TINNERS ARMS, Cornwall

26   DRIFTWOOD SPARS, Cornwall

32   THE PLUME OF FEATHERS, Cornwall

36   THE RISING SUN, Cornwall

40   DARTMOOR INN, Devon

46   BICKLEY MILL, Devon

52   THE MASONS ARMS, Devon

56   TARR FARM INN, Somerset

64   THE FARMERS INN, Somerset

70   THE ROCK INN, Somerset

74   LORD POULETT ARMS, Somerset

78   THE DEVONSHIRE ARMS, Somerset

82   THE WOOKEY HOLE INN, Somerset

86   THE MANOR HOUSE INN, Somerset

90   THE QUEEN'S ARMS, Somerset

98   THE WHEELWRIGHTS ARMS, Somerset

102   THE WHEATSHEAF, Somerset

106   THE SHAVE CROSS INN, Dorset

110   THE EUROPEAN INN, Dorset

114   THE STAPLETON ARMS, Dorset

120   THE MUSEUM INN, Dorset

124   THE BATH ARMS, Wiltshire

128   THE SWAN, Wiltshire

134   THE CASTLE INN, Wiltshire

140   SPREAD EAGLE INN, Wiltshire

144   THE HORSE & GROOM, Wiltshire

150   THE PEAR TREE INN, Wiltshire

154   THE GEORGE AND DRAGON, Wiltshire

158   THE COMPASSES INN, Wiltshire

164   THE KING'S ARMS, Gloucestershire

168   THE AMBERLEY INN, Gloucestershire

172   THE GREEN DRAGON, Gloucestershire

178   THE VILLAGE PUB, Gloucestershire

182   THE BATHURST ARMS, Gloucestershire

186   THE PUESDOWN INN, Gloucestershire

192   EIGHT BELLS, Gloucestershire

196   HORSE AND GROOM, Gloucestershire

200   WESTCOTE INN, Gloucestershire

206   INDEX

208   ACKNOWLEDGEMENTS

Inn Location Map

1   **THE OLD COASTGUARD HOTEL**
    Cornwall

2   **THE GURNARD'S HEAD**
    Cornwall

3   **THE TINNERS ARMS**
    Cornwall

4   **DRIFTWOOD SPARS**
    Cornwall

5   **THE PLUME OF FEATHERS**
    Cornwall

6   **THE RISING SUN**
    Cornwall

7   **DARTMOOR INN**
    Devon

8   **BICKLEY MILL**
    Devon

9   **THE MASONS ARMS**
    Devon

10 **TARR FARM INN**
    Somerset

11 **THE FARMERS INN**
    Somerset

12 **THE ROCK INN**
    Somerset

13 **LORD POULETT ARMS**
    Somerset

14 **THE DEVONSHIRE ARMS**
    Somerset

15 **THE WOOKEY HOLE INN**
    Somerset

16 **THE MANOR HOUSE INN**
    Somerset

17 **THE QUEEN'S ARMS**
    Somerset

18 **THE WHEELWRIGHTS ARMS**
    Somerset

19 **THE WHEATSHEAF**
    Somerset

20 **THE SHAVE CROSS INN**
    Dorset

21 **THE EUROPEAN INN**
    Dorset

22 **THE STAPLETON ARMS**
    Dorset

23 **THE MUSEUM INN**
    Dorset

24 **THE BATH ARMS**
    Wiltshire

25 **THE SWAN**
    Wiltshire

26 **THE CASTLE INN**
    Wiltshire

27 **SPREAD EAGLE INN**
    Wiltshire

28 **THE HORSE & GROOM**
    Wiltshire

29 **THE PEAR TREE INN**
    Wiltshire

30 **THE GEORGE AND DRAGON**
    Wiltshire

31 **THE COMPASSES INN**
    Wiltshire

32 **THE KING'S ARMS**
    Gloucestershire

33 **THE AMBERLEY INN**
    Gloucestershire

34 **THE GREEN DRAGON**
    Gloucestershire

35 **THE VILLAGE PUB**
    Gloucestershire

36 **THE BATHURST ARMS**
    Gloucestershire

37 **THE PUESDOWN INN**
    Gloucestershire

38 **EIGHT BELLS**
    Gloucestershire

39 **HORSE AND GROOM**
    Gloucestershire

40 **WESTCOTE INN**
    Gloucestershire

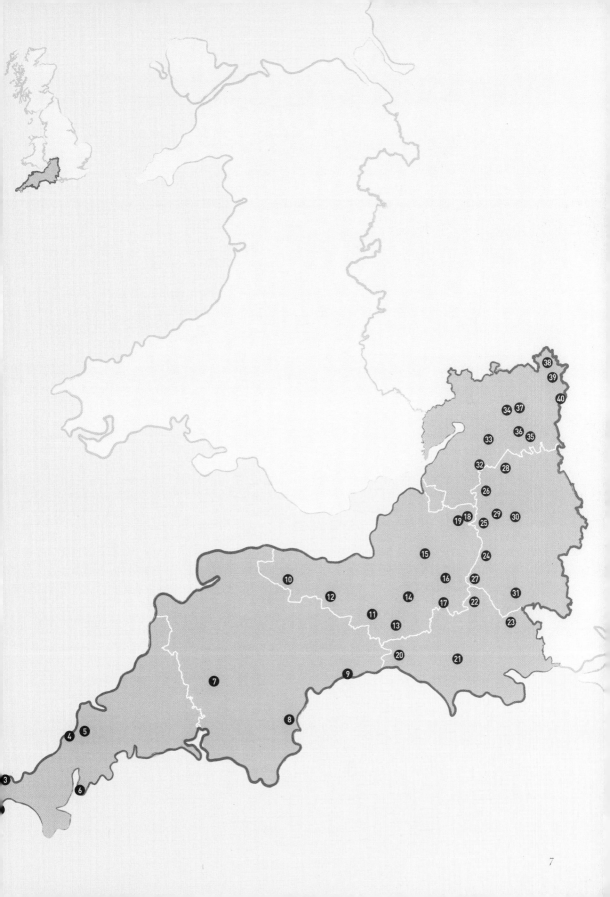

Welcome to...
Room At The Inn

The South West is an area of great natural beauty, embracing Devon's lush pastures and Cornwall's rugged cliffs, the serene and rolling landscape of Dorset, the flatness and huge skies of the Somerset Levels and Gloucestershire's idyllic Cotswold scenery. It's a rich rural land, with an abundance of good things to eat and drink, and famed for its delightful villages, cosy country pubs and historic inns.

Not long ago the thought of staying overnight in one of these pubs or inns would conjure up images of cheaply furnished bedrooms, the smell of stale smoke, food and beer, and basic shared bathrooms at the end of chilly, dimly lit corridors. How things have changed over the last decade! Just flicking through this colourful collection of stylish West Country inns, it's clear to see that pubs are fast becoming our new breed of country hotels and restaurants.

Many of the inns listed in these pages are owned by chef/patrons who have previously plied their trade in top restaurants, or there's a talented and ambitious chef at the stove cooking imaginative modern British and European dishes. You'll find chalkboard or daily printed menus championing local, seasonal produce, be it fish and shellfish from day boats at Brixham, Falmouth and Lyme Regis, traceable farm-reared meats like Ruby Red Devon beef and Exmoor lamb, locally shot game or organic vegetables from allotment holders in the same village. Even the time-honoured ploughman's lunch and cheeseboard selections offer exciting regional farmhouse cheeses like Sharpham Rustic and Cornish Yarg. One or two have taken their commitment to support local producers a step further by opening small produce shops in adjoining buildings, and a few even hold their own weekly small-scale farmers' markets in the pub car park.

There have also been major improvements in the range and quality of both wine and beer. Gone are the days when there was only one red and one white wine by the glass and a basic list to choose from. Wines are now carefully selected to match the style of food being created in the kitchen. Chalked-up lists blend Old and New World wines, include wines from the many excellent small vineyards across the South West of England, offer decent tasting notes, classic vintages and often up to 20 different wines by the glass. You'll also find scores of interesting and often outstanding hand-pumped ales from local independent micro-breweries, from tip-top Sharp's Doom Bar in Cornwall, to Blindman's Buff in Somerset and Uley Pig's Ear brewed in Gloucestershire, and you must try the range of heady scrumpy or West Country cider.

So, having wined and dined well, just climb the stairs to sleep in a cosy and well-equipped bedroom. The furnishings, fabrics, cosseting extras and swish bathrooms once only found in posh hotels are now the norm in the classy inns within these pages. You'll find soothing heritage colours, plasma TV screens, digital radios, fresh coffee, home-made biscuits, goose down duvets and pillows and Egyptian cotton sheets on big beds, and spotless bathrooms kitted out with claw-foot baths, storm showers, fluffy bathrobes, under-floor heating and top toiletries. Bliss!

To aid your rest and relaxation on a weekend break in the West Country we've included details on the best places to visit, from National Trust properties and select museums to glorious gardens and timeless villages. Ideas to keep active types amused range from balloon trips and where to play golf to information on local cycle rides and where you can hire a classic car for the day. Upmarket shops are not forgotten: we guide you to the best shopping towns, key antique shops, galleries and clothing boutiques and, perhaps, a local farm shop or deli to find those all-important edible goodies and gifts to take home.

The final ingredient to a relaxing weekend away is a good country walk, the best way to get to know the area. So, having tucked into a hearty breakfast you can follow the suggested rural ramble. All of the mapped walks are between 3 and 8 miles long and within easy reach of the inn, some even pass the door. You'll find detailed directions, essential notes on the terrain, and the relevant Ordnance Survey map to take with you.

Walking in Safety

Each of the inns featured in this book has a specially selected walk that will guide visitors around a nearby place of interest. Before you embark on any of the walks, read the righthand panel giving at-a-glance practical information about the walk, including the distance, how much time to allow, terrain, nature of the paths, and where to park your car.

All of the walks are suitable for families, but less experienced family groups, especially those with younger children, should try the shorter walks. Route finding is usually straightforward, but the maps are for guidance only and we recommend that you always take the relevant Ordnance Survey map with you.

The Risks

Although each walk has been researched with a view to minimising any risks to walkers, it is also good common sense to follow these guidelines:

• Be particularly careful on cliff paths and in hilly terrain, where the consequences of slipping can often be very serious.
• Remember to check the tidal conditions before walking on the seashore.
• Some sections of the walk routes are by, or cross, busy roads. Take care here, and remember that traffic is a danger even on minor country lanes.
• Be careful around farmyard machinery and livestock.
• Be prepared for the consequences of changes in the weather, and check the forecast before you set out.
• Ensure everyone is properly equipped with suitable clothing and a good pair of boots or sturdy walking shoes. Take waterproof clothing with you and a torch if you are walking in the winter months.
• Remember that the weather can change quickly at any time of the year, and in moorland and heathland areas, mist and fog can make route-finding much harder. In summer, take account of the heat and sun by wearing a hat, sunscreen and carrying enough water.
• On walks away from centres of population you should carry a mobile phone, a whistle and, if possible, a survival bag. If you do have an accident requiring emergency services, make a note of your position as accurately as possible and dial 999.
• Many of the routes in this book are suitable for dogs, but observing your responsibility to other people is essential. Keep your dog on a lead and under control.

⇢	Walk Route		Built-up Area
❶	Route Waypoint		Woodland Area
	Adjoining Path	🚻	Toilet
☼	Viewpoint	P	Car Park
•	Place of Interest	🛏	Picnic Area
⌂	Steep Section		

The Old Coastguard Hotel

Cornwall

The Inn

Mousehole is a pretty, higgledy-piggledy fishing village and the Old Coastguard a real delight. Don't be put off by the old-fashioned façade. Those in the know head for the enticing bar – all wood floor, smart brown leather bucket chairs, white walls and contemporary canvasses – where picture windows make the most of the stunning view over Mount Bay. Or, if the sun's shining, bag a table on the terrace, which gives on to a sub-tropical garden leading down to a small, rocky beach. The restaurant is a continuation of the bar, stylish and good-looking.

It's the perfect seaside retreat: the bedrooms deliver wide-screen sea views and many have their own terrace, with the peace disturbed only by the cry of seagulls and the breaking of waves. Each room has a clean, simple, up-to-date look – white walls and crisp white bed linen reflecting the light, pale wood furniture, cream-coloured armchairs and flat-screen TVs with a wide range of channels are standard, as are simple modern bathrooms.

The Old Coastguard Hotel, The Parade, Mousehole, Cornwall TR19 6PR

The Essentials

Time at the Bar!
11am-11pm
Food: 12-2.30pm, 6-9.30pm

What's the Damage?
Main courses from £10

Bitter Experience:
Sharp's Doom Bar

Sticky Fingers:
Children welcome; children's
menu at lunchtime

Muddy Paws:
Dogs welcome in the bar

Zzzzz:
20 rooms, £90-£170

Anything Else?
Terrace, garden, car park

The Food

With beef, lamb, pork and bacon sourced from farms and butchers in
nearby St Just, fish from Newlyn down the road, lobster from small boats
in Mousehole harbour, locally grown fruit and vegetables, Cornish cheeses,
and real ale from Sharps Brewery in Rock, North Cornwall, the kitchen
ticks all the local, seasonal boxes. Newlyn crab sandwiches for lunch taken
on the terrace are a wonderful summer treat, but if the weather drives you
inside, the well-spaced, white-clad tables in the two-tiered restaurant are
arranged to maximise the view.

Fish is a strength, dinner bringing grilled whole megrim sole teamed,
perhaps, with crab, paysanne vegetables and hollandaise sauce, or there
could be turbot with mussel nage and shellfish foam. Meatier options might
be chicken and ham hock terrine ahead of roast chump of new season lamb
(with creamed potato, summer vegetables and wild mushrooms), while
vegetarians can opt for saffron and chive gnocchi with roast beetroot and
baby spinach. For dessert, dark chocolate torte with chocolate ice cream is
hard to resist, and there's a user-friendly wine list to match.

What To Do

Shop

BOSAVERN FARM SHOP
Everything sold here is either home-grown or home-reared; organic veg, grass-fed Hereford beef, free-range pork and eggs, too. One of Rick Stein's Food Heroes.
St Just, Penzance, Cornwall TR19 7RD
01736 786739

ENYS WARTHA DELI
Specialising in all things Cornish, this packed deli is a foodie's paradise, with almost everything in the shop home-produced by the owners. Take home a basketful of delicious cakes, cheese and smoked fish, pâtés and pies.
28 Market Jew Street, Penzance, Cornwall TR18 2HR
01736 367375

LIGHTHOUSE GALLERY
Contemporary artists from Cornwall and the Scilly Isles are represented in this lovely, light gallery. Choose from paintings, glass, jewellery and ceramics.
25 Causeway Head, Penzance, Cornwall TR18 2SP
01736 350555
www.lighthouse-gallery.com

THE ROUND HOUSE & CAPSTAN GALLERY
Smack on the beach and built of wood and granite, the Round House contained the capstan that was used for hauling boats out of the water. It is now a unique gallery displaying work by local artists who draw their inspiration from Penwith's rugged and atmospheric landscape.
Sennen Cove, Land's End, Cornwall TR19 7DF
01736 871859
www.round-house.co.uk

Visit

ST IVES
This is a beautiful, bustling town that tumbles down to two fantastic beaches. There's a full day's worth of sightseeing, but must-dos are the Tate Gallery on the sea front – a spectacular contemporary building full of light – and Barbara Hepworth's sculpture garden, which is an absolute jewel, with a stunning sculpture round every corner.
Tate Gallery
Porthmeor Beach, St Ives, Cornwall TR26 1TG
01736 796226
www.tate.org.uk/stives
Barbara Hepworth Museum & Sculpture Garden
Barnoon Hill, Cornwall TR26 1AD
01736 796226
www.tate.org.uk/stives/hepworth

ST MICHAEL'S MOUNT
Take a short boat trip or wait for low tide and walk across the causeway to this iconic rocky island crowned by a medieval church and castle. Once there, explore the Victorian underground railway and sub-tropical hanging gardens.
Marazion, Penzance, Cornwall TR17 0HS
01736 710507
www.stmichaelsmount.co.uk

TRENGWAINTON GARDEN
A picturesque stream runs the length of the garden, and paths lead up to a terrace and summerhouses with marvellous views across Mount Bay to the Lizard. The walled gardens contain many rare species indigenous to this part of Cornwall, and enormous tree ferns.
Madron, Penzance, Cornwall TR20 8RZ
01736 363148
www.nationaltrust.org.uk

Activity

GOLF
You'll get a fabulous sea view from every hole on this scenic par 70, 18-hole course perched above the Atlantic, surrounded by Iron and Bronze Age settlements and old mine workings.
Cape Cornwall Golf & Country Club
St Just, Penzance, Cornwall TR19 7NL
01736 788611
www.capecornwall.com

MINACK OPEN-AIR THEATRE
The inspiration and life's work of Rowena Case, the theatre is in a spectacular location perched above the sea at Porthcurno. There are daytime as well as evening performances, and don't miss the stunning gardens. There's a shop and good cafe, too.
Porthcurno, Penzance, Cornwall TR19 6JU
01736 810181
www.minack.com

SURFING
Hang ten and chase the riptides on stunning Porthmeor beach. You'll get first-class tuition and be amazed at how quickly you pick up the surfer moves.
St Ives Surf Centre
Porthmeor Beach, St Ives, Cornwall TR26 1JZ
01736 793366
www.st-ives.uk.com/surfing

The Walk - Merry Maidens At Lamorna Cove

A coastal and inland walk passing an ancient stone circle along the way.

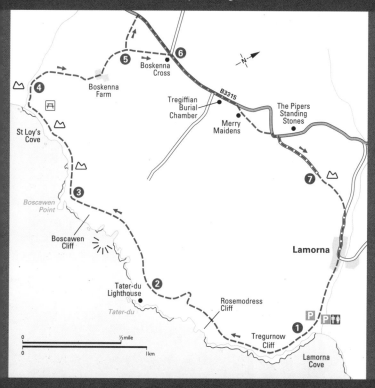

Walk Details

LENGTH: 6 miles (9.7km)

TIME: 3hrs 30min

ASCENT: 558ft (170m)

PATHS: Good coastal footpaths, field paths and rocky tracks

SUGGESTED MAP: aqua3 OS Explorer 102 Land's End

GRID REFERENCE: SW 450241

PARKING: Lamorna Cove

❶ From the far end of the seaward car park, at the end of the terrace above Lamorna Cove, follow the coast path through short rocky sections. Continue along the path past the tops of Tregurnow Cliff and Rosemodress Cliff.

❷ Pass above the entrance ramp and steps to Tater-du Lighthouse. Pass large residence (right); where the track bends right, keep left along the coast path, at signpost.

❸ Descend steeply (take care when muddy) from Boscawen Point to St Loy's Cove. Cross the section of boulders (may be slippery when wet). Follow the path inland through dense vegetation and by the stream. Cross a private drive then climb steeply uphill. Cross the stile on to the track, turn right over the stile and follow the path through trees.

❹ By the wooden signpost and an old tree, go right and cross the stream on large boulders; follow the hedged-in path left. Shortly, by a wooden signpost, go right and up to a surfaced lane. Turn left; follow the lane uphill. At a junction with a bend on another track, keep ahead and uphill. At Boskenna Farm buildings follow the lane left; keep ahead.

❺ From the lane, at entrance drive to bungalow on right, right of way goes through a field gate, then cuts across a field corner to a stile in the wire fence. Beyond, right of way (no path) leads diagonally across field to top righthand corner, where a stile leads into a lay-by with a granite cross at the edge. An alternative route is to continue along the farm lane; turn right along a public road, taking care, to a lay-by.

❻ Follow the road to Tregiffian burial chamber on the right, then walk to Merry Maidens stone circle. From the circle continue to the field corner, cross the stile and follow the path diagonally right across the next field towards the buildings. Cross over the stile on to the road, then down the righthand of 2 lanes (surfaced, 'No Through Road' sign).

❼ Where the lane ends, keep ahead on to the public bridleway. Follow the track downhill to reach the public road. Turn right and walk down the road, with care, passing Lamorna Wink Inn, to the car park.

The Gurnard's Head
Cornwall

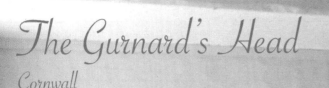

The Inn

An early 17th-century coaching inn standing on the windswept coastal road that runs between St Ives and Land's End, The Gurnard's Head shines out like a beacon of warmth and hospitality amid a patchwork of fields and ancient farms. Brothers Charles and Edmund Inkin have transformed the original building into a fabulous pub with rooms in much the same way that they made The Felin Fach Griffin the must-visit pub of the Brecon Beacons. The Inkins' motto is 'the simple things in life done well', and this extends to all aspects of the running of The Gurnard's Head.

Its stunning location and views of the Atlantic make it popular with walkers, tourists and city dwellers looking for tranquillity. The ensuite bedrooms are simply and tastefully decorated: the handmade beds are so comfortable that the owners regularly get asked if they're for sale, and they're made up with the softest white linen. Each room, like the rest of the pub, is lined with old books and local pictures and maps, which enhances the feeling that guests are staying with old friends.

The Essentials

Time at the Bar!
12-11.30pm
Food: 12.30-2.30pm, 6.30-9pm

What's the Damage?
Main courses from £9.50

Bitter Experience:
St Austell Tribute,
Skinner's Betty Stogs

Sticky Fingers:
Children welcome, small portions
available

Muddy Paws:
Dogs welcome in the bar

Zzzzz:
7 rooms, £72.50-£125

Anything Else?
Patio, garden, car park

The Food

With the Atlantic a mere 500 metres away, it's hardly surprising that locally caught fish is one of the highlights on the menu at The Gurnard's Head. The head chef Matt Williamson works hard to cut down food miles wherever possible, and this means that much of the seasonal produce used in the kitchen has actually been grown or raised on the doorstep. At lunchtime, there's a chalkboard menu offering a handful of options, all of them under £10 and always featuring hearty broths and soups, stews, sandwiches, home-made pork pies and fish and chips.

In the evening, the menu rarely stretches beyond five starters and five main courses. Keen local sourcing is evident in dishes such as smoked Cornish pilchards served with pickled beetroot and horseradish ice cream; The Gurnard's fish stew with new potatoes and aioli; and rabbit and porcini cannelloni – the latter served with Gilly's leaves (a reference to the woman who supplies the pub with salad). All can be washed down with well-chosen wines or beers from the Cornish brewers St Austell or Skinner's.

What To Do

Shop

ST IVES GALLERIES

Reflecting the long history of St Ives as a centre for artists, the town is packed with art galleries and shops selling hand-made artistic goodies. Countless specialist outlets make the town's narrow streets and lanes a treasure trove for those searching for a stunning painting, ceramics, or a one-off piece of pottery, sculpture, jewellery and a wealth of other crafts, to take home.

Tourist Information Centre 01736 769297

www.stives-cornwall.co.uk

VICARAGE FARM SHOP

Specialists in rare-breed pork (Duroc and Large Black) and lamb (Moorits), all raised locally, this well-stocked farm shop also gathers in produce from further afield, including a good range of delicious Cornish farmhouse cheeses. Their own-farm Aberdeen Angus beef is a mainstay; a wide range of unusual preserves and other foods is also available.

Underlane, Helston, Cornwall TR13 0EJ

01326 340484

www.vicaragefarmshop.com

Visit

GOONHILLY SATELLITE EARTH STATION

The very first transatlantic television pictures were received here on this remote Cornish moor on the Lizard Peninsula. Amazingly, Goonhilly Downs is still the world's biggest satellite station; a visitor centre and tour reveal the inside story of the space-age technology in operation here.

Helston, Cornwall TR12 6LQ

0800 679593

www.goonhilly.bt.com

MINACK THEATRE

The unique, open-air, cliff-side setting of the theatre is worth the visit in its own right. An extremely varied programme of plays and events – everything from *Of Mice and Men* to *Robin Hood* to *His Dark Materials* to performances by town bands – ensures that there's something on here virtually every day throughout the summer.

Porthcurno, Lands End, Cornwall TR19 6JU

01736 810181

www.minack.com

ST MICHAEL'S MOUNT

Reached by foot across the causeway at low tide, by boat at high water, St Michael's Mount is an iconic priory-cum-mansion capping a rocky island in Mount's Bay, near Penzance, lived in today by a modern family. An ancient cobbled path leads visitors up to the medieval castle battlements from where the view over Penzance Bay is superb. The craggy garden has a wealth of rare and unusual plants and a hanging sub-tropical garden.

Marazion, Penzance, Cornwall TR17 0HS

01736 710507

www.stmichaelsmount.co.uk

TATE ST IVES

One of Britain's leading abstract and modern art complexes, celebrating the St Ives School and worldwide contemporary art. It incorporates the nearby Barbara Hepworth Museum and Sculpture Garden at Barnoon Hill, once home to the renowned sculptress.

Porthmeor Beach, St Ives, Cornwall TR26 1TG

01736 796226

www.tate.org.uk/stives

Activity

FLYING AT LAND'S END

Flying lessons from Land's End Airport, with flights over the coast and countryside of Penwith, give you the chance to pilot the aircraft (you can even take a friend). Leisure flights are also available. The airport is also the base for scheduled day-return flights to the Isles of Scilly. You can combine a flight-out and boat-back excursion from the island of St Mary's.

Land's End Airport, St Just, Penzance, Cornwall TR19 7RL

For lessons: 01736 788771

www.landsendairport.co.uk

For Isles of Scilly: 0845 710 5555

www.ios-travel.co.uk

GEOLOGY TOURS

Interesting half-day or day trips, led by a professional geologist, can be arranged to introduce non-specialists to the extraordinary geology of the Penwith Peninsula. These trips help to explain the area's natural landscapes as well as exploring its tin-mining heritage.

07887 556245

www.cornwallgeology.co.uk

MARINE DISCOVERY

Appreciate a mariner's view of West Cornwall on a trip into Mount's Bay and along the rugged Penwith peninsula in a semi-rigid inflatable boat. Locations visited include some of the offshore reefs that make this coast so treacherous and a sight of Wolf Rock Lighthouse, built to warn against these hazards. Porpoise, sunfish and huge but harmless basking sharks may be seen.

Penzance Harbour, Cornwall

01736 874907

www.marinediscovery.co.uk

The Walk - The Tinners' Trail from Pendeen

A stroll through Cornwall's tin- and copper-mining country.

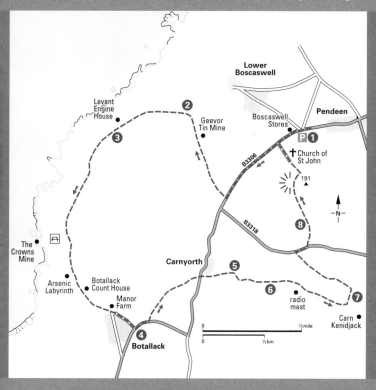

Walk Details

LENGTH: 5 miles (8km)

TIME: 4hrs

ASCENT: 328ft (100m)

PATHS: Coastal footpath, field paths and moorland tracks

SUGGESTED MAP: aqua3 OS Explorer 102 Land's End

GRID REFERENCE: SW 383344

PARKING: Free car park in centre of Pendeen village, opposite Boscaswell Stores, on the B3306

❶ Turn left out of the village-centre car park and follow the road to reach the entrance of Geevor Tin Mine. Walk down the drive towards the reception building and keep to its left down the road between the buildings, signposted 'Levant'.

❷ Just beyond the buildings, turn left along the narrow path that soon bears right and becomes unsurfaced track between walls. Turn left at the huge boulder and head towards the very tall chimney stack ahead. Continue across broken ground to the National Trust's Levant Engine House.

❸ Follow the bottom edge of Levant car park and then take the rough track to reach Botallack Count House. Keep on past Manor Farm and shortly reach the public road at Botallack.

❹ Go left at the main road (watch out for fast traffic), then turn left along Cresswell Terrace to reach the stile. Follow the field paths to enter the old mining village of Carnyorth. Cross the main road, then follow the lane opposite. Turn right once you reach the junction, to arrive at a solitary house.

❺ Keep left of the house, go over the stile and cross the field to the opposite hedge to reach the hidden stile. Follow the path leading through the small fields towards the radio mast. Cross a final stile onto a rough track.

❻ Go left, then immediately right at the junction. Keep on past the radio mast, then follow the path through gorse and heather to the rocky outcrop of Carn Kenidjack (not always visible when misty).

❼ At the junction abreast of Carn Kenidjack, go back left along the path past the small granite parish boundary stone, eventually emerging on the road. Turn right and, in about 140yds (128m), go left along the obvious broad track opposite the house.

❽ Keep left at the junction. By 2 large stones on the left, bear off right along the grassy track. Go left over the big stone stile directly above the Church of St John, built by the mining community in the 1850s, and descend to the main road. Turn right to return to the car park.

21

The Tinners Arms

Cornwall

The Inn

The Tinners Arms was built in 1271 to house the masons constructing St Senara's church next door. Totally unspoilt, the stone-built inn is set in glorious countryside a short distance from the coastal path (hence its popularity with walkers) and is a real get-away-from-it-all place with no mobile phone signal and no TV. In fine weather, the lovely sheltered courtyard to the front and suntrap terrace at the back come into their own; at other times, the low-ceilinged public bar, with its exposed stone walls, pitch pine panelling and a large log fire, is the focal point. There's also a smaller bar with a pool table, plus a dining room.

Light, airy bedrooms are on the first floor of a separate house a few steps across the courtyard: there are two ensuite doubles plus a pair of singles sharing a bathroom. All are simply decorated in a fairly traditional manner and are very well maintained, with spotless bathrooms and pretty countryside views. Breakfast is a friendly affair, served downstairs in a cottagey kitchen at a communal table.

The Essentials

Time at the Bar!
11am-11pm
Food:12-2.30pm, 6-9pm

What's the Damage?
Main courses from £8.25

Bitter Experience:
St Austell's Tinners Ale,
Sharp's Doom Bar, Special

Sticky Fingers:
Children welcome; children's menu

Muddy Paws:
Dogs welcome in the bar

Zzzzz:
4 rooms, £40-£70

Anything Else?
Terrace, garden, car park

The Food

This may not be the most elegant place, but there's a laudable effort to source local produce, with blackboards listing fish and vegetarian specials. The quality of the simple, homely food has people flocking here, especially in high summer. Home-cooked local ham, egg and chips, and Cornish cheese ploughman's typify the sort of dishes to expect at lunchtime, along with cheese or ham sandwiches and such dishes as fish pie, cottage pie and vegetarian lasagne – great fodder for walkers, good value, too, and well matched by the cracking Tinners Ale on tap.

In the evening, expect to find home-cured salmon with horseradish cream, or tomato, mozzarella and basil salad among the starters, and main courses ranging from confit of duck with orange and ginger to sirloin steak with tomatoes and mushrooms, chips and mixed salad. Portions are generous, and the irresistible home-made tarts and cakes offered for pudding at both lunch and dinner might need to be vigorously walked off; the selection of locally made ice creams and sorbets is a lighter choice.

What To Do

Shop

THE GREAT ATLANTIC GALLERY

Rich in the mining, farming and fishing industries, St Just retains its unique character. Local artists are well represented at this gallery, where you can buy photography, paintings, ceramics, sculpture, jewellery and limited edition prints.

5 Bank Square, St Just, Cornwall TR19 7HH

01736 788911

www.greatatlantic.co.uk/gallery

LENTERNS BUTCHERS

Recently named retail butcher of the year, Simon Lentern stocks only local organic meat from farms where animal welfare is top priority. Take home the speciality, hog's pudding, aka Cornish black pudding.

1 Chapel Street, Penzance, Cornwall TR18 4AJ

01736 363061

QUAYSIDE FISH

This award-winning fishmonger's right on the harbour at Porthleven sells only line-caught fish, and it specialises in both smoked fish and shellfish, including haddock, salmon, trout and prawns.

The Harbourside, Porthleven, Cornwall TR13 9JU

01326 562008

www.quaysidefish.co.uk

TATE ST IVES

Located right on the beach at Porthmeor, The Tate Gallery is always worth a visit to see current as well as permanent exhibitions. The gallery shop is full of items by well-known local artists.

Porthmeor Beach, St Ives, Cornwall TR26 1TG

01736 796226

www.tate.org.uk/stives

Visit

GEEVOR TIN MINE

Set among stunning Atlantic coastal scenery, Geevor was a working mine until 1990, employing 400 people in a labyrinth of mines reaching far out under the sea. Exhibits enable visitors to appreciate the fascinating process of mining and extracting tin.

Pendeen, Penzance, Cornwall TR19 7EW

01736 788662

www.geevor.com

NEW MILLENNIUM GALLERY

The largest privately owned gallery in St Ives, the New Millennium is a wonderfully large, light space, exhibiting the fruit of 20 years of collecting abstract and innovative pieces of artwork.

Street-an-Pol, St Ives, Cornwall TR26 2DS

01736 793121

www.newmillenniumgallery.co.uk

PENDEEN LIGHTHOUSE

Dramatically positioned on a jagged stretch of coastline, the Pendeen lighthouse has saved countless ships and lives over the past 100 years. Now fully automated, you can take a tour inside; it's also a great place from which to spot seals, kestrels and buzzards.

Pendeen Watch, Penzance, Cornwall TR19 7ED

01736 788418

WAYSIDE FOLK MUSEUM

Sixty years ago, Colonel 'Freddie' Hirst started gathering ephemera unique to Zennor, which resulted in this quaint, eclectic museum, with over 6,000 items relating to the lives of local people.

Zennor, Cornwall TR26 3DA

01736 796945

Activity

BOAT TRIP

Explore Cornwall's granite coast in a boat, and see seals, dolphins, porpoises, St Michael's Mount and the extraordinary Minack Theatre from a unique perspective.

Marine Discovery Penzance, 5 Gulval Cross, Penzance, Cornwall TR18 3BN

01736 874907

www.marinediscovery.co.uk

GOLF

This natural links course is on the southern edge of St Ives, with breathtaking scenery across the bay to the Atlantic. It's not a championship course but a challenging one!

West Cornwall Golf Club, Church Lane, Lelant, St Ives, Cornwall TR26 3DZ

01736 753401

www.westcornwallgolfclub.co.uk

SEA FISHING

Your skipper will ensure a great day at sea – all tackle and refreshments are provided on his 38ft (12m) boat. On a good day, expect to land cod, pollock and conger eel.

Bite Adventure, The Workshop, Back Lane, Marazion, Penzance, Cornwall TR17 0HE

01736 759528

www.biteadventures.com

SURFING

The combination of Atlantic surges and the warm Gulf Stream will ensure a great surfing experience, whether you're a beginner or a pro and especially under professional tuition from experienced surfers at the Shore Surf School at St Ives.

Shore Surf School, 46 Mount Pleasant, St Ives, Cornwall TR27 4LE

01736 755556

www.shoresurf.com

The Walk - Church Paths and Coastguard Ways

A long coastal walk following old church and coastal paths around St Ives.

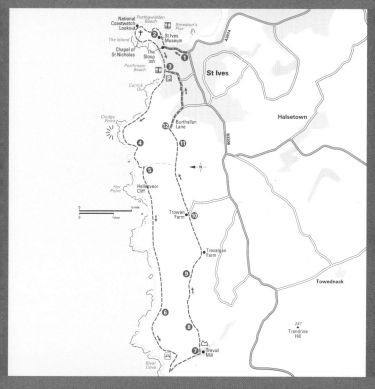

Walk Details

LENGTH: 8 miles (12.9km)

TIME: 3hrs

ASCENT: 394ft (120m)

PATHS: Coastal path, can be quite rocky. Field paths, some stiles. Very scenic coast and small inland fields

SUGGESTED MAP: aqua3 OS Explorer 102 Land's End

GRID REFERENCE: SW 522408

PARKING: Upper Trenwith car park St Ives or Porthmeor Beach, Smeaton's Pier and Porthmeor car park

❶ Walk along the harbour towards Smeaton's Pier. Before reaching the pier entrance, turn left (Sea View Place). Where the road bends, keep ahead into Wheal Dream. Turn right past St Ives Museum; follow the walkway to Porthgwidden Beach.

❷ Cross the car park above the beach; climb to National Coastwatch lookout. Go down the steps, behind the building at the back, then follow footway to Porthmeor Beach. Go along the beach to the car park.

❸ Go up the steps beside the public toilets; turn right along the track leading past the bowling and putting greens. Continue walking to Carrick Du and Clodgy Point.

❹ From the square-cut rock on Clodgy Point, walk uphill and through the low wall. Follow path right and across boggy area. In 0.5 mile (800m) go left at the junction.

❺ Reach the T-junction with the track just past the National Trust sign ('Hellesveor Cliff'). Turn right; follow coast path. (The short version of the walk goes left and inland.)

❻ Keep right at the junction past the old mine stack and shed (left). Continue to River Cove. On the other side, go left at the junction and inland through the woods.

❼ At the junction, go left over cattle grid; follow signs past Trevail Mill. Go through a metal gate and climb.

❽ Cross the track; follow the path opposite. Shortly go left over the stile by the black-and-white pole. Follow the field edges over stiles.

❾ Follow righthand edge of the field containing parish boundary stone. Cross 2 stiles; at the hedge corner, bear right across field; continue to Trevalgan Farm. Cross behind farm to stile; continue to Trowan Farm.

❿ Go left over the stile just before the house; turn right. Go through the farmyard to the lane; turn left then right, over the stile. Follow the field paths over more stiles.

⓫ Go over the stile and through a metal gate, pass the field gap, then go left and down the hedged-in path. Cross a stile and pass between hedges to Burthallan lane.

⓬ Turn right to reach T-junction with main road. Turn left; follow the road downhill to Porthmeor Beach and the start of the walk.

Driftwood Spars

Cornwall

Driftwood Spars, Trevaunance Cove, St Agnes, Cornwall TR5 0LE

The Inn

There is a feeling of space and a welcome for all at this solid 17th-century inn, a stone's throw from lovely Trevaunance Cove where good surfing and safe swimming can be enjoyed from the sandy beach. The beams in the ceilings of the two large bars include 'spars' (large poles used for the mast) salvaged from wrecked ships and framed photographs that capture the sea-faring Cornish life of bygone days. Here, a pint of landlord Gordon Treleaven's legendary Cuckoo Ale, brewed in his microbrewery just across the road, is the perfect antidote to a long drive or a hot day on the beach.

The local brew is guaranteed to make your toes tap to the live music played every Friday and Saturday evening. Get there early, grab a barrel seat and be prepared to be treated as one of the locals in this lively and unpretentious environment.

Stay the night here and there are 15 crisp, bright, nautically themed bedrooms to choose from – many have wonderful sea views, all are ensuite. There's no doubt that Driftwood Spars is a hidden gem in a beautiful and bustling part of the Cornish coast.

The Essentials

Time at the Bar!
11am-11pm
Food: 12-2.30pm, 6.30-9.30pm (all day in summer)

What's the Damage?
Main courses from £15

Bitter Experience:
Driftwood Cuckoo Ale, Sharp's Own and Doom Bar

Sticky Fingers:
Children welcome; small portions available

Muddy Paws:
Dogs welcome

Zzzzz:
15 rooms, £43-£49

Anything Else?
Terrace, garden, car park

The Food

The Atlantic air causes hearty appetites, so while the bar menu has a something-for-everyone appeal – from light snacks such as red onion and anchovy tartlet topped with parmesan, through salads, baguettes, ploughman's and pies, to good-value mains along the lines of seared loin of swordfish with Mediterranean salsa or lamb steak marinated in rosemary and garlic – look to the Spindrift restaurant to up the culinary stakes. This is where old Cornwall gives way to the new, with oak flooring and chunky wooden tables and chairs, all bathed in a healthy dose of bright sea light.

The ambitious menu features a wealth of seasonal fish and shellfish dishes as well as locally grown produce. Start your meal with delicious black tiger gambas and chorizo or grilled goats' cheese with raspberry and walnut dressing before moving on to whole roasted sea bass stuffed with apricot and hazelnuts and herb butter, or brochette of monkfish marinated in fresh chillies, ginger and Moroccan spices.

Finish with the heavenly white chocolate profiteroles or a Cornish cheeseboard and you'll be ready for the soft mattress waiting for you upstairs.

What To Do

Shop

ATLANTIS SMOKED FISH

Stop here for high-class smoked fish, meats and cheeses from a long-established local foods business using modern and traditional smoking processes. The goods are on sale in their little shop in Grampound.

Fore Street, Grampound, Truro, Cornwall TR2 4SB

01726 883201

www.atlantisfoods.co.uk

ST AGNES POTTERY

Craft workshop using local clays to produce an eclectic range of functional pottery, exhibition pieces and decorative pots, many finished with glazes developed at the pottery. The pretty town has many other galleries, set beside lanes dropping to Trevaunance Cove.

Vicarage Road, St Agnes, Cornwall TR5 0LT

01872 553445

SPINDRIFT GALLERY

An ultra-modern gallery drawing together the best of contemporary Cornish artists working in oils, watercolours and acrylics. Other exhibitors show their range of ceramics, glass, porcelain and jewellery. Portscatho village has more art galleries, craft and antique shops.

8 The Quay, Portscatho, Truro, Cornwall TR2 5HF

01872 580155

www.spindrift-gallery.co.uk

Visit

CAMEL VALLEY VINEYARD

In the sheltered middle valley of the River Camel, good soils and reliable sun produce international award-winning still and sparkling wines. Daily tours (in season) around the vineyard, plus wine tasting.

Nanstallon, Bodmin, Cornwall PL30 5LG

01208 77959

www.camelvalley.com

GWEEK SEAL SANCTUARY

This long-established rescue and rehabilitation centre provides care for injured seals, most of which are returned to the wild – though some are long-term residents, too traumatised to fend for themselves. Also home to sea-lions and otters.

Gweek, Helston, Cornwall TR12 6UG

01326 221361

www.sealsanctuary.co.uk

NATIONAL MARITIME MUSEUM

Celebrate and investigate Cornwall's long maritime heritage at this quayside museum overlooking one of Britain's greatest natural harbours at Falmouth. There are exhibits on traditional and modern craft and navigation skills. Underwater viewing gallery.

Discovery Quay, Falmouth, Cornwall TR11 3QY

01326 313388

www.nmmc.co.uk

TRERICE

A picture-perfect manor virtually unchanged since Elizabethan times. It houses an excellent collection of furniture, glass, ceramics and an extensive collection of clocks.

Kestle Mill, Newquay, Cornwall TR8 4PG

01637 875404

www.nationaltrust.org.uk

Activity

BISSOE TRAMWAYS CYCLE HIRE

The harbour at Portreath was a major centre for exporting tin ore, carried there on former tramroads and mineral railways. These are now at the heart of a cycle network exploring mid-Cornwall's industrial heritage and peaceful countryside. Hiring a cycle by the hour or the day is the perfect way to explore this half-hidden world.

Old Conns Works, Bissoe, Truro, Cornwall TR4 8QZ

01872 870341

www.cornwallcyclehire.com

PERRANPORTH BEACH

Mile after mile of windswept beaches between Perranporth and Newquay are tailor-made for kite-based adrenalin sports. Buggy-surfing, land-boarding and kite-surfing are just some of the on-beach or in-water activities for which instruction is available. Surf-schools teaching 'traditional' techniques also thrive here.

01637 831383

www.mobiusonline.co.uk

SEGUE CHARTERS

Falmouth Bay and the waters off The Lizard Peninsula are home to a wealth of sealife. Take the opportunity to go cetacean watching: porpoises and perhaps even killer whales, as well as sunfish and basking sharks, are regularly seen during the summer. In a different mode, Segue Charters also operates exciting deep-sea wreck-fishing expeditions or shark angling days; fish of more than 500lbs patrol these waters.

01326 312116

www.seguecharters.co.uk

The Walk - *Cliffs and a High Hill*

A bracing walk along the cliffs at St Agnes, then inland to the top of St Agnes Beacon.

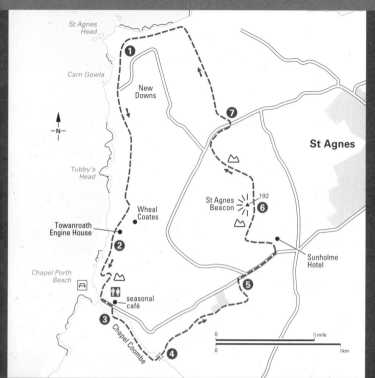

Walk Details

LENGTH: 5 miles (8km)

TIME: 3hrs

ASCENT: 623ft (190m)

PATHS: Good coastal footpaths and inland tracks

SUGGESTED MAP: aqua3 OS Explorer 104 Redruth & St Agnes

GRID REFERENCE: SW 699512

PARKING: St Agnes Head. There are parking spaces along the clifftop track. Start the walk from any one of these

❶ Join the coastal footpath from wherever you park along the cliff top. Follow the stony track across the little promontory of Tubby's Head, the former Iron-Age settlement. Branch off right on to the narrower path about 100yds (90m) before old mine buildings (these are the remains of the Wheal Coates mine). Cross the stone stile and continue on the path to Towanroath mine Engine House.

❷ About 50yds (46m) beyond Towanroath Engine House, branch off right at the signpost and descend to Chapel Porth Beach.

❸ Cross the stream at the back corner of the car park and then follow the path up Chapel Coombe next to the stream. Pass below the mine building and, where the path forks among trees, go left through the wooden kissing gate.

❹ Cross the bridge, then turn right onto the track. Continue along the grassy track and at the point where the track narrows, keep well ahead at the fork. Keep alongside the field and on to the track; now turn left over the wooden stile by the gate onto the track. After around 50yds (46m), reach the junction with the wide track. Turn left and continue to the public road.

❺ Turn right along the public road, and keep ahead at the junction. In 200yds (183m), next to the entrance to the Sunholme Hotel, continue up the stony track on the left. After 50yds (46m), at the junction, go left and follow the path rising to the obvious summit of 629ft (192m) St Agnes Beacon, used traditionally for the lighting of signal fires and celebratory bonfires. The views from the top of the Beacon reach as far as the tors of Bodmin Moor.

❻ From the summit of the Beacon, follow the lower of 2 tracks, heading northwest, down towards the road. Just before you reach the road turn right along the narrow path, skirting the base of the hill, eventually emerging at the road by a seat.

❼ Cross over and follow the track opposite, across New Downs, directly to the edge of the cliffs, then turn left at the junction with the coastal path and return to the clifftop parking spaces.

The Plume of Feathers

Cornwall

The Inn

The white-painted Plume of Feathers is a textbook example of the wonders that can be worked when bringing back to life a run-down boozer. While the interior has been completely overhauled and opened up; it has been done without stripping it of an ounce of character. There's still a cheerful, rambling feel, and lots of deft touches: the original ceiling of heavy planks and timbers has been retained, and there's a dining area that uses a glassed-over well as a table. Thick stone walls and tiny windows may restrict natural light, but pale colours, soft lighting and bright modern prints create a comfortable look.

Bedrooms are found in what were once outbuildings at the back – names such as the Boot Room and the Hay Loft hint at the former uses they were put to. All rooms have the Plume's trademark modern wrought-iron beds covered with crisp white duvets, and offer a mix of spotlessly maintained bath or shower rooms. The spacious suites include double sofa beds (ideal for families), while the very large Tack Room has room for a king-size double and two proper single beds.

The Plume of Feathers, Mitchell, Truro, Cornwall TR8 5AX

The Essentials

Time at the Bar!
9am–12 midnight
Food: 12–5pm 6–10pm

What's the Damage?
Main courses from £7.50

Bitter Experience:
Changing guest beers, Sharp's Doom
Bar and Eden Ale, Skinner's Ales

Sticky Fingers:
Children welcome; half
portions served

Muddy Paws:
Dogs welcome in the bar

Zzzzz:
7 rooms, £70–£100

Anything Else?
Garden, car park

The Food

At heart, The Plume of Feathers remains a local, reserving a space at the bar for drinkers, but the food is a major draw. The kitchen gives due deference to regional produce – a cornerstone of the cooking style is fish – yet the menu looks beyond the back yard for inspiration, giving the food a modern, cosmopolitan flavour and reflecting sunnier climes. Consistent delivery keeps the place afloat, with the kitchen moving deftly through a repertoire of contemporary dishes such as fresh River Fowey mussels with chorizo and basil, confit duck leg with sautéed potatoes, fine green beans and a sherry vinaigrette, and chargrilled Cornish porbeagle shark with coconut rice and a pineapple and mango salsa.

But if you find yourself in the mood for something simpler, such as salmon and cod fishcake with home-made tartare sauce, chargrilled beef burgers in a toasted foccacia with red onion jam and fries, or a Caesar salad, you certainly won't put the kitchen off its stroke. Desserts range from sticky toffee pudding via Cornish ice cream to pannacotta laden with fresh local raspberries and chocolate sauce.

What To Do

Shop

KINGSLEY VILLAGE
Showcasing the best of the region's produce, you will find all things Cornish under one roof in this huge, family-run enterprise.

Penhale, Fraddon, Cornwall TR9 6NA

01726 861111

www.kingsleyvillage.com

KITTOW BROS.
Butchers since the 1800s, the fifth generation of Kittows prepare and sell quality meat, including their famous sausages – choose from wild boar and venison, champagne and mushroom, pork, apple and Lerryn cider.

1–3 South Street, Fowey, Cornwall PL23 1AR

01726 832639

www.kittowsbutchers.co.uk

PADSTOW
There are numerous great shops in this ancient harbour town.

Blue Wing Gallery

2 Hornabrook Place, Padstow, Cornwall PL28 8DY

01841 533999

www.blue-wing.co.uk

Rick Stein's Deli

South Quay, Padstow, Cornwall PL28 8BY

01841 533218

www.rickstein.com

SOUTH TORFREY FARM
This organic farm raises small flocks of chickens in mobile houses – a slow-growing French breed is used. The mature birds are processed on site, dry-plucked and hung for a few days. You can also buy eggs and Longhorn beef.

Golant, Fowey, Cornwall PL23 1LA

01726 833126

www.southtorfreyfarm.com

Visit

EDEN PROJECT
The world-renowned Eden Project is about connecting plants, people and the environment. It's a living demonstration of regeneration, housed in a series of spectacular geodesic domes.

Bodelva, St Austell, Cornwall PL24 2SG

01726 811911

www.edenproject.com

LANHYDROCK
One of the most fascinating and complete Victorian houses in the country, Lanhydrock is full of period atmosphere. The garden has a stunning collection of magnolias, rhododendrons and camellias, and 364 acres of park and woodland sweeping down to the River Fowey.

Bodmin, Cornwall PL30 5AD

01208 265950

www.nationaltrust.org.uk

TRERICE HOUSE & GARDENS
This delightful, small, secluded Elizabethan manor house was built in 1571, with fine fireplaces, ceilings, furniture and clocks. Famed for its barrel-roofed great chamber, it also has lovely flowering gardens and an old Cornish apple orchard, as well as an experimental Tudor garden.

Kestle Mill, Newquay, Cornwall TR8 4PG

01637 875404

www.nationaltrust.org.uk

WHEAL COATES TIN MINE
Standing dramatically on the cliff top is the Towanroath engine house once belonging to the Wheal Coates mine. It's one of Cornwall's instantly recognisable landmarks, and has become an iconic image.

St Agnes, Cornwall

Activity

HORSE RIDING ON BODMIN MOOR
There are several choices of stunning terrain to ride across on horseback: woodland, moorland and, one of the most popular, the Blisland Trail, which involves a gentle journey to the picturesque village of Blisland and lunch in the local pub.

Hallagenna Farm, St Breward, Bodmin, Cornwall PL30 4NS

01208 851500

www.hallagenna.co.uk

STEAM TRAIN RIDE
Let the train take the strain! This is a delightful steam train journey through stunning countryside, travelling on the country's steepest heritage track.

Bodmin & Wenford Railway

General Station, Bodmin, Cornwall PL31 1AQ

0845 125 9678

www.bodminandwenfordrailway.co.uk

WATER SPORTS
Watergate Bay is a mecca for water sport junkies – learn to kite surf, wave-ski, ride a land board or master a traction kite. You could do a lot worse than to start the day off with a fabulous Fifteen fry-up breakfast at Jamie Oliver's restaurant, also at Watergate Bay.

Extreme Academy

Watergate Bay, Cornwall TR8 4AA

01637 860543

www.watergatebay.co.uk

The Walk - Giant Steps and Staircases

A coastal walk exploring Bedruthan Steps and Park Head.

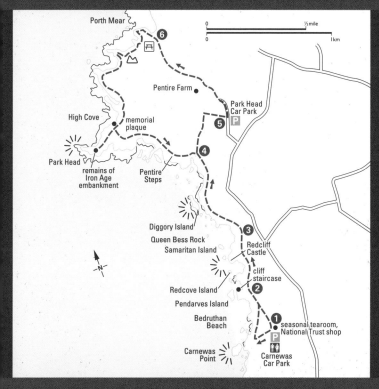

Walk Details

LENGTH: 4.5 miles (7.2km)

TIME: 2hrs 30min

ASCENT: 131ft (40m)

PATHS: Coastal paths and field paths. Coast path very close to unguarded cliff edges in some places. Take care in windy weather and with children and dogs. 1 stile

SUGGESTED MAP: aqua3 OS Explorer 106 Newquay & Padstow

GRID REFERENCE: SW 850691

PARKING: National Trust car park at Carnewas

1 From the car park, go through the gap in the wall on the right of the National Trust shop; shortly, bear left at the junction. Continue to the crossing of the paths; go straight across and down the grassy path to Carnewas Point (there are dramatic views from here). Return to the crossing; follow the path left along the cliff edge. (Heed the warning notices.) At the junction with the cobbled path, go left and descend to the dip at Pendarves Point.

2 At the junction in the dip, go down left to the top of the cliff staircase. On re-ascending the staircase, go back uphill to the junction with the coast path and turn left past the National Trust sign ('Carnewas'). Follow the coast path along the

fence and below the parking area with the picnic tables above.

3 Pass Redcliff Castle; where the path forks by the signpost, follow either to where they rejoin. Keep right of the stone wall with the tamarisk trees, to the wooden kissing gate. Continue along the clifftop to the set of wooden gates on the right.

4 Go right and pass through the smaller gate; follow the permissive footpath along the field edges. Just before you reach the buildings at Pentire, turn right through the gate and follow the field edges to the Park Head car park.

5 Turn left; go left down the surfaced lane. Before the Pentire buildings go through the gate on

the right ('Porthmear Beach and Park Head'). Bear left across the field to the stile and gateway. Bear right down the next field to the kissing gate in the bottom corner. Go through the gate, then follow the path through the wetland to reach the coast path above Porth Mear.

6 Go left; follow the coast path uphill then round Park Head. Take care near the cliff edges. At the memorial plaque above High Cove, divert to the promontory of Park Head itself. Return to the plaque and follow the coast path south to Point 4. Retrace your steps to Point 2, in the dip above the start of the cliff staircase. Follow the cobbled walkway uphill and back to Carnewas car park.

The Rising Sun

Cornwall

The Inn

With its edge-of-harbour setting and an atmosphere that generates a cheerful holiday feeling – especially if the sun is shining and you've bagged a table on the suntrap front terrace – this comfortable inn has an upmarket and cared-for atmosphere. It's a popular place that successfully combines providing enterprising food alongside its role as a village local. While there are traditional touches in the spacious bar, the driftwood-style tables, plump, comfy sofas and armchairs, and soft pastel shades create a stylish colonial feel. This theme continues in the restaurant, where paddle fans and a glassed-in terrace make an elegant statement.

The eight bedrooms are traditionally decorated as befits a seaside hotel, with crisp white covers on the beds, pale walls, floral curtains, comfortable armchairs or sofas and gleaming modern bathrooms. All the rooms are named after famous Cornish gardens. Just three – Heligan, Cotehele and Trelissick – are sea-facing, while Glendurgan has partial sea views. Trebah is ideal for families, as it offers two interconnecting rooms.

The Food

Food is a major attraction here, with as many raw materials sourced locally as possible, and everything cooked freshly to order. Bar food includes some special sandwiches – treats like hand-picked white crabmeat with mayo – or there could be jacket potatoes and a ploughman's of two locally made cheeses with pickled onions, apple and real ale chutney. Elsewhere, there's a crowd-pleasing list that rolls out the likes of local mussels cooked in white wine and cream with fresh herbs and crusty bread, goes on to pan-fried scallops and bacon teamed with a cherry tomato salad or grilled pork sausages with potato purée, fried onions and red wine sauce, and finishes with a brandy snap basket of local ice cream with pineapple compote.

In addition, the restaurant offers a short choice two- or three-course set menu that could bring succulent rump of lamb niçoise with an olive tapenade and dressed leaves salad ahead of butter-baked breast of chicken on a spinach and leek risotto with a red wine jus, and vanilla bavarois with poached rhubarb for afters.

The Essentials

Time at the Bar!
10am-11pm
Food: 12-2.30pm, 6-9.30pm

What's the Damage?
Main courses from £8

Bitter Experience:
St Austell's Tribute, HSD and Tinners

Sticky Fingers:
Children welcome; children's menu

Muddy Paws:
Dogs welcome in the bar

Zzzzz:
8 rooms, £65-£85 per person

Anything Else?
Terrace, small car park

What To Do

Shop

ANTIQUES

Old School Antiques specialises in purveying fine furniture and clocks, while at Ruby Antiques, one of the largest dealers in the West Country, you'll find a large selection of good-quality chairs, sofas, chaises longues and mirrors.

Old School Antiques
Church Road, Penryn, Cornwall TR10 8DA
01736 375092

Ruby Antiques
Grays Wharf, Penryn, Cornwall TR10 8AE
01326 379322

CORNISH FARMHOUSE CHEESES

This well-stocked farm shop sells an interesting range of cows', goats' and ewes' milk cheeses – you can watch them being made and taste the goods before you buy. Unsurprisingly, the shop is one of Rick Stein's Food Heroes.

Menallack Farm
Treverva, Falmouth, Cornwall TR10 9BP
01326 340333
www.cornishfarmhousecheeses.com

CORNISH SMOKED FISH COMPANY

This great little fish shop, located right on the quayside, sells a plethora of traditionally oak-smoked fish – sea trout, salmon, mackerel, mussels and eels.

Charlestown, St Austell, Cornwall PL25 3NY
01726 72356

THE SQUARE GALLERY

There's a very good range of original Cornish contemporary art available in this friendly, inviting gallery, with paintings, prints, ceramics, sculpture, jewellery and textiles on show.

5 The Arcade, St Mawes, Cornwall TR2 5DT
01326 270720

Visit

GLENDURGAN GARDEN

Running down to the tiny village of Durgan and its tranquil sandy beach and rock pools, the garden has fine trees and plants, with glorious wild flowers carpeting the valley slopes. There's also a fantastic laurel maze.

Manwan Smith, Falmouth, Cornwall TR11 5JZ
01326 250906
www.nationaltrust.org.uk

LOST GARDENS OF HELIGAN

The now world-famous gardens span 80 acres, including a Georgian walled flower garden and huge vegetable garden. The Northern Summer House has views to St Austell and St Michael's Mount.

Pentewan, St Austell, Cornwall PL26 6EN
01726 845100
www.heligan.com

PENDENNIS CASTLE

With a stunning backdrop of the Fal estuary and Falmouth, Pendennis was built in the 1500s by Henry VIII to counter threats from France. Explore centuries of war-time history – or just relax, and take in the scenery with a cream tea.

Falmouth, Cornwall TR11 4LP
01326 316594
www.english-heritage.org.uk

TRELISSICK GARDEN

Beautifully set at the head of the Fal estuary, Trelissick has panoramic sea views, woodland walks and a unique collection of exotic plants. There's an interesting art and craft gallery and a cafe.

Trelissick Garden, Feock, Truro, Cornwall TR3 6QL
01872 862900
www.nationaltrust.org.uk

Activity

FERRY RIDE

Explore Cornwall from the sea, and take the ferry from Roseland to Truro, or along the dramatic coastline to Falmouth, where *Poldark* was filmed.

King Harry's Ferries
Feock, Cornwall TR3 6QJ
01872 862312
www.kingharryscornwall.co.uk

GOLF

Good things often come in small packages. Set in the magnificent grounds of the Killiow Estate, this is a picturesque 18-hole parkland course over only 4,000 yards, but it's a testing course in a tranquil setting with mature trees and natural water features.

Killiow Golf Club
Kea, Truro, Cornwall TR3 6AG
01862 240915

WATERSPORTS

Learn to sail, windsurf or drive a power boat on Cornwall's beautiful Roseland peninsula.

Roseland Paddle & Sail
Merrose Farm, Portscatho, Truro, Cornwall TR2 5EL
01872 580964

The Walk - *Guns and Guiding Lights*

Visit a church, lighthouse and gun battery at St Anthony Head.

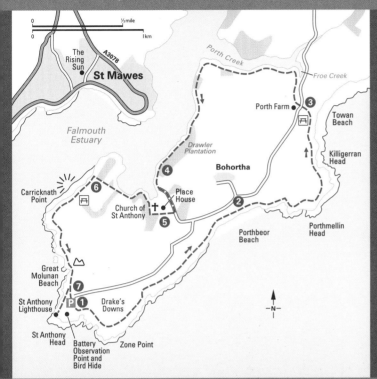

Walk Details

LENGTH: 6.5 miles (10.4km)

TIME: 4hrs

ASCENT: 230ft (70m)

PATHS: Excellent coastal and creekside footpaths. May be muddy in places during wet weather, 12 stiles

SUGGESTED MAP: aqua3 OS Explorer 105 Falmouth & Mevagissey

GRID REFERENCE: SW 848313

PARKING: National Trust St Anthony Head car park. Alternative parking on the route at Porth Farm (Point 3, SW 868329)

1 Leave St Anthony Head car park at the far end; keep ahead along the lane past the row of holiday cottages (left). Follow the coast path, parallel with the old military road alongside Drake's Downs, to where it passes above Porthbeor Beach at the junction with the beach access path.
2 Follow the coastal path round Porthmellin Head and Killigerran Head to Towan Beach. When you reach the junction with the beach access path, turn left and start walking inland. Bear left before the gate and go through the roofed passageway to the road.
3 Cross the road and through the gapway ('Porth Farm'), then down the surfaced drive. Turn into the entrance to the National Trust

car park, bear left along the path, ('Place via Percuil River'). Cross over the footbridge, turn right and follow the edge of Froe Creek to the stile into the woods. Follow the path alongside Porth Creek and through Drawler Plantation, ignoring the side paths ('Bohortha').
4 Pass the jetty for St Mawes ferry. Continue to the kissing gate and on to the road end in front of Place House. Go left along the road and climb uphill.
5 Turn right and cross the stile by the red gate ('Church of St Anthony and St Anthony Head'). Follow the path past gravestones to the church (control dogs here). Go up the steps opposite the church door and follow the path uphill. Bear right and at the

T-junction with the track, turn right. Follow the track ahead; at the bend, bear left. Cross the stile by the gate; follow the field edge uphill. Cross stile (seat to left) and keep ahead and downhill until the water's edge.
6 Turn left and follow the coastal path around Carricknath Point. Once past Great Molunan Beach, cross the causewayed dam above the quay; at the junction, keep right and follow the coast path signs. At the junction with surfaced track from the left, keep ahead to reach St Anthony Lighthouse.
7 Return to the junction and climb the steep track to the car park. Halfway up, another track leads right to the Battery Observation Post and bird hide above Zone Point.

Dartmoor Inn

Devon

The Inn

Karen and Philip Burgess and their staff imbue this 16th-century roadside coaching inn with warmth and personality. It's set against the backdrop of Dartmoor's spectacular landscape, just a short drive from Lydford Gorge, and is in great walking country. Inside, the relaxed, laid-back, lovingly restored and refurbished interior is made up of a rambling succession of wood- and slate-floored dining rooms, many with their own open fire or wood-burning stove, while a tiny bar dispensing pints of Otter Ale or Dartmoor Best Bitter keeps the pub tradition alive.

This is rural chic at its best, with a French country feel; the soft colours, lamps, and an eclectic mix of furnishings and tasteful bric-a-brac, which is picked up in the three bedrooms upstairs. All are spacious and highly individual. One, decorated in powder blue, is dominated by a lovely cream-painted French provincial-style bed; another has a high-beamed ceiling hung with a chandelier. All of the bedrooms have antique pieces, plus modern and very well-equipped bathrooms, while sofas and Roberts radios are standard issue – TVs, however, are available on request.

The Essentials

Time at the Bar!
11am-3pm, 6-11pm (closed Sun evening, Mon lunchtime)
Food: 12-2.30pm, 6-10pm

What's the Damage?
Main courses from £9

Bitter Experience:
Otter Ale, Dartmoor Best Bitter

Sticky Fingers:
Children welcome; children's menu on request

Muddy Paws:
Dogs welcome in the bar

Zzzzz:
3 rooms, £115

Anything Else?
Terrace, car park

The Food

The kitchen at the Dartmoor Inn is committed to using first-class ingredients sourced from the very best suppliers in Devon and Cornwall. Regularly changing menus list some comfortingly familiar traditional dishes alongside a range of imaginative modern ones, with the overall standard of skill, quality of ingredients and presentation being well above average for a country inn. Light bites in the bar may include devilled sprats with a mustard dressing, fish and shellfish cakes with a tomato sauce, and fish and chips served with deliciously different green mayonnaise.

In the evening the choice extends to Cornish crab and saffron risotto with parmesan, or avocado and asparagus salad with pea shoots and balsamic wine vinegar, while main courses may consist of croustade of hake and sea bass with saffron and leeks, and slow-cooked shank of lamb with thyme and shallots. Similarly, chargrilled rib steak with herb butter and Maris Piper chips is a classic done well.

There could be warm caramelised rhubarb cake with clotted cream for dessert, and an exceptionally well-chosen wine list at ungreedy prices proves a happy match to the food. There's a lovely walled patio for summer dining.

Dartmoor Inn, Lydford, Okehampton, Devon EX20 4AY

What To Do

Shop

COUNTRYMAN CIDER

Housed in the 15th-century stables block of a former coaching inn on the Devon side of the Tamar Valley, this traditional cider producer uses apples from local farms to make a range of craft ciders, plus cider brandy and country wines. Mead is also sold at the farm shop. Short tours and tastings are available.

Felldownhead, Milton Abbot, Tavistock, Devon PL19 0QR

01822 870226

POWDERMILLS POTTERY

A range of unusual and collectible wares produced by craftsmen and women mainly based on Dartmoor and in south Devon. Pottery is made on the premises, plus textiles, baskets and a range of delicious honey and chocolates.

Postbridge, Dartmoor, Devon PL20 6SP

01822 880263

www.powdermillspottery.com

SOUTH WEST CRAFTS

Deep in the heart of Tavistock, a craft gallery concentrating on established artists in the south west as well as displaying work from newcomers. You'll find bronze sculpture by Charlotte Marlow, ceramics by Peter Swanson, hand-made cushions and bags with traditional and contemporary designs by Ann-Marie Stone and fine silver jewellery made by Ann Powell. Wander around town and you'll come across several other art galleries and craft artisans specialising in Dartmoor-related subjects and works.

Church Lane, Tavistock, Devon PL19 8AA

01822 612689

www.southwestcrafts.co.uk

Visit

BUCKLAND ABBEY

Sir Francis Drake's former family home celebrates his life and achievements. The abbey dates from the 13th century and has some fine plasterwork and a series of galleries. Much of it was incorporated into a grand country house by Sir Richard Grenville – another of England's naval heroes – who subsequently sold the building to Drake. The grounds include a large herb garden, a tithe barn and craft workshops.

Yelverton, Devon PL20 6EY

01822 853607

www.nationaltrust.org.uk

DARTMOOR PRISON

It began as a holding point for French captives during the Napoleonic Wars and has seen riots and mutinies, chain-gangs, crime, punishment – and rehabilitation – in its long and disturbing history. Find out more and view fascinating memorabilia such as the original convict 'arrow' suit of the 1850s, at this unusual visitor centre.

Heritage Centre, Princetown, Devon PL20 6RR

01822 892130

www.dartmoor-prison.co.uk

MORWELLHAM QUAY

Explore the history of the Dartmoor copper mining industry at these renovated quays and old buildings set deep in the Tamar Valley at Great Consols Mine. Interpretive materials re-create the busy site at its height in the 1860s – including a tram trip into one of the old mines.

Tavistock, Devon PL19 8JL

01822 832766

www.morwellham-quay.co.uk

Activity

CANOEING

The Tamar Valley is an Area of Outstanding Natural Beauty and one of the most unusual and highly exhilarating ways to experience it is by Canadian canoe, starting from one of the ports and villages nestling in the wooded valley. Either a full- or a half-day trip (depending on the state of the tide) will probably reward you with a glimpse of a seal or even an otter as you glide past trees, quays and remote cottages well away from any roads.

Canoe Tamar

0845 430 1208

www.canoetamar.co.uk

FALCONRY

Find out all about the feeding and nesting habits of birds of prey and owls before taking the opportunity to fly one of these magnificent creatures yourself. The art of falconry can be savoured on a half- or full-day flying experience on the wild moors of western Dartmoor.

High Willsworth Farm, Peter Tavy, Tavistock, Devon PL19 9NB

01822 810112

www.totaltravel.co.uk (follow link)

TAVISTOCK TROUT FISHERY

A series of five lakes just outside Tavistock regularly yields enormous rainbow trout to dedicated fly-fishers who know the waters – fish touching 30lbs (14kg) have been caught here. You don't have to be an expert to try your hand: fly-fishing tuition can be arranged for absolute beginners and all the necessary equipment is provided.

Parkwood Road, Tavistock, Devon PL19 9JW

01822 615441

www.tavistocktroutfishery.co.uk

The Walk - On Dartmoor's Highest Tors

An ancient oak woodland and views of Yes Tor at Meldon Reservoir.

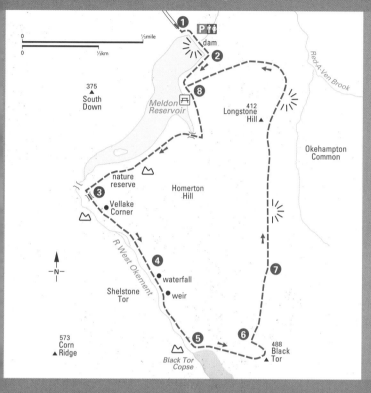

Walk Details

LENGTH: 4.25 miles (6.8km)

TIME: 2hrs 45min

ASCENT: 722ft (220m)

PATHS: Grassy tracks and open moorland

SUGGESTED MAP: aqua3 OS Outdoor Leisure 28 Dartmoor

GRID REFERENCE: SX 563917

PARKING: Car park at Meldon Reservoir (voluntary contributions)

① Walk up the stone steps by the toilets, go through the gate and turn left on the tarmac way towards the dam, ('Bridleway to Moor'). Cross over the dam here.

② Turn right along the track. The stile on the right leads to the waterside picnic area. Don't cross the stile, but leave the track here to go straight on, following the edge of the reservoir through the side valley and over the footbridge. The narrow path undulates to a steepish descent at the end of the reservoir to meet the broad marshy valley of West Okement River. Corn Ridge at 1,762ft (537m) lies ahead.

③ Cross the footbridge; take the path along the left edge of the valley, keeping to the bottom of the slope on the left. The path broadens as it travels uphill and becomes grassy as it rounds Vellake Corner above the river below right.

④ At top of the hill, the track levels; you can glimpse Black Tor Copse ahead. Follow the river upstream, past the waterfall and weir, right of the granite enclosure, and along the left bank through open moorland to enter Black Tor Copse.

⑤ Retrace your steps to emerge from the trees and veer right around the copse edge, walking uphill and aiming for the left outcrop of Black Tor on the ridge above. Walk through the bracken to the tor; there is no definite path here, but it's straightforward. The outcrop on the right rises to 1,647ft (502m).

⑥ Return to the grassy area north of tor. Turn right to continue away from the river valley behind, aiming for track visible ahead over Longstone Hill. To find the track go slightly downhill from tor to small stream. Turn left, then right towards 3 granite blocks marking the track.

⑦ Intermittent track runs straight across open moor (good views of the quarry ahead). Where Red-a-Ven Brook Valley appears below right, enjoy the view of Row Tor, West Mill Tor and Yes Tor. High Willhays, Dartmoor's highest tor, lies just out of sight to the right. The track veers left around the end of the hill and drops back to the reservoir.

⑧ Turn right to rejoin the track back over dam and back to the car park.

Bickley Mill

Devon

Bickley Mill, Stoneycombe, Kingskerswell, Newton Abbot, Devon TQ12 5LN

The Inn

Turn left for Kingskerswell at Two Mile Oak Cross on the A381 south of Newton Abbot to locate this 13th-century flour mill tucked in among narrow lanes in a hidden valley. The building was converted to an inn in 1971 and, more recently, spruced up and transformed by David and Tricia Smith into a stylish dining pub-with-rooms. Posh parasols adorn the decked terrace, while the secluded terrace, surrounded by tropical plants and trees, draws the summer crowds for alfresco pints of local Teignworthy Reel Ale or jugs of Pimms.

Rustic-chic sums up the decor in the rambling bar and dining areas, so expect glowing winter log fires, deep, striped sofas in cosy nooks, a mix of seagrass and wood flooring, chunky wooden tables, cushioned settles, and big, bold paintings on panelled walls. Original features abound throughout the nine simply decorated bedrooms, where you'll find old pine furnishings and wooden beds with quality cotton sheets and smart, coffee-coloured throws and cushions. The bathrooms are gradually being upgraded – all are spotlessly clean with good toiletries.

The Essentials

Time at the Bar!
11.30am-3pm, 6.30-11pm
(12-8pm Sun)
Food: 12-2pm, 6.30-9pm
(9.30pm Fri & Sat; 12-2.30pm Sun)

What's the Damage?
Main courses from £8.95

Bitter Experience:
Teignworthy Reel Ale, Otter Ale

Sticky Fingers:
Children welcome; children's menu

Muddy Paws:
Dogs allowed in the bar

Zzzzz:
9 rooms, £65-£80; single £50

Anything Else?
Garden, decked terrace, car park

The Food

Bill Gott's cooking draws inspiration from the Mediterranean and beyond, with the likes of Asian crab cakes with sweet chilli and lime sauce, and Mediterranean vegetable, artichoke and black olive lasagne with tallegio cheese making an appearance on his seasonally changing menu. Along with the good value 'Best of British' menu, which offers, for example, Lancashire hotpot, and chicken, leek and ham pie, as well as weekly fish specials, there's something to suit all tastes.

Gott sources meat from local farms, and fish from Brixham, perhaps gurnard, pan-fried with a mushroom and parsley sauce, whole brill served with a pea mint butter, and baked sea bass with anchovy butter. At lunch, tuck into chicken and bacon Caesar salad, smoked haddock and leek fishcake with caper and horseradish mayonnaise, or a rare roast beef and red onion marmalade sandwich. Evening main courses may include sea bream with roast beetroot, French bean and feta salad, and chargrilled rib-eye steak with fat chips. Leave room for sticky ginger pudding with vanilla ice cream, or rum and raisin cheesecake.

What To Do

Shop

BRIXHAM MARKET BAZAAR

This eclectic Sunday market has something for everyone, from antiques, artwork, pottery and textiles to bric-a-brac, memorabilia and a wealth of local produce.

Harbourside, Brixham, Devon

INDIGO BLUE ART GALLERY

A stylish contemporary gallery housing a stunning collection of original works, limited edition prints, sculpture, ceramics and bronzes, by both renowned and new artists.

294 Torquay Road, Preston, Paignton, Devon TQ3 2ER

01803 551347

www.indigoblue4art.com

TOTNES

Totnes is a mecca for foodies – throw a stone and you are bound to hit a good butcher's, cheese shop, fishmonger's or grocer's. The oddly named Riverford Goes To Town is an organic 'convenience' store, the urban outpost of the Watson family's nearby farm shop, where you'll find meat, poultry, fruit, veg and wine. The Ticklemore Cheese shop sells local artisan cheeses, including those from Sharpham. Cranch's Sweet Shop is packed with tooth-rotting goodies you haven't seen for years: sherbert lemons, pear drops and midget gems.

Riverford Goes To Town

38 High Street, Totnes, Devon TQ9 5YR

01803 868380

Ticklemore Cheese

1 Ticklemore Street, Totnes, Devon TQ9 5EJ

01803 865926

Cranch's Sweet Shop

35 Fore Street, Totnes, Devon TQ9 5HN

01803 864437

Visit

BRADLEY MANOR

This delightful medieval manor house has an impressive collection of pre-Raphaelite pictures and Arts and Crafts furniture.

Newton Abbot, Devon TQ12 6BN

01626 354513

www.nationaltrust.org.uk

COCKINGTON

A picture-postcard village, with narrow lanes opening out onto 'chocolate box' thatched cottages, old English gardens and tea rooms for classic cream teas. There's a Norman church, and Cockington Court, an impressive manor house. You'll get a good lunch at the stunning Drum Inn, which was designed by Lutyens.

Drum Inn, Cockington, Devon TQ2 6XA

01803 690264

GREENWAY

Agatha Christie's glorious, award-winning garden on the banks of the Dart estuary is a delightful haven of tranquillity, with an important collection of trees and shrubs featured in the BBC's *Hidden Gardens*. There's a very good cafe.

Galmpton, Brixham, Devon TQ5 0ES

01803 842382

www.nationaltrust.org.uk

UGBROOKE PARK

Set in a tranquil romantic valley, with a history covering 900 years, this impressive house was designed by Robert Adam, with the grounds landscaped by Capability Brown. The interior is outstanding, with fine furniture, painting and needlework.

Chudleigh, Devon TQ13 0AD

01626 852179

www.ugbrooke.co.uk

Activity

CYCLING

Enjoy superb coastal views on the route between Torquay and Brixham, or go off road on the trails just outside Cockington village – Simply the Bike will furnish you with guides and routes.

Simply the Bike

100–102 Belgrave Road, Torquay, Devon TQ2 5HZ

01832 200024

www.simplythebike.co.uk

OUTDOOR FILMS

Watch your favourite films under the stars, from cult classics to independent shorts. Bring your own wine and seating, or drive in and watch from the comfort of your car. Log on to the website for programme and location details.

Skylight Open Air Cinema

Available at 9 locations across the West Country

www.skylightcinema.co.uk

STEAM TRAIN RIDE

Experience unspoilt Devon from the comfort of a vintage steam train. The South Devon Railway line hugs the beautiful River Dart between Buckfastleigh and Totnes for 7 miles. Period uniforms, original station buildings and vintage motors complete the picture.

South Devon Railway

The Station, Dart Bridge Road, Buckfastleigh, Devon TQ11 0DZ

0845 345 1420

www.southdevonrailway.org

Bickley Mill, Stoneycombe, Kingskerswell, Newton Abbot, Devon TQ12 5LN

The Walk - *Around A Medieval Mansion*

A walking tour of the Dartington Hall Estate.

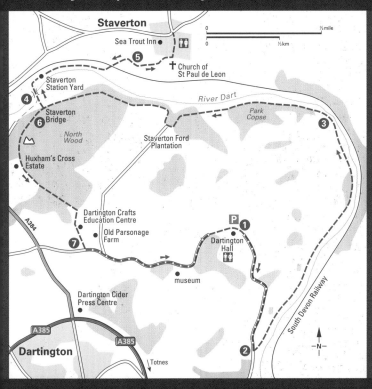

Walk Details

LENGTH: 5 miles (8km)

TIME: 2hrs 30min

ASCENT: 164ft (50m)

PATHS: Fields, woodland tracks and country lanes, 4 stiles

SUGGESTED MAP: aqua3 OS Explorer 110 Torquay & Dawlish

GRID REFERENCE: SX 799628

PARKING: Opposite entrance to Dartington Hall

NOTE: All paths on Dartington Hall Estate are permissive unless otherwise marked

❶ From the car park, turn left and walk downhill. Follow the pavement to the River Dart.

❷ Turn left over the stile and follow the river northwards (this area can be very muddy after rain). Pass over the stile, through the strip of woodland and over another stile into the meadow. At the end, cross the stile to reach the wooded track.

❸ Walk along the river edge of the next field (Park Copse is to the left). At the end of the field, cross the stile into Staverton Ford Plantation. Where the track veers left, go through the gate in the wall ahead, then turn right to follow the wooded path back towards the river. Keep on the path as it runs parallel with the river, becoming broad woodland track through North Wood. When you begin to see buildings through the trees on the right, leave the track and walk downhill to reach the metal gate and the lane.

❹ Turn right to cross Staverton Bridge. At the level crossing, turn right to pass through Staverton Station yard into the park-like area between the railway and the river. Follow the path across the single-track railway and walk on to the lane by Sweet William Cottage.

❺ Turn right and follow the lane to the end. Go ahead on the small path to pass the Church of St Paul de Leon, who was a 9th-century travelling preacher. Turn left at the lane to pass the public toilets and, if you need a break, go left at the junction to the Sea Trout Inn. After your break, retrace your steps to the metal gate past Staverton Bridge.

❻ Turn immediately right to rejoin the track. Follow the track until it runs downhill and bends to the left. Walk towards the gate on the right. Turn left on the narrow concrete path. Keep on the concrete path, which leaves the woodland and runs between the wire fences to the concrete drive at Dartington Crafts Education Centre. Follow the drive to reach the road.

❼ Turn left to pass Old Parsonage Farm. Keep on the road back to Dartington Hall, passing the gardens and the ruins of the original church (right), until you reach the car park on your left.

HOTEL

RESTAURANT

BAR FOOD

The Masons Arms

Devon

The Inn

Approach 'chocolate box' Branscombe through plunging narrow lanes (be prepared to reverse!) to find the creeper-clad inn deep in National Trust land and just a 10-minute stroll through fields to a pebbly beach and miles of stunning coastal path walks. The old stone building dates from the 14th century and occupies most of the village centre, with its neighbouring terraces of quaint cottages housing most of the inn's bedrooms, making it the perfect place to relax and unwind. Beyond the sun-trap front terrace, with its unusual thatched parasols, you'll find a cracking bar, which retains a strong period feel with its ancient ship's beams, worn slate floors, old settles and a huge inglenook fireplace, which not only warms the bar but also cooks the spit-roast joints of lamb and beef.

Stay in one of the quaint and compact beamed rooms in the inn or opt for one of the converted thatched cottages, where pretty rooms offer a mix of reproduction and antique furnishings, bold fabrics, big comfortable beds, fresh flowers and valley or sea views. The most luxurious have splendid four-poster beds, deep sofas and first-class bathrooms – Cottage 12 even has a private terrace and parking space.

The Essentials

Time at the Bar!
11am-11pm
Food: 12-2pm, 7-9pm

What's the Damage?
Main courses from £9.50;
fixed-price dinner £27.50

Bitter Experience:
Masons Ale, Otter Bitter,
Branoc ales, guest beers

Sticky Fingers:
Children welcome in the bar
and rooms

Muddy Paws:
Dogs welcome in the bar

Zzzzz:
22 rooms, £80-£165

Anything Else?
Terrace, garden, car park

The Food

Branscombe beach draws the crowds in summer, so expect the terrace, rustic bar and beamed restaurant to throng with drinkers and diners quaffing local Branoc ales or farm cider and tucking into some top-notch food. Locally grown produce, especially excellent fish and crab landed on the beach, and beef and lamb reared in the village, feature on changing menus.

From ploughman's lunches and crab sandwiches, the choice in the bar extends to smoked haddock and leek chowder, and steamed mussels with garlic, lemon and coriander. Main courses may take in garlic roasted lamb shank, venison and mushroom pudding with red wine jus, seafood mixed grill, and West Country lobster and spring onion risotto. For pudding, try the dark chocolate tart with chocolate sauce. Dinner taken in the restaurant is a fixed-price affair, perhaps commencing with ham hock and baby onion terrine with home-made piccalilli, continuing with confit of aromatic duck leg on truffle oil mash with pear compote, and concluding with caramelised banana and maple syrup tart tatin with toffee ice cream, or a board of West Country cheeses.

What To Do

Shop

EXETER FARMER'S MARKET
This is one of TV chef's Rick Stein's favourite food markets, where you can buy a range of speciality cheeses, organic meat and vegetables, game, bread, cakes and pastries.

Fore Street/South Street, Exeter, Devon
01392 665757

HAYMAN'S BUTCHERS
Take home some award-winning sausages from this artisan butcher's, as well as meaty delights such as pressed brisket, steak and kidney pudding, home-cured ham and bacon. The shop has the distinction of being one of Rick Stein's Food Heroes.

6 Church Street, Sidmouth, Devon EX10 8LY
01395 512877
www.haymansbutchers.co.uk

HONITON ANTIQUES
Just a few miles from the coast, Honiton has become known as the antiques capital of the Southwest. A walk down the high street will reward you with any number of good antique dealers, selling everything from French painted furniture, clocks and lace to teddy bears, tin soldiers and chandeliers.

The Grove Antiques Centre
55 High Street, Honiton, Devon EX14 8PW
01404 43377
www.groveantiquescentre.com

Honiton Antique Toys
38 High Street, Honiton, Devon EX14 1PJ
01404 41194

Jane Strickland & Daughters
Godford Mill, Awliscombe, Honiton, Devon EX14 1PW
01404 44221
www.jsdantiques.co.uk

Visit

A LA RONDE
A quirky, 16-sided house built by cousins Jane and Mary Parminter on their return from a grand tour of Europe in 1796. It contains mementos from their travels, an extraordinary feather frieze and shell-encrusted gallery. Stunning views over the Exe estuary.

Summer Lane, Exmouth, Devon EX8 5BD
01395 265514
www.nationaltrust.org.uk

BICTON PARK
An extraordinary glass palm house, an Italian garden designed by Versailles landscaper Le Nôtre, a fernery and a shell house.

East Budleigh, Budleigh Salterton, Devon EX9 7BJ
01395 568465
www.bictongardens.co.uk

THE OLD BAKERY
When it closed in the late 1980s, The Old Bakery was the last traditional working bakery in Devon.The original baking equipment has been preserved and you can see it now in the enchanting tea room.

Branscombe, Devon EX12 3DB
01392 881691
www.nationaltrust.org.uk

OTTERTON MILL
There's something for everyone here – art gallery, restaurant, working water mill and bakery, as well as music venue. Nestled beside the River Otter in a beautiful valley a mile from the coast, Otterton is a great place to shop, eat and listen!

Summer Lane, Budleigh Salterton, Devon EX9 7HG
01395 568521
www.ottertonmill.com

Activity

FOSSIL HUNTING
Explore Devon's Jurassic coast – you're sure to unearth an ammonite or two with the assistance of experienced father-and-son fossil-hunting team Brandon and Ian Lennon. Meet them at the Millennium Clock at the bottom of Broad Street, Lyme Regis.

Brandon and Ian Lennon
07944 664757

GOLF
Axe Hill Golf Club is a stunning 18-hole course, with breathtaking views over Lyme Bay and the Axe Valley. This family-run outfit is a little gem of a club, where you're sure to get a warm welcome.

Squires Lane, Axmouth, Devon EX12 4AB
01297 24371

SEA FISHING
Take to the sea and bag yourself some mackerel off the coast of Beer, a quiet, quaint fishing village with a delightful beach.

Kim Aplin
01297 21955

TRAM RIDE
Seaton Tramway has been running since the early 1950s, and the 3-mile trip through the Axe Valley to Colyford is charming. You'll pass through the ancient town of Colyton (a Saxon village with a wonderful maze of narrow streets, quaint shops and some fine art galleries) and, if you're lucky, you'll observe some of the abundant wading bird life en route.

Seaton Tramway, Riverside Depot, Harbour Road, Seaton, Devon EX12 2NQ
01297 20375
www.tram.co.uk

The Walk - Along The East Devon Cliffs

A stroll along the Devonshire coast near Branscombe.

Walk Details

LENGTH: 6.25 miles (10.1km)

TIME: 3hrs 30min

ASCENT: 492ft (150m)

PATHS: Coast path (one steep ascent), country lanes, 14 stiles

SUGGESTED MAP: aqua3 OS Explorer 115 Exeter & Sidmouth

GRID REFERENCE: SY 167890

PARKING: Unsurfaced car park at Weston

1 From the car park, take the track over the stile on to the East Devon Heritage Coast path ('Weston Mouth'). After 0.5 mile (800m), at the stile and gate, go straight on; veer left across the field; join the coast path at another stile.

2 Go left, steeply uphill (wooden steps), to top of Weston Cliff. A kissing gate leads on to Coxe's Cliff; the path runs diagonally away from the coast via a deep combe towards another stile in the top left corner of the field. Cross the next field and stile on to grassland above Littlecombe Shoot.

3 Pass the coast path marker ahead and 2 stands of gorse (left). Turn diagonally left, away from the cliff, towards a gap in the gorse hedge. Head for the gate in top left corner of next field; turn left down the track to a lane at Berry Barton.

4 Turn right down the lane to the Fountain Head pub. Turn right again down the valley, passing thatched cottages and St Winifred's Church (right). Continue downhill past the post office and Forge to St Branoc's Well and the village hall.

5 Turn right opposite Parkfield Terrace down a lane ('Branscombe Mouth'). Shortly, the farm gate leads to a well-signposted path through a field to a footbridge and gate. Go through the next meadow and gate. Turn right over the wooden bridge and gate to Branscombe Mouth.

6 Turn immediately right through the kissing gate to join the coast path signs uphill beneath the coastguard cottages (now private). Go through the open gateway and left into the woods via the stile. Ignore the paths left and right until, after 2 stiles and 0.5 mile (800m), a signpost points left between grassy hummocks towards the cliffs.

7 Follow the coastal footpath signs to rejoin the cliff edge, over the stile on to Littlecombe Shoot. Retrace your steps over 2 stiles to Coxe's Cliff, then take the stile and kissing gate on to Weston Cliff. Turn immediately right through a kissing gate into wildflower meadow.

8 Pass the cottage and outbuildings (right) over 2 stiles and on to the track leading to the tarmac lane. Go left to Weston and your car.

Tarr Farm Inn

Somerset

The Essentials

Time at the Bar!
11am-11pm
Food: 12-3pm, 6.30-9.30pm

What's the Damage?
Main courses from £12

Bitter Experience:
Exmoor Ale, Gold and Wild Cat

Sticky Fingers:
Children over the age of 10 welcome

Muddy Paws:
Dogs welcome; overnight stay £8

Zzzzz:
9 rooms, £65 per person per night

Anything Else?
Garden, car park

The Inn

Combine a stylish appearance with a warm, attentive and pleasingly informal atmosphere, add a mix of restaurant, hotel and traditional pub, and you have an ideal place to visit. That's Tarr Farm, which dates from the 16th century and is set in its own wooded 40 acres just a short stroll from the ancient Clapper Bridge at Tarr Steps. In summer, jaw-dropping views out over the valley and river mean that garden tables are at a premium. Inside, there's a comfortable feel to the traditional-looking beamed bar with its mix of slate floor, window seats, benches and various bits and bobs, while the smart dining room has polished oak and pine tables.

The lavish bedrooms are impressive, too. Light, contemporary and showing considerable attention to detail, they include beds made up with fine Egyptian cotton sheets, spacious bathrooms with power showers and full-size baths, as well as fluffy bathrobes and towels, satellite TV alongside DVD and CD players. There are home-made biscuits and fresh milk in the fridge, broadband access and desk space, even an iron and ironing board. And it's all very peaceful.

Tarr Farm Inn, Tarr Steps, Dulverton, Exmoor National Park, Devon TA22 9PY

The Food

While the dining room has all the right period trimmings, the food is a fresh blast of modern ideas, with the sound kitchen emphasising quality, locally sourced produce wherever possible. So, expect braised Exmoor meatballs served on a pea pancake with onion jus, or pumpkin soup with parmesan and sautéed wild mushrooms among starters. Chump of Exmoor lamb with dauphinoise potatoes, red onion confit and rosemary and lamb sauce, and braised, roasted belly of pork with celeriac mash show the meatier range of main courses. Fish from Cornwall is something of a speciality – perhaps poached fillet of brill with roasted shallots, crispy pancetta and a rich shiraz sauce, or seared fillet of sea bass with pressed leek terrine, mussel and chervil sauce.

Chocolate mocha tart with vanilla and orange-scented mascarpone or baked lemon cheesecake with a tuile biscuit filled with blackberry compote might stand out among ice creams and sorbets on the dessert list, but the selection of West Country cheeses – say, a St Endellion brie or Cornish yarg – make a great savoury alternative.

What To Do

Shop

BICKLEIGH MILL

This 18th-century working water mill is a great shopping venue. There's a good restaurant, too, set in pretty grounds with lovely walks.

Bickleigh, Tiverton, Somerset EX16 8RG
01884 855419
www.bickleighmill.com

HINDON ORGANIC FARM

An idyllic setting for a farm on 500 acres of the National Trust's Holnicote Estate, selling home-reared organic meat.

Minehead, Exmoor, Somerset TA24 8SH
01643 705244
www.exmoororganicmeat.co.uk

LANTIC GALLERY

A light and airy space, exhibiting and selling an eclectic selection of modern paintings, ceramics, sculpture, jewellery and glass.

38 Gold Street, Tiverton, Somerset EX16 6PY
01884 259888
www.lanticgallery.co.uk

SOUTH MOLTON

A pretty market town, with great shops. Try the Moorland Larder for Exmoor trout and venison, the Melchior chocolate factory, and for all your gardening and DIY needs, Mole Valley Farmers.

Moorland Larder
113 East Street, South Molton,
Devon EX36 3DB
01769 573554

Melchior Chocolates
Tinto House, Station Road, South Molton,
Devon EX36 3LL
01769 574442

Mole Valley Farmers
Station Road, South Molton,
Devon EX36 3BH
01769 573431

Visit

DUNSTER CASTLE

A picture-book romantic castle in a dramatic hilltop location. The gardens are terraced with sub-tropical plants, and you'll find the National Collection of strawberry trees here, a lovely Mediterranean garden, and the famous Dunster lemons. Don't miss the amazing oak staircase and ornate gothic plasterwork inside the castle.

Dunster, Minehead, Somerset TA24 6SL
01643 821314
www.nationaltrust.org.uk

GAULDEN MANOR GARDENS

A small but charming historic manor house, Gaulden is set in a beautiful valley between the Quantock hills. There's a 'secret' garden beyond the Monks' fish pond planted entirely with white flowers, where hundreds of butterflies visit.

Tollan, Lydeard St Lawrence, Taunton,
Somerset TA4 3PN
01984 667213

KNIGHTSHAYES COURT

A romantic Victorian country house with gothic-style splendours inside, and celebrated formal gardens with lily ponds and humorous topiary.

Bolham, Tiverton, Devon EX16 7RQ
01884 254665
www.nationaltrust.org.uk

SELWORTHY

Selworthy is a perfect time-capsule English village. All Saints church, on the side of a hill, has a staggering view of the Vale of Porlock – inside is a painted nave ceiling and 18th-century gallery.

All Saints Church, Selworthy,
Somerset TA24 8TJ
01643 862452

Activity

FOSSIL HUNTING

Watchet is a delightful small harbour town with a maritime history going back two millennia. On the beach between Watchet and Warren Bay, alabaster can be found in the cliffs. It's also a rich fossil-hunting area – author Daniel Defoe was very impressed with both the quality and quantity of ammonites he found here!

STEAM TRAIN RIDE

Take a nostalgic journey on a steam train through stunning countryside and glimpse the cliffs and coast of the Bristol Channel.

West Somerset Railway
The Railway Station, Minehead,
Somerset TA24 5BG
01643 704996
www.west-somerset-railway.co.uk

TROUT FISHING

Set in the unrivalled surroundings of Exmoor National Park, this is a quiet, secluded spot for a bit of fishing. Expect to land rainbow, blue and tiger trout.

Combe Sydenham Fisheries
Monksilver, Somerset TA4 4JG
01984 656273, 07795 096020
www.somersetfishing.co.uk

WATERSPORTS

There's plenty to occupy you at Wimbleball Lake – true watersports enthusiasts can try their hand at canoeing, windsurfing or sailing, while others may enjoy a pleasant stroll through the surrounding woodland and meadows.

Wimbleball Lake, Brompton Regis,
Dulverton, Somerset TA22 6NW
01398 371460
www.swlakestrust.org.uk

The Walk - Bronze-Age Trackways at Tarr Steps

A walk that visits one of the world's 'oldest' bridges.

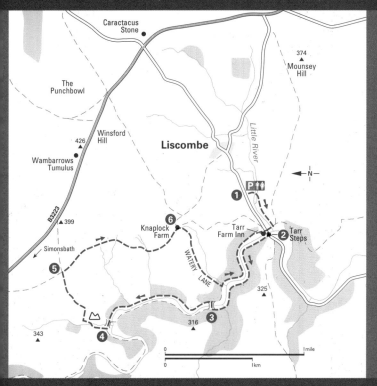

Walk Details

LENGTH: 5.25 miles (8.4km)

TIME: 2hrs 30min

ASCENT: 700ft (210m)

PATHS: Riverside paths and field tracks, some open moor, no stiles

SUGGESTED MAP: aqua3 OS Outdoor Leisure 9 Exmoor

GRID REFERENCE: SS 872323

PARKING: Just over 0.25 mile (400m) east of Tarr Steps – can be full in summer. (Parking at Tarr Steps for disabled people only)

❶ Leave the bottom of the car park by the footpath on the lefthand side ('Scenic Path'). This leads down to the left of the road to Little River, crossing 2 footbridges to Tarr Steps, over the River Barle, ahead.

❷ Cross Tarr Steps, turning upstream at the far side ('Circular Walk'). Follow the river bank path past the wire footbridge. After 0.75 mile (1.2km) cross the side-stream via the stepping stones, then reach the footbridge over the river.

❸ Cross the river, and continue upstream (the river is now left). After 0.75 mile (1.2km) the path crosses a wooden footbridge, then divides at a signpost.

❹ Turn right, uphill ('Winsford Hill'). The wide path goes up through the woods with the stream on the right. Where it meets the track, turn briefly right to ford the stream; continue uphill on the narrower signed path. At the low bank with beech trees turn right to the gate; follow the foot of the field to the tarred lane. Go up to the cattle grid on to open moor. Bear right on a faint track heading up between the gorse bushes. After 250yds (229m) reach the 4-way signpost.

❺ Turn right ('Knaplock') and slant down to the hedge corner. Follow the hedge briefly, then take the path that slants gradually up into the moor. After 170yds (155m) the sign points back down towards moor-foot banking. Beech bank crosses ahead: aim for the lower end, where soft track leads forward, with occasional blue paint-spots. After 0.25 mile (400m) the track turns downhill, then back to the left (it becomes firmer as it reaches Knaplock Farm).

❻ At the farm buildings turn downhill ('Tarr Steps'), on to the muddy farm track. Where this turns off into the field, continue ahead on the stony track, Watery Lane. After an initial descent this becomes a smooth path down to the River Barle. Turn left, downstream. When the path rises above the river, look for the fork on the right ('Footpath'). This rejoins the river to pass through open field. Cross the road and turn left up the scenic path to return to your car.

✳ Tarr Steps on the River Bale, Exmoor National Park, Devon

The Farmers Inn

Somerset

The Inn

To locate this isolated inn, come off the M5 at junction 25 and take the A358 south for a mile, then head right at the Nag's Head and follow the brown 'inn' signs for two miles down winding narrow lanes, deep into unspoilt Somerset countryside. Taunton is just over the hill, but you wouldn't believe it as you take in the amazing views across the Somerset Levels.

Tom and Debbie Lush have injected new life into this rambling 16th-century inn, smartening up the rustic bar with scrubbed oak tables and placing squashy leather sofas around the roaring log fire, and creating a civilised yet relaxed dining area, beyond which you will find a flower-decked terrace with posh benches and brollies just right for sunny days.

Decide to stay the night and you will be hard-pressed to know which of the five bedrooms to choose. Some are large, others are vast, yet all have been kitted out with style and good taste with their antique furnishings, polished wooden floors and gleaming bathrooms with deep claw-foot baths. For a sophisticated continental feel and views across sheep-grazed fields to the Quantock Hills, book the Quantock Room.

The Essentials

Time at the Bar!
12-3pm, 6-12pm
Food: 12-2pm (2.30pm Sat-Sun),
7-9pm (9.30pm Thu-Sun)

What's the Damage?
Main courses from £10.75

Bitter Experience:
Otter Ale, Sharp's Doom Bar

Sticky Fingers:
Children welcome; small portions
available

Muddy Paws:
Dogs welcome in the bar

Zzzzz:
5 rooms, £70-£120

Anything Else?
Terrace, garden, car park

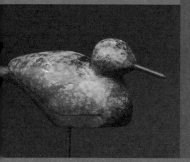

The Food

In keeping with the upscale refurbishment of the pub and the addition of the chic bedrooms, both the quality of the food and the style of cooking have improved markedly. You'll find a daily-changing menu that lists imaginative modern British dishes, prepared with some skill, with the focus firmly on seasonal local produce. Start with home-made bread and olives, then follow with butternut squash and root ginger soup, potted smoked trout pâté with soda bread and mixed leaves, or whole grilled sardines served with Napoli sauce and focaccia bread.

If you are in the mood for fish, there may be home-made fishcakes with roasted Mediterranean vegetables, parsley sauce and fries, or pan-fried monkfish with braised leeks and a pancetta, cream and fennel-seed sauce, with meatier mains including rib-eye steak with baked garlic and red onion and rosemary jus, or pan-fried chicken with mushroom and thyme jus.

Finish with the mouthwatering dark chocolate and mint mousse with pistachio anglaise. A refreshing pint of Otter Ale tapped straight from the barrel and a selection of excellent wines by the glass add to the appeal.

What To Do

Shop

SHEPPY'S CIDER

There was a time when each farm made its own cider in this neck of the woods – no longer, though at Three Bridges, the Sheppys have maintained a tradition that began in the early 1800s. The 370 acres farmed here produce award-winning ciders that you can take home to enjoy. You can sample the wares in the cafe, tour the orchards, and stock up in the shop, which also sells the farm's wonderful home-reared Longhorn meat.

Three Bridges, Bradford-on-Tone, Taunton,
Somerset TA4 1ER
01823 461233
www.sheppyscider.com

TAUNTON ANTIQUES MARKET

With more than 130 dealers, this is one of the West Country's biggest markets, and you'll find a huge range of desirables here, from Victorian silver to 20th-century ceramics. Once you've browsed for bargains, you can take a breather in the Market Cafe which sells good coffee and home-made cakes.

27-29 Silver Street, Taunton,
Somerset TA1 3DH
01823 289327

Visit

COLERIDGE COTTAGE

Samuel Taylor Coleridge lived here with his family for three years from 1797. In the house you can see his writing ephemera, pictures of friends and family, and letters penned in his distinctive handwriting. His good friends William Wordsworth and his sister Dorothy were regular visitors, and it was on one such occasion that Coleridge and Wordsworth went on one of their nocturnal walks, and Coleridge's *The Rime of the Ancient Mariner* took shape. Walk along The Coleridge Way, starting at the cottage, to see the isolated farm house where he wrote the opium-inspired symbolic poem *Kubla Khan*.

35 Lime Street, Nether Stowey, Bridgwater,
Somerset TA5 1NQ
01278 732662
www.nationaltrust.org

HESTERCOMBE GARDENS

The gardens at Hestercombe were designed by Sir Edwin Lutyens and planted by Gertude Jekyll, and you'll see beautiful stonework, an orangery and pergolas. As well as the formal gardens, there are 40 acres of 18th-century landscaped parkland with woodland walks, temples, cascades and breathtaking views across the Vale of Taunton to the Blackdown Hills. The contemporary visitor centre has a plant centre, gift shop and cafe serving good home-made meals.

Cheddon Fitzpaine, Taunton,
Somerset TA2 8LG
01823 413923
www.hestercombegardens.com

STUART INTERIORS AT BARRINGTON COURT

Specialising in medieval, Tudor and Georgian interior design, Stuart Interiors are a well-established architectural design company with their showrooms at Barrington Court, a National Trust Elizabethan manor house – be inspired by what they do and steal ideas for your own home. Take a stroll round the Gertrude Jekyll-inspired garden while you're here; it is laid out in a series of walled rooms, including the White Garden, the Rose and Iris Garden and the Lily Garden. There is also a well-stocked arboretum and a kitchen garden that supplies the restaurant with home-grown ingredients. Plants and garden produce are on sale in the shop and make great take-home memories.

Barrington Court, Ilminster,
Somerset TA19 0NQ
01460 240349
www.stuartinteriors.ltd.uk

Activity

GOLF

Burnham & Berrow Golf Club has an idyllic 18-hole championship course built into sandy dunes – you'll find the layout challenging, with ravine-like valleys for fairways, and lots of natural hollows and humps. Burnham hosts one of the qualifying events for the British Open Championships, so work on your handicap and you may walk out with the giants!

Burnham & Berrow Golf Club,
St Christopher's Way, Burnham-on-Sea
Somerset TA8 2PE
01278 783137
www.burnham-on-sea.com/golf

TAUNTON RACES

If you enjoy the 'sport of kings', why not have a little flutter at the youngest National Hunt racecourse in Britain? The Taunton racecourse is beautifully located, with views out towards the wooded slopes of the Blackdown Hills.

Orchard Portman, Taunton,
Somerset TA3 7BL
01823 337172
www.tauntonracecourse.co.uk

The Walk - Woodlands at Blackdown Hills

Prior's Park Wood is at its best with autumn's colours or spring's bluebells.

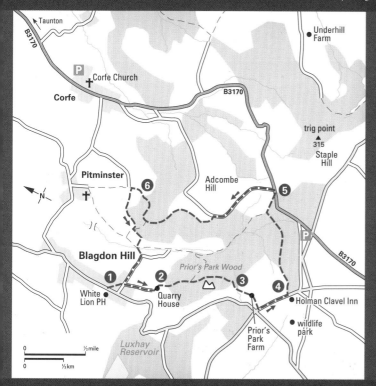

Walk Details

LENGTH: 5 miles (8km)

TIME: 2hrs 40min

ASCENT: 700ft (210m)

PATHS: Rugged in Prior's Park Wood, otherwise comfortable, 7 stiles

SUGGESTED MAP: aqua3 OS Explorer 128 Taunton & Blackdown Hills

GRID REFERENCE: ST 211182

PARKING: Roadside pull-off between post office and White Lion, at Blagdon Hill

❶ The walk starts at the phone booth opposite the White Lion, a handsome 17th-century inn. Cross the stile and follow along the left edge of the triangular field to another stile into Curdleigh Lane. Cross into ascending Quarry Lane. Bend left between the buildings of Quarry House, on to the track running up into Prior's Park Wood.

❷ From mid-April, Prior's Park Wood is delightful with bluebells and other wild flowers. It is also aglow with the reds and golds of autumn (but possibly muddy) in late October and November. Where the main track bends left and descends slightly, keep uphill on a smaller one. This track eventually declines into muddy trod, slanting up and

leftwards to reach a small gate at the top edge of the wood.

❸ Pass along the wood's top edge to reach the gate. Red-and-white poles mark the line across the next field that leads to another gate. After 50yds (46m) turn right, between the buildings of Prior's Park Farm to its access track and road. Turn left and follow the road with care (this is a fairly fast section) towards the Holman Clavel Inn.

❹ Just before the inn turn left onto the forest track. Where the track ends a small path runs ahead, zig-zagging down before crossing the stream. At the wood's edge turn right up a wider path to the B3170.

❺ At once turn left on the lane ('Feltham'). After 0.5 mile (800m), a

wide gateway on the left leads to an earth track. This runs along the top of Adcombe Wood then down inside it, giving a very pleasant descent.

❻ Once below the wood follow the track downhill for 180yds (165m). Look for a gate with a signpost on the lefthand side. Now go through the gate and follow the hedge on the right to a stile and footbridge, then bend left, below the foot of the wood, to another stile. Ignore the stile leading into the wood on the left, but continue along the wood's foot to the next field corner. Here a further stile enters the wood but turn right, beside the hedge, to the concrete track. Turn left – the track becomes Curdleigh Lane, leading you back into Blagdon Hill once more.

The Rock Inn

Somerset

The Inn

True to its name, a third of this half-timbered former smithy and coaching inn is carved out of the rock, with parts of it visible in the bar next to the open fire. Set in a stunning green valley beside the babbling River Tone on the southern fringe of Exmoor, the inn dates back over 400 years and has been comfortably upgraded by Matt Harvey and his mother Joanna Oldman, who also owns a farm in the valley. Expect a laid-back feel in the rustic bar, with its worn wood floor, scrubbed tables and local farmers downing pints of Exmoor Gold. Steps lead to the small dining room, a cosy space with a handful of chunky tables topped with church candles and Riedel glasses.

Rooms at the inn are traditional, some simply kitted out with modern pine, others with big brass beds with smartly tiled modern bathrooms; all have plasma screens, Egyptian cotton sheets, and are very comfortable. One room boasts a wood-burning stove, leather sofa, antique pine bed, and a swish bathroom with walk-in power shower.

The Rock Inn, Waterrow, Taunton, Somerset TA4 2AX

The Food

Expect good country cooking using top-notch produce sourced from local farms, Exmoor shoots and select suppliers, notably superb Angus beef from the family farm, free-range pork reared in the village and locally grown seasonal soft fruits. The constantly changing menu lists pub favourites – lasagne and salad – alongside more inventive meals, such as a starter of fresh pea and mint soup with cheese and onion bread, or a well-presented main course of Somerset lamb chump, served with onion and rosemary purée and a red wine and redcurrant jus.

Delicious alternatives may take in Angus beef, red wine and baby onion pie, pork fillet with Dijon mustard, scrumpy cider and cream sauce, or fresh fish delivered daily from Brixham, perhaps sea bass with red and yellow pepper confit, Ladram Bay lobster, or beer-battered haddock with chips and home-made tartare sauce. Leave room for home-made rhubarb and custard cheesecake and wash down with a decent house wine.

The Essentials

Time at the Bar!
12-3pm, 6-11pm
Food: 12-2.30pm, 6.30-9.30pm
(7-9pm Sun)

What's the Damage?
Main courses from £7.50

Bitter Experience:
Otter Ale, Cotleigh Tawny,
Exmoor Gold

Sticky Fingers:
Children welcome; children's menu
and half portions available

Muddy Paws:
Dogs allowed in the bar

Zzzzz:
8 rooms, £70; single £40

Anything Else?
Car park

What To Do

Shop

FARMERS' MARKET
All the products sold at the stalls lining this pretty market square are fresh, and locally grown and reared – fruit and vegetables, meat, bread and pastries, eggs and much more.

Pannier Market, Tiverton, Devon
www.tiverton-market.co.uk

LYNG COURT FARM
Lyng Court produces organic lamb and beef from Normandy breeds on the Somerset Levels. Reared naturally on grass and home-grown barley, meat is available directly from the farm, but call first to reserve your order.

West Lyng, Taunton, Somerset TA3 5AP
01823 490510

QUINCE HONEY FARM
This family-run farm, founded in 1949, has 1,500 beehives set on rolling hills, providing distinctive heather honey, as well as various honey-related goodies: ice cream, chutney, marmalade and skincare products. You can safely watch the bees doing their work!

North Road, South Molton, Devon EX36 3AZ
01769 572401

www.quincehoney.co.uk

SHAKSPEARE GLASS
Here, the memorably named Will Shakspeare makes his beautiful, three-dimensional hand-blown glass pieces in a workshop with a gallery attached. His work is world-renowned, and you can choose from jewellery, bowls, vases and wall hangings. He also shows work by other glass artists.

Riverside Place, Taunton, Somerset TA1 1JJ
01823 333422

www.shakspeareglass.co.uk

Visit

CLEEVE ABBEY
There is evidence of around 800 years of history at this picturesque Cistercian abbey, representing the most complete and unaltered set of monastic cloister buildings in England. Especially interesting are the gatehouse and the 15th-century refectory, with its glorious angel roof and unusual painted chamber. The great dormitory is renowned as one of the finest examples of its kind in the country.

Washford, Somerset TA23 0PS
01984 640377

www.english-heritage.org.uk

COLERIDGE COTTAGE
The poet Samuel Taylor Coleridge moved to this modest house in 1796 with his wife Sara and young son David, and it was here that he wrote *Kubla Khan* and *The Rime of the Ancient Mariner*. His great friends William and Dorothy Wordsworth lived close by, where they walked in the countryside and wrote some of their best-known poetry.

35 Lime Street, Nether Stowey, Bridgwater, Somerset TA5 1NQ
01278 732662

www.nationaltrust.org.uk

DUNSTER
There are over 200 listed buildings in this medieval village near the coast. Visit Dunster Castle in its dramatic hilltop location overlooking Exmoor and the Bristol Channel, and the Old Yarn Market in the High Street, a reminder of Exmoor's wool and cloth trade.

Dunster Castle
Dunster, Minehead, Somerset TA24 6SL
01643 821314

www.nationaltrust.org.uk

Activity

HORSE RACING
Taunton Racecourse is the youngest National Hunt course in the country, and definitely one of the most attractive, with outstanding views across the course to the wooded slopes of the Blackdown Hills.

Taunton Racecourse
Orchard Portman, Taunton, Somerset TA3 7BL
01823 337172

www.tauntonracecourse.co.uk

HORSE RIDING
This pony centre is dedicated to the promotion and conservation of Exmoor ponies, and you can have a great day's trekking in magnificent countryside, enjoying the wildlife and flora at a leisurely pace.

Exmoor Pony Centre
Ashwick, Dulverton, Somerset TA22 9QE
01398 323093

www.moorlandmousietrust.org.uk

STEAM TRAIN RIDE
Recapture the magic of the 1950s branch line country railway – there are 20 miles of glorious Somerset scenery to take in as the train rolls back the years beside the Quantock hills to the Bristol Channel coast.

West Somerset Railway
The Railway Station, Minehead, Somerset TA24 5BG
01643 704996

www.west-somerset-railway.co.uk

TROUT FISHING
Enjoy a day's fly fishing in Exmoor National Park on a privately owned estate in 600 acres of woodland.

Combe Sydenham Fisheries
Monksilver, Somerset TA4 4JG
01984 656273, 07795 096020

www.somersetfishing.co.uk

The Walk - Wiveliscombe and the River Tone

A pretty village and a wooded riverside on the edge of the Brendons.

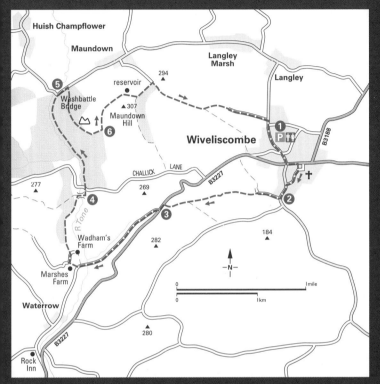

Walk Details

LENGTH: 6 miles (9.7km)

TIME: 3hrs 15min

ASCENT: 1,000ft (300m)

PATHS: Tracks, a quiet lane, a few field edges, 1 stile

SUGGESTED MAP: aqua3 OS Explorer 128 Taunton & Blackdown Hills

GRID REFERENCE: ST 080279

PARKING: North Street, Wiveliscombe

❶ Turn left out of the car park into the Square; head down the High Street and turn left at the traffic lights (Church Street). Turn right, down the steps under the arch, to Rotton Row. Continue to South Street; turn left along pavement.
❷ At end of 30mph limit turn.right, into lane; go ahead through gate with footpath sign. Cross the stile ahead, and bottom edges of 2 fields. Stile in hedge ahead has grown over, so head up to left to gateway before returning to foot of field to reach farm buildings. Go up lefthand edge of field above to a gate on to B3227.
❸ Turn left, then right into lane heading downhill. After 0.75 mile (1.2km) it crosses River Tone and bends left at Marshes Farm. Keep

ahead, on track marked by broken bridleway sign. Do not turn right here into track towards Wadham's Farm; keep uphill to deeply sunken lane. Turn right, descending towards farm, but at 1st buildings turn left (track runs up River Tone). With houses visible ahead, turn right at T-junction; cross the footbridge and turn left to Challick Lane.
❹ The continuing track upstream is currently beside the River Tone: polite enquiry at the farm will let you through between the buildings. The track continues upstream through the pleasant woodland to Washbattle Bridge.
❺ Turn right, along the road, for 200yds (183m). The signed forest road leads uphill on the right. At

the highest point, with the pheasant fence alongside, bear left on to the wide path that continues uphill. At the wood edge cross the bottom corner of the field to the woodland opposite, then turn uphill alongside to reach the gate.
❻ Go through the gate and turn left, with the hedge beside it on the left. The next gate opens on to a hedged track which turns right, and passes the reservoir at the summit of Maundown Hill. At the top of the tarred public road turn right on to the track that becomes a descending, hedged path. At a signposted fork turn left on to the contouring path. Soon the lane leads down into the town, with the car park near by on the right.

Lord Poulett Arms

Somerset

The Inn

Set in a village full of scenic charm, the handsome Lord Poulett Arms bears the character of many years of service. Unstuffy and relaxed, the imaginatively restored interior mixes Osborne & Little with Farrow & Ball, while flagstones, wooden floors, polished antique tables, several open fires and evening candles create a classy, comfortable look. The balance between the pub (the bar delivers Branscombe brewery ales straight from the cask and is popular with locals and their dogs) and food is just about right.

Bedrooms have style and simple good taste, juxtaposing exposed stone with contemporary wallpapers, while handsome beds and quality fabrics take centre stage. A Victorian roll-top and an old slipper bath are placed eccentrically in two of the rooms; another has its private bathroom across the corridor – dressing gowns are provided. Thoughtful touches include home-made biscuits, organic apple juice, cafetières, fresh milk and Roberts radios.

The Food

You wouldn't expect such a modern twist on food in so classic an interior, but the kitchen delivers an eclectic menu. All sorts of influences show up among starters – grilled Capricorn goats' cheese with pickled rhubarb and almonds, or brown crab and smoked haddock fishcake with sweet chilli mayonnaise – while mains include pan-roasted tenderloin of pork with Chantenay carrots, baby leeks and a Somerset cider brandy sauce.

The kitchen uses the best in raw materials. Herbs are grown organically in the garden while other ingredients are as local as can be: port-braised hare, for example, served with parsnip purée; and free-range meat that comes from trusted suppliers on the Somerset/Dorset border. Everything is handled with aplomb. Puddings include bread and butter pudding with vanilla ice cream and a raspberry purée, locally made ice creams and a fine selection of West Country cheeses, and there's a decent wine list, too. This is the kind of idyllic country inn that woos urbanites from the glamour of the city.

The Essentials

Time at the Bar!
12-3pm, 6.30-11pm. Food: 12-2pm, 7-9pm

What's the Damage?
Main courses from £9

Bitter Experience:
Branscombe Vale Branoc, guest ales

Sticky Fingers:
Children welcome, smaller portions available

Muddy Paws:
Dogs welcome in the bar

Zzzzz:
4 rooms, £88

Anything Else?
Garden, car park

What To Do

Shop

THE OLD FORGE FOSSIL SHOP

A large and spacious shop stocked with a unique range of fascinating fossils and minerals from all over the world. A complete service is available, including restoration work, cleaning, reformulating and casting. The shop also sells amber jewellery and unusual gifts.

15 Broad Street, Lyme Regis,
Dorset DT7 3QE
01297 445977
www.fossilshop.net

THE SOMERSET GUILD OF CRAFTSMEN

Situated in the picturesque old Wessex capital of Somerton, the guild is one of the oldest in the country and enables members to sell their work to customers looking for something that is individual.

Market Place, West Street, Somerton,
Somerset TA11 7LX
01458 274653
www.somersetguild.co.uk

MARTOCK GALLERY

A small, friendly business stocking prints by most of the country's leading artists and also offering a complete framing service.

Water Street, Martock, Somerset
01935 823254
www.martockgallery.co.uk

DODGE & SON

Antique dealers and interior furnishers for nearly a century: exceptional antiques, garden furniture, reproductions and interior fabrics and sofas.

28-33 Cheap Street, Sherborne,
Dorset DT9 3PU
01935 815151
www.dodgeandson.com

Visit

FORDE ABBEY & GARDENS

Completed in 1148, Forde Abbey flourished as a Cistercian monastery for 400 years until the Dissolution, when it began its career as a private residence. A unique opportunity to see both the monastic and state rooms, as well as 30 acres of spectacular award-winning gardens.

Forde Abbey, Chard, Somerset TA20 4LU
01460 220231
www.fordeabbey.co.uk

THE PHILPOT MUSEUM

This award-winning little museum offers a great insight into the history of Lyme Regis as a port, the geology of the Jurassic coast and the development of geology as a science, as well as links with famous writers connected with this area such as Henry Fielding, Jane Austen and John Fowles.

Bridget Street, Lyme Regis, Dorset DT7 3QA
01297 443370
www.lymeregismuseum.co.uk

MONTACUTE HOUSE

A superb Elizabethan house built of the local golden Ham Hill Stone; its architecture is an exquisite pastiche of Gothic tradition and new Renaissance ideas that were arriving from the continent at the time of its completion in 1601. The house is filled with historic treasures and a fantastic collection of 17th-century textile samples and artworks on loan from the National Portrait Gallery. It was also the location for the film of Jane Austen's *Sense and Sensibility*.

Montacute, Somerset TA15 6XP
01935 823289
www.nationaltrust.org.uk

Visit

BARRINGTON COURT GARDEN

Gertrude Jekyll influenced the creation of this beautiful formal garden, laid out in a series of walled rooms that surround a fine Tudor manor house. Stroll through the White Garden and on into the Rose and Iris Gardens.

Barrington Court, Ilminster,
Somerset TA19 0NQ
01460 241938
www.nationaltrust.org.uk

Activity

GOLF

The Windwhistle Golf Club offers a well-designed 18-hole course.

Cricket St Thomas, Chard,
Somerset TA20 4DG
01460 30231
www.windwhistlegolfclub.co.uk

SAILING

Saltsail Charters offer sailing with a qualified, experienced skipper on day trips, weekends or longer on a well-equipped cruiser/racer yacht.

Saltsail Charters, Weymouth, Dorset
01297 32169
www.saltsailcharters.co.uk

HORSE RIDING

Horseback riding tailored to suit all levels and abilities.

Hill View Riding Centre, Sunnyside Farm,
Crewkerne, Dorset
01460 72731

FOSSIL HUNTING TOUR

Take a walk along Dorset's Jurassic coast with geology expert Chris Pamplin and discover what has been moving and shaking on Planet Earth for the last 400 million years.

www.fossilwalks.com

The Walk - From Thorncombe to Forde Abbey

The going is fairly easy through this area renowned for its soft fruit.

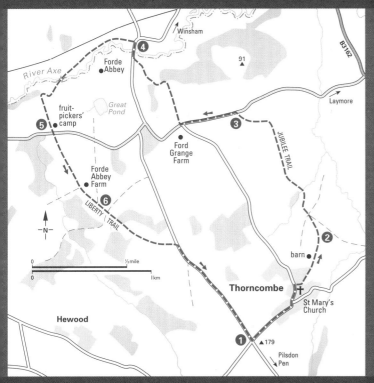

Walk Details

LENGTH: 5 miles (8km)

TIME: 2hrs 30min

ASCENT: 443ft (135m)

PATHS: Field paths, country lanes, 18 stiles

SUGGESTED MAP: aqua3 OS Explorer 116 Lyme Regis & Bridport

GRID REFERENCE: ST 373029

PARKING: At crossroads south-west of Thorncombe

INFORMATION: This walk is over the county border in Dorset

❶ From the crossroads turn left (north-east) and walk down into Thorncombe. Turn left up Chard Street and take the footpath on the right through the churchyard. Now bear right down the lane, then left on the gravel track beside the wall, opposite Goose Cottage. Cross the stile into the field, pass barn on left, then go straight on down the hedge.
❷ Cross the stile in the corner; go straight across the field. Cross the stile and bear diagonally right, down to the corner of the next field. Cross the stile, then cross the 2nd stile on your right. Ford the stream and bear left, up the field. Cross the stile on the left; continue up. Cross another stile on the right; bear right round the edge of the field. The track veers

right through the hedge. Cross 2 more stiles; continue straight on. By the trough turn left over a pair of stiles; go straight ahead up the field edge. Go through the gate and bear right, towards the house.
❸ Emerge through the gate on to the road; turn left. At the junction turn right on to the path; head for the woods. Turn left before the edge of the woods; at the corner go right, through the gate. Head diagonally left to the bottom corner, opposite Forde Abbey gates. Cross stile; turn right on the road to cross River Axe.
❹ Turn immediately left on to the footpath; follow it past the back of the Abbey. At the far corner cross a footbridge over the river; bear right towards the lone cedar, then left up

the slope to stile ('Liberty Trail'). Cross, then walk along top of the woods. Cross stile; bear left across the fields towards another cedar.
❺ Meet the road by the fruit-pickers' camp. Go across, through a gate and up the field. Towards the top righthand corner bear right through the gate; keep on this line. Cross a pair of stiles in the corner, pass Forde Abbey Farm on the left and keep straight on by the hedge. Cross the stile and walk down track.
❻ At the junction of tracks keep straight on. Where the track forks bear left, go through the gate and left across the field. Cross the stile in the hedge; turn right up the road. Follow the road for 0.5 mile (800m) to return to your car.

The Devonshire Arms

Somerset

The Inn

The impressive Devonshire Arms is at odds with its rural village setting, but the coat of arms displayed prominently over the porticoed front door gives a clue to the building's origins – this was once a hunting lodge belonging to the Dukes of Devonshire. Inside, a colour scheme of light wood (stripped floorboards, chunky tables), terracotta, stone and leather sets a rather elegant tone, but despite the urbane, sophisticated look you are made to feel very welcome. A log fire crackles in the bar in winter, fronted by leather sofas for cosy laid-back lounging, but in fine weather head out to the sheltered courtyard or the large terraced garden for peerless alfresco eating.

The bedrooms are full of thoughtful touches that reflect the owner-managed approach. Digital TV, cafetières with fresh coffee and tasteful, neutral colour schemes are common to all, as are quality beds and bed-linen. The rooms at the front with views over the village green are the most spacious, but smaller rooms overlooking the garden are equally charming. Bathrooms are a mix of bath and shower – there's even a Victorian roll-top – and all are impressively maintained.

The Devonshire Arms, Long Sutton, Langport, Somerset TA10 9LP

The Essentials

Time at the Bar!
12-3pm, 6-11pm
Food: 12-2.30pm, 7-9.30pm
(9pm Sunday)

What's the Damage?
Main courses from £12.95

Bitter Experience:
Teignworthy Reel Ale, Bath Ales SPA,
Pot Holes

Sticky Fingers:
Children welcome; children's menu

Muddy Paws:
Dogs welcome in the back bar

Zzzzz:
9 rooms, £75-£130

Anything Else?
Terrace, garden, car park

The Food

Tasty, consistently well-cooked food draws people from miles around. Lunch in the bar can be as simple as cream of parsnip and stilton soup served with hunks of locally baked granary bread, or chargrilled beef salad with horseradish dressing, while other highlights include ploughman's of Keen's cheddar and Somerset brie, or a traditional bangers and mustard mash with red onion gravy. Impressive, too are the refreshingly low prices with a set lunch coming in at under £10.

The cooking offers a well judged mix of the familiar and the gently inventive, best seen at dinner (served in the elegant dining room) in dishes like crab crème brûlée with fennel and rocket salad, and mains of roasted wood pigeon with bacon, caramelised button onions and thyme jus, or slow-cooked shoulder of Somerset lamb.

Puddings are a must, whether a ginger sticky toffee pudding with lime leaf ice cream or crème fraîche and black pepper pannacotta with strawberry sorbet. The wine list features some interesting bottles.

What To Do

Shop

THE COURTHOUSE

Craftspeople from Somerset and beyond display and sell a range of hard and soft craftworks, including pottery, textiles and paintings.

Market Place, West Street, Somerton, Somerset TA11 7LX

01458 274653

www.somersetguild.co.uk

HECKS CIDER

One of the longest established smaller producers, Hecks Cider makes a range of ciders from Somerset orchards, together with cider brandies and aperitifs and the rare perry cider (made from pear juice). The mill shop stocks locally made cheeses and preserves.

9-11 Middle Leigh, Street, Somerset BA16 0LB

01458 442367

www.hecksfarmhousecider.co.uk

MUCHELNEY POTTERY

John Leach is the latest in an acclaimed family lineage of potters and designers to produce both functional and decorative pottery at this rural retreat with gallery.

Muchelney, Langport, Somerset TA10 0DW

01458 250324

www.johnleachpottery.co.uk

SOMERSET LEVELS BASKET & CRAFT CENTRE

Making the most of local materials, artisans utilise the copious willow carrs of The Levels to produce basketware, furniture, sculpture and houseware. Rush, seagrass and cane products add a global feel.

Lyng Road, Burrow Bridge, Bridgwater, Somerset TA7 0SG

01823 698688

www.somersetlevels.co.uk

Visit

FLEET AIR ARM MUSEUM

Discover the little-known history of the Fleet Air Arm – part of the navy's airforce. A Fairey Swordfish and a Concorde, for example, at this busy airbase bring operations to life – from WWI to the present day.

Yeovilton, Ilchester, Somerset BA22 8HT

01935 840565

www.fleetairarm.com

PEAT MOORS CENTRE

A look at how culture, lifestyle and industry – including peat digging over thousands of years – have shaped the Somerset Levels. At the heart of the centre is a reconstruction of Glastonbury Lake Village, an Iron Age settlement.

Shapwick Road, Westhay, Glastonbury, Somerset BA6 9TT

01458 860697

www.somerset.gov.uk/cultureheritage

WELLS CATHEDRAL

The West Front of the cathedral has the largest collection of medieval statuary in Britain. Within is a treasure trove of architectural gems and stained glass; look out, too, for the astronomical clock with its jousting knights. The clever swans that can be seen swimming on the moat of the adjoining Bishop's Palace have been trained to ring a bell whenever they want to be fed.

Cathedral Green, Wells, Somerset BA5 2UE

01749 832210

www.wellscathedral.org.uk

Activity

BIRDWATCHING

The Levels are one of England's prime wild bird sites. The RSPB has several reserves, the largest is at Greylake: 5,000 acres of flood-plain grassland, ditches, reeds and open water with hides in place for birdwatching. You'll see mainly waterbirds, but with many other species, resident or passing. Regular events and walks also introduce visitors to the land mammals that make a home here.

Greylake RSPB Reserve, Bridgwater, Somerset

01458 252805

www.rspb.org.uk

CYCLING

Langport is at the heart of the Somerset Levels, an area with a wealth of peaceful lanes ideal for easy cycling through wildlife-rich countryside and characterful ancient villages. The River Parrett Centre is the ideal starting place.

Bow Bridge Cycles, Westover, Langport, Somerset TA10 9RB

01458 250350

www.southsomerset.gov.uk (follow links)

MIDDLEMOOR WATER PARK

This 20-acre lake has facilities for waterskiing, wakeboarding, jetskiing and other waterborne activities. Tuition is available for beginners; equipment can be hired by more experienced users.

The Causeway, Woolavington, Bridgwater, Somerset TA7 8DN

01278 685578 www.middlemoor.co.uk

The Walk - *In Praise of Apples at East Lambrook*

A gentle ramble around the fields and fragrant apple orchards of Somerset.

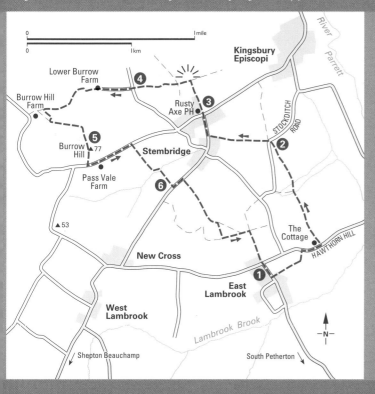

Walk Details

LENGTH: 4.75 miles (7.7km)

TIME: 2hrs 30min

ASCENT: 350ft (110m)

PATHS: Little-used field paths (some possibly overgrown by late summer), 24 stiles

SUGGESTED MAP: aqua3 OS Explorer 129 Yeovil & Sherborne

GRID REFERENCE: ST 431190

PARKING: Street parking in East Lambrook village

❶ Head into the centre of the village, eventually turning left onto the track. After passing one field, the track leads left to the lane (Hawthorn Hill). Turn right to The Cottage, where the gate with the stile leads into the orchard on your left. Follow the left edge and the next field. Cross the following field, keeping 70yds (64m) from the left edge, to the gate. Bear right to the stile-with-footbridge and the orchard. At the far end the gate leads onto Stockditch Road.
❷ Turn left for 40yds (37m), onto an overgrown track. The edge of another orchard leads to 2 stiles and a footbridge. Follow the left edges of 2 fields to the road; turn right to reach the Rusty Axe pub.

❸ Keep ahead, onto the track, past the houses. On crossing the crest, turn left on the green track. At the next field follow the hedge on left (ignoring the waymarker for a different path). Two stiles lead into a long field with the stumps of a former orchard. Keep to left of house to join the quiet country lane.
❹ Cross into the tarred driveway of Lower Burrow Farm; follow waymarkers between the farm buildings. Bear left, slanting uphill, to the gateway. Cross the next field to the double stile. Inside the next field bear right to the gate and stile. Burrow Hill Farm is one field ahead. Turn left, up the side of the field and across top to the gate. Go up field to poplars and summit of Burrow Hill.

❺ Drop to the lane at Pass Vale Farm and then turn left for 0.25 mile (400m) to the waymarked field gate on the right. Follow the left edges of 2 fields to the footbridge with the brambly stile. Turn left beside the stream to another brambly stile and turn right to lane.
❻ Turn left to the gate on the right ('East Lambrook'). Follow the left edges of 3 fields, then bear left over the stile and footbridge to the 2nd bridge beyond. In the next large field, follow the waymarkers down the righthand side and across the far end to the orchard. Do not cross the obvious stile out of the orchard but turn right, to its far end, where the lane leads you back into East Lambrook and your car.

The Wookey Hole Inn

Somerset

The Inn

Wookey Hole is a thriving all-year-round tourist spot, and this wonderful village inn caters for everyone. From the outside, the early Victorian black-and-white building looks like a typical village boozer, but the large, funkily decorated interior indicates otherwise. Bright colours are pitched against softer tones, and lots of windows and skylights (some with stained glass) make for an interesting open-plan interior with light wood tables and chairs well spaced over wood or stone floors. It's a surprisingly relaxing spot for an early evening pint of Cheddar Potholer, but at weekends, when the place is busy, the atmosphere is electric.

Upstairs are five bedrooms decorated in muted colours, with contemporary furnishings and lighting, arresting art and big bathrooms, three of them shower only. There's an interesting mix of old and new – a Victorian roll-top bathtub here, a low-slung coffee table incorporating a glass chess set there – and the overall effect is of understated style. All rooms have digital TVs, books and board games, as well as all the expected extras.

The Essentials

Time at the Bar!
12-11pm
Food: 12-2.30pm 7-9.30pm
(no food Sun evening)

What's the Damage?
Main courses from £12.50

Bitter Experience:
Cheddar Potholer, Glastonbury
Mystery Tor

Sticky Fingers:
Children welcome; small
children's menu

Muddy Paws:
Well-behaved dogs welcome

Zzzzz:
5 rooms, £90-£100

Anything Else?
Garden, car park

The Food

On entering, the dining area is the first thing you see: a smartly arranged area with tables laid with white cloths and fresh flowers, and in winter, a fire blazing in an elegant fireplace – it's quite a foil to the funky bar. The menu reflects the eclecticism of the decor, opening with the likes of spicy vegetable samosas with wasabi crème fraîche and piccalilli, or salmon and coriander fish cake with basil, aioli and tomato chutney. Main course dishes range from succulent pan-fried swordfish with black noodles, vegetable stir-fry and sweet chilli and soy sauce to oven-roasted lamb rump served with a balsamic and thyme jus, wilted spinach, fondant potato and vine cherry tomatoes. Puddings include an unusual dark chocolate and chilli tart with lime and mango sorbet.

Lunch in the bar is simpler, with balsamic pepper and red Leicester cheese bruschetta, a spiced lamb burger topped with chilli cheddar and tomato chutney, or peppered rib-eye steak with home-cut fries being typical offerings. Children get their own lunchtime menu and a bulging box of toys.

What To Do

Shop

CHEDDAR GORGE CHEESE COMPANY

No trip to Somerset would be complete without taking home a hunk of the real thing! You can watch the process – cheese here is still hand-made – and buy the finished product. The range is wide – choose from the award-winning Vintage Cheddar, Natural Blue, or Especially Strong for the hardcore cheeseophiles. There's a good choice of jars of pickles, too, for the perfect ploughman's.

The Cliffs, Cheddar Gorge, Somerset BS27 3QA

01934 742810

www.cheddargorgecheese.co.uk

WELLS MARKET

There's not much you can't source at the twice-weekly market – jewellery, plants, organic fruit and vegetables, olives, books and pottery – but your nose will lead you first to Morgan Delights Bakers, as the smell of fresh-baked bread and pies wafts across the square. One of Rick Stein's favourites.

Market Place, Wells, Somerset

01749 673091

WELLS TRADING POST

A fascinating emporium of new and second-hand goods housed in a former 12th-century mill. You'll find all sorts of treasures, from old garden tools, costume jewellery and reclaimed pine to Art Deco furniture and bric a brac, as you explore the labyrinth of rooms over three floors.

Old Priory Mill, West Street, Wells, Somerset BA5 2HH

01749 671454

www.wellstradingpost.com

Visit

CHEDDAR CAVES & GORGE

Go underground and experience the spectacular natural phenomenon of Cheddar's cathedral-like caverns. Marvel at the million-year-old subterranean rivers, stunning stalactites and stalagmites and the famous Cheddar Man, the UK's oldest complete skeleton – 9,000 years old on his last birthday. There's plenty to see above ground, too; you may be lucky enough to spot nesting peregrine falcons and the feral Soay sheep employed to keep the grass cropped.

Cheddar, Somerset BS27 3QF

01934 742343

www.cheddarcaves.co.uk

WELLS

Wells has the distinction of being the smallest city in Europe and it is a lively, charming place with some interesting shops and cafes, but most people agree that the jewel in its crown is the Cathedral and Bishop's Palace. The magnificent West Front of the Cathedral is carved with hundreds of statues in the warm yellow stone. Don't miss the chime of the unique medieval Wells clock, with its jousting knights. Vicar's Close is an intact medieval street, leading to the Bishop's Palace, which is a spectacular moated stronghold surrounded by beautiful well-tended gardens.

Bishop's Palace & Gardens

Wells, Somerset BA5 2PD

01749 678691

www.bishopspalacewells.co.uk

Wells Cathedral

Cathedral Green, Wells, Somerset BA5 2UE

01749 832210

www.wellscathedral.org.uk

Activity

CLIMBING, CAVING & KAYAKING

Under full instruction from qualified instructors head underground and explore the Mendip Hill caves, climb the natural limestone rock faces around Cheddar Gorge, and take to the water to learn the basic skills of kayaking. All equipment is provided, and there's also the chance to go raft building, abseiling and shooting.

Aardvark Endeavours

Broadway House, Axbridge Road, Cheddar, Somerset BS27 3DB

01934 744878

www.aardvarkendeavours.com

DEEP SEA FISHING

Take to the waters at Burnham on Sea for a day's fishing. The unique tides in the Bristol Channel guarantee an interesting catch, particularly in the summer months. Kelly's Hero will kit you out with everything you need for a day out – but it's up to you to catch the fish.

Kelly's Hero

23 Alstone Lane, West Huntspill, Alstone, Somerset TA9 3DS

01278 785000

STEAM TRAIN RIDE

Go on a relaxed trip back in time along the delightful Strawberry Line, which winds through the glorious Mendip Hills, aboard a proper old steam train. Treat yourself to a good old-fashioned Sunday lunch on the *Mendip Belle*, and really wallow in some old-style travel nostalgia.

East Somerset Railway

Cranmore Railway Station, Cranmore, Shepton Mallet, Somerset BA4 4PQ

01749 880417

www.eastsomersetrailway.com

The Walk - *Ebbor Gorge - Coleridge's Inspiration*

The sublime limestone gorge that inspired Samuel Taylor Coleridge.

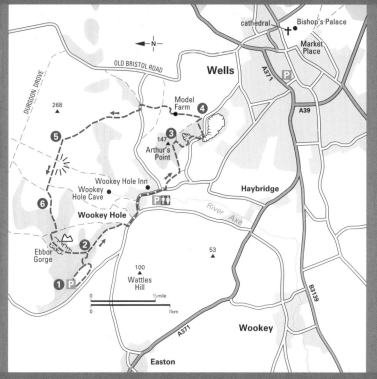

Walk Details

LENGTH: 4.75 miles (7.7km)

TIME: 2hrs 30min

ASCENT: 700ft (210m)

PATHS: Small paths and field edges, with a rugged descent, 9 stiles

SUGGESTED MAP: aqua3 OS Explorer 141 Cheddar Gorge

GRID REFERENCE: ST 521484

PARKING: Lane above Wookey Hole (optional, small fee)

❶ From the notice-board at the top end of the car park, descend the stepped path. After the clearing, turn left ('The Gorge'). Wide path crosses stream to another junction.

❷ Turn right, away from the gorge; follow valley down to road. Turn left, passing through the village of Wookey Hole. At the end of the village, the road bends right; take kissing gate on left ('West Mendip Way' waymarker post). After 2 more kissing gates turn left up spur to stile and top of Arthur's Point.

❸ Bear right into woods again. Beware: hidden in the brambles ahead is the top of the quarry crag; turn right, down to stile. Go down field edge to kissing gate; bear left between boulders back into the wood. After a sharp rise bear right, to join Lime Kiln Lane below, which bends left with the path on the left diverting through the bottom of the wood. This emerges at the end of the short field track; follow it down to the footpath signpost.

❹ Turn sharp left on a track that passes through Model Farm. Follow the track through the farm, turning right by houses to continue to a track to Tynings Lane. Turn left to the signposted stile on your right. Go up with the fence right, then bear left to the gate with the stile. Go straight up the next, large field, aiming for the gateway with the tractor ruts. The track leads up through the wood and field to the gate. Slant upwards in the same direction to another gate next to the stile 100yds (9.1m) below the field's top left corner.

❺ The path runs along the tops of 3 fields with view across the Levels to the left. With the stile on right and gate and horse trough in front, turn downhill with the fence on the right; follow the fence to the stile leading into Ebbor Gorge Nature Reserve.

❻ A 2nd gate leads into wood. At the junction with red arrow and sign ('Car Park') pointing forward, turn right into valley and go down – it narrows to rocky gully. At foot of gorge turn right ('Car Park'). You are now back at Point 2 of outward walk. Cross the stream, turn left at the T-junction to the wood's edge and back right to the car park.

The Manor House Inn

Somerset

The Inn

The setting of this 17th-century inn is apparently everything anyone could wish for: off the beaten track (but well signposted) in a pretty Somerset village. The ancient and lovely interior is in superb condition. With exposed brick walls, worn slate floors, polished tables, candles and open fires, the owners have got the relaxed, informal rustic feel exactly right. Similarly, the pleasant, chatty bar functions superbly, playing its part in creating a model country inn with bright, on-the-ball staff dispensing real ales such as Butcombe Bitter and Otter Ale.

The Manor House is the sort of place that tempts you to stay even if you hadn't intended to, and the three pleasant, traditionally styled bedrooms housed in an old mews at the back of the inn do not disappoint. Named after racehorses trained in the village, they have a cosy and cottagey feel, with floral curtains, cream bedspreads, scatter cushions and soft lighting (but up-to-date flat-screen TVs, too), and offer a mix of comfortable twin and double beds. It's a cosy look that contrasts well with the modern style of the pristine bathrooms.

The Manor House Inn, Ditcheat, Shepton Mallet, Somerset BA4 6RB

The Essentials

Time at the Bar!
11am-11pm
Food:12-2pm, 7-9.30pm. Not Sun eve.

What's the Damage?
Main courses from £6.95

Bitter Experience:
Butcombe Bitter, Otter Ale,
Lovington Brewery ales

Sticky Fingers:
Children welcome;
half portions served

Muddy Paws:
Dogs welcome in the bar

Zzzzz:
3 rooms, £50-£90

Anything Else?
Garden, terrace, car park

The Food

Match a restaurant that offers a stylish space and makes the most of its ancient setting with a kitchen delivering cooking with a modern edge, and you have a place that is well worth a detour. Emphasis is placed on the quality sourcing of local raw materials, and the menu flits between tried-and-tested pub favourites (breaded brie wedges with mixed leaves and cranberry sauce, home-made pie of the day, mixed grills, or steak with a choice of creamy garlic, brandy and peppercorn, or port and stilton sauces) and some modern gutsy cooking of, say, pan-fried pigeon breast on wild mushroom risotto with port and redcurrant sauce.

Elsewhere there could be confit of duck on a bed of pickled red cabbage and port sauce, braised rabbit and bacon lardons on a grainy mustard mash with a port and blackberry sauce, or breast of chicken wrapped in streaky bacon and stuffed with goats' cheese and sun-blushed tomatoes, served with a rich red wine jus. Chocolate brownie with vanilla ice cream is an unbeatable way to finish, and the formidable wine list (including 16 by the glass) garners the praise it deserves.

What To Do

Shop

AVALON VINEYARD
Nestling on a hillside overlooking the Vale of Avalon, Glastonbury Tor and Somerset Levels, Avalon Vineyard produces Pennard organic mead, wine and cider, hand-produced on a small scale. You're invited to taste before you buy!

The Drove, East Pennard, Shepton Mallet, Somerset BA4 6UA
01749 860393
www.pennardorganicwines.co.uk

HIGHER ALHAM FARM
Organic unpasteurised buffalo milk is the basis of Francis Wood's mozzarella cheese – the main variety is Junas, based on an old mountain recipe, similar to pecorino. You can watch the cheese being made, and buy buffalo meat.

West Cranmore, Shepton Mallet, Somerset BA4 6DD
01749 880221
www.buffalo-cheese.co.uk

WELLS RECLAMATION COMPANY
You'll find everything you need in this fascinating 5 -acre yard, from doors, windows, iron and brasswork to garden statues.

Coxley, Wells, Somerset BA5 1RQ
01749 677087
www.wellsreclamation.com

WESTCOMBE FARM
The milk for Westcombe's award-winning traditional cheddar is taken from just 3 herds grazed on lush Somerset pastures – the 100 rounds of cheese are hand-made and aged for 20 months.

Evercreech, Shepton Mallet, Somerset BA4 6ER
01749 831300
www.farmhousecheesemakers.com

Visit

BISHOP'S PALACE & GARDENS
This stunning palace has been the home of the Bishop of Bath & Wells for 800 years. There are 14 acres of garden, and springs, from which the city takes its name. Visit the Bishop's private chapel, the Great Hall and the gatehouse, and see the portcullis beside which the famous mute swans ring a bell for food.

Wells, Somerset BA5 2PD
01749 678691
www.bishopspalacewells.co.uk

GLASTONBURY ABBEY
Set in 36 acres of peaceful parkland in the centre of Glastonbury, this was the first Christian sanctuary in the country, visited by Joseph of Arimathea and Saints David and Patrick. Award-winning museum.

Abbey Gatehouse, Magdalene Street, Glastonbury, Somerset BA6 9EL
01458 832627
www.glastonburyabbey.com

LYTES CAREY MANOR
This charming intimate golden stone house has a 14th-century chapel and Tudor great hall, and was home to the famous medieval herbalist Henry Lyte.

Charlton Mackrell, Somerton, Somerset TA11 7HU
01458 224471
www.nationaltrust.org.uk

MILTON LODGE GARDENS
Milton Lodge has a Grade II listed Arts and Crafts terraced garden, with views over Wells Cathedral and the Vale of Avalon. See, too, the 18th-century arboretum.

Old Bristol Road, Wells, Somerset BA5 3AQ
01749 672168
www.miltonlodgegardens.co.uk

Activity

BALLOONING
For sheer exhilaration and romance, take a hot-air balloon flight over the stunning countryside, with a glass of champagne at dusk.

Aerosaurus Balloons
Wheathill Golf Club, Lovington, Somerset TA11 7HG
01963 240667
01404 823102
www.ballooning.co.uk

GOLF
Wells Golf Club is a challenging, well-presented course in delightful parklands, with panoramic views over the city and cathedral.

Wells Golf Club
East Horrington Road, Wells, Somerset BA5 3DS
01749 675005
www.wellsgolfclub.co.uk

HORSE RACING
Set in the heart of the Somerset countryside, Wincanton Racecourse is known for its friendly atmosphere and hospitality. Expect the best of jump racing here, with some of the country's finest horses and jockeys.

Wincanton Racecourse
Wincanton, Somerset BA9 8BJ
01963 323444
www.wincantonracecourse.co.uk

STEAM TRAIN RIDE
Founded in 1974 by wildlife artist David Shepherd, the East Somerset Railway is set in a beautiful part of the countryside. The original station building has a restaurant, shop and gallery, and there's also a museum.

Cranmore Railway Station, Cranmore, Shepton Mallet, Somerset BA4 4PQ
01749 880417
www.eastsomersetrailway.com

The Walk - Golden Wool at Bruton

A walk around and above beautiful Bruton, a typical Somerset wool town.

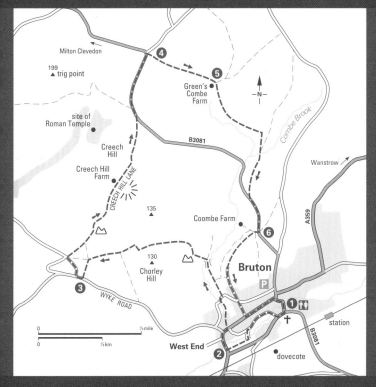

Walk Details

LENGTH: 4.5 miles (7.2km)

TIME: 2hrs 15min

ASCENT: 500ft (150m)

PATHS: Enclosed tracks, open fields, an especially muddy farmyard

SUGGESTED MAP: aqua3 OS Explorer 142 Shepton Mallet

GRID REFERENCE: ST 684348

PARKING: Free parking off Silver Street, 50yds (46m) west of church; larger car park in Upper Backway

❶ With the church to your left and the bridge to your right, head down Silver Street to the car park in Coombe Street. The old packhorse bridge over the River Brue leads into Lower Backway. Turn left for 350yds (320m), ignoring the arch leading towards the footbridge; take the path between the railed fences to reach the 2nd footbridge. Turn right along the river to West End.

❷ Turn right over the river and right again into the end of the High Street; immediately turn uphill on to walled path ('Mill Dam'). At the lane above turn right along the track ('Huish Lane'). Just after the footbridge fork left: the hedged track is steep and muddy, bending right then left to the lane (Wyke Road).

❸ Turn right, then right again; after 220yds (201m) turn right past farm buildings on to uphill track (Creech Hill Lane), which becomes a hedged tunnel, then emerges at Creech Hill Farm. Pass along the front of the farm and out to the B3081. Turn left over hill crest to triangular junction.

❹ Turn right for 40yds (37m) to the public bridleway sign and gate on the right. Go down combe below; at foot keep left of Green's Combe Farm and above intermittent wall; turn down through the gate between the farm buildings.

❺ Continue down the farm's access track for 0.25 mile (400m) until it bends right. Keep ahead through the field gate with the blue waymarker, on to the green track. After 200yds

(183m), beside 3 stumps, turn downhill, to the left of hazels, to the gate. Pass through the small wood to the gate and waymarked track. When this emerges into open field, follow the fence above to join the B3081. Turn left, uphill, to Coombe Farm entrance.

❻ Ignoring stile on left, go through an ivy-covered wall gap, then down the driveway; turn left on to the wide path under sycamores. The path rises, with the bank on the left. At open grassland, keep to left edge to descending path that becomes St Catherine's Lane. Weavers' cottages are on the right as street descends into Bruton. Turn left along High Street. At end turn right down Patwell Street to Church Bridge.

The Queen's Arms

Somerset

The Queen's Arms, Corton Denham, Somerset DT9 4LR

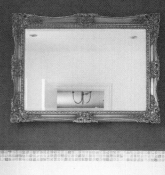

The Inn

Drive down winding narrow lanes through stunning countryside to find this 18th-century pub hidden away in a sleepy village. The simple stone façade and the slate sign by the door stating 'We like muddy boots and dogs' set the informal feel of this revamped and revitalised village local. The slate- and wood-floored bar is patrolled by the resident labrador and is filled with a refreshing mix of farm workers, walkers and the local gentry. Here, you can sink into a deep leather armchair by the glowing fire, sup a pint of local Butcombe ale and tuck into one of the irresistible home-made pork pies – bliss after an invigorating country walk.

Bedrooms are all contemporary rustic chic where great care has been taken with the fabrics – think squashy, rose-patterned bedspreads, Egyptian cotton bedlinen and silk curtains. Even the beanbags are suede. Bathrooms are swish, modern affairs – choose from a rainstorm shower, cast iron bath (lilac!) or a twin-headed shower for showering à deux. Only the most hard of heart will fail to be enchanted by the views of the church, sheep-grazed fields and distant rolling hills.

The Food

The contemporary-style lunch and dinner menus change weekly to reflect the availability of local produce which includes succulent lamb reared in the village, Old Spot pork from the Piddle Valley, fish from the Dorset coast and organic vegetables.

Lunch is a hearty affair and could consist of English sausages served with hearty chive mash and red onion gravy, a ploughman's lunch with Montgomery cheddar, or a wholesome bowl of broth packed with pearl barley, ham and vegetables. Robust British dishes are simply cooked and presented to allow the flavours to shine through. In the evening, start with chicken liver pâté with Cumberland sauce, followed by classic jugged hare, roast local partridge with game sauce, or pork tenderloin stuffed with figs.

Puddingophiles should really consider the pressing need for building in a healthy country walk in the rolling Somerset countryside to their stay at The Queen's Arms. Only this could possibly justify the steamed syrup sponge with home-made custard or gooey chocolate pudding with chocolate chip ice cream.

The Essentials

Time at the Bar!
12–3.30pm, 6–11pm (all day weekends)
Food: 12-3pm, 6-10pm (9.30 Sunday)

What's the Damage?
Main courses from £9.70

Bitter Experience:
Butcombe, Timothy Taylor Landlord

Sticky Fingers:
Children welcome in bar and overnight; children's menu

Muddy Paws:
Dogs welcome in bar

Zzzzz:
5 rooms, £75–£120

Anything Else?
Terrace, car park

The Queen's Arms, Corton Denham, Somerset DT9 4LR

What To Do

Shop

DODGE & SONS

Dodge & Sons have been trading in antiques for more than 80 years – they also have a modern interior design shop selling fabrics by Colefax and Fowler and Jane Churchill, and Zoffany wallpapers. With more than 100 similarly independent shops, you'll find everything from hand-made chocs, Georgian silverware and modern art to kitchenware and delis.

28-33 Cheap Street, Sherborne, Dorset DT9 3PU

01935 815151

www.dodgeandson.com

EAST LAMBROOK MANOR GARDENS NURSERY

Known as 'the home of English cottage gardening', Lambrook was created in the 1930s by owner Marjorie Fish who would dig up plants and give them to interested visitors. In time, she set up a nursery, and people came from far and wide to buy her rare 'gems'. You can now choose from more than 800 specialist plants. In the award-winning tea shop everything is home-made and locally sourced.

South Petherton, Somerset TA13 5HH

01460 240328

www.eastlambrook.co.uk

SWAN GALLERY

Specialist art gallery established in 1982 where you'll find a wealth of antique works of art from the 18th, 19th and 20th centuries. This is the place for antique maps and prints, original oils and watercolours.

51 Cheap Street, Sherborne, Dorset DT9 3AX

01935 814465

www.swangallery.co.uk

Visit

MONTACUTE HOUSE

An Elizabethan manor house glittering with thousands of tiny windows, Montacute stands in 300 acres of parkland and incorporates part of the National Portrait Gallery. Here you'll find 17th-century textile samplers, fine 17th- and 18th-century furniture, and the smallest ensuite bathroom you've ever seen – Lord Curzon installed a bijou bath behind a wood panel in his bedroom in the early 1900s. Outside are two 'pudding houses', from a time when guests at dinner parties would savour their dessert in the garden.

Montacute, Somerset TA15 6XP

01935 823289

www.nationaltrust.org

HAYNES MOTOR MUSEUM

This museum houses the UK's largest collection of iconic cars, from Fords to Ferraris. There are 350 cars and bikes in 10 exhibition halls: the Red Room has 50 beautiful red sports cars from around the world. Don't miss the nostalgic 1950s and 60s classics, Bentleys, Rollers and super-modern cars. Buy memorabilia from the shop and top off your afternoon by indulging in a West Country cream tea in the cafe.

Sparkford, Yeovil, Somerset BA22 7LH

01963 442784

www.haynesmotormuseum.com

THOMAS HARDY'S HOUSE

Hardy was born in 1840 in this idyllic cob and thatch cottage built by his grandfather and almost unaltered since the family left. He lived here until he was 22 and in this period wrote *Under the Greenwood Tree*, in which he describes the cottage in detail, and *Far From the Madding Crowd*. He would sit at a window seat in a small room upstairs to write, overlooking his beloved Black Down. The traditional cottage garden has superb displays of lupins, lavender and lilies.

Higher Bockhampton, Dorchester, Dorset DT2 8QJ

01297 561900

www.nationaltrust.org

Activity

RACING AT WINCANTON

Saturday meetings provide some of the best jump racing of the National Hunt season, featuring some of the country's top horses. Thursday racing includes Irish Day with pints of the black stuff and live Irish music – with seven bars you won't need to go thirsty.

Wincanton, Somerset BA9 8BJ

01963 323444

www.wincantonracecouse.co.uk

HORSE RIDING

You are deep in Thomas Hardy's fictionalised Wessex here, and what better way to discover his beloved county than on horseback. Go back in time to explore the woodland bridleways, gently rolling clay pastures and patchwork-quilt fields vividly depicted by Hardy in his novel *Tess of the D'Urbevilles*.

Pound Cottage Riding Centre

Luccombe Farm, Milton Abbas, Blandford Forum, Dorset DT11 0BD

01258 880057

The Walk - *Cadbury Castle as Camelot?*

South Cadbury's hill fort gives wide views of Somerset and a glimpse of pre-history.

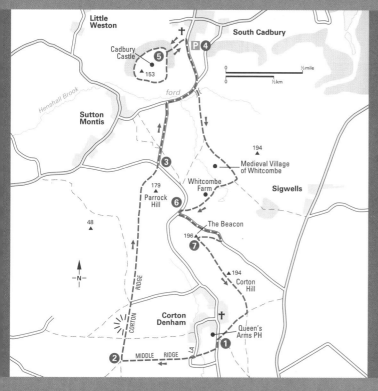

Walk Details

LENGTH: 6.75 miles (10.9km)

TIME: 3hrs 30min

ASCENT: 1,000ft (300m)

PATHS: Well-used paths, 6 stiles

SUGGESTED MAP: aqua3 OS Explorer 129 Yeovil & Sherborne

GRID REFERENCE: ST 635224

PARKING: The Queen's Arms car park, or Cadbury Castle car park (free), south of South Cadbury (point 4)

1 From The Queen's Arms turn left on the road, between high banks for 110yds (100m) to the stile ('Middle Ridge Lane'). Keep left of the trees to the field gate, with stile beyond leading into lane. Go onto the stony track that climbs to the ridgeline.
2 Turn right; walk along Corton Ridge with the hedge on your right and the view on your left. After 650yds (594m) Ridge Lane starts on the right, but go through the small gate on the left to continue along the ridge. After the small gate, the green path bends around the flank of Parrock Hill. With Cadbury Castle now on your left, ignore the 1st green track down to the left. Shortly the main track turns down left into the hedge end and a waymarked

gate. From this point a hedged path leads you down to reach the road.
3 Cross into the road ('South Cadbury'). Shortly turn right, again for South Cadbury; follow the road around the base of Cadbury Castle to reach the adjacent car park.
4 Turn right out of the car park to the 1st house in South Cadbury. The track leads up to Cadbury Castle. The ramparts and top of the fort are access land; stroll around at will.
5 Return past car park. After 0.25 mile (400m), pass a side road on the left, to a stile signposted 'Sigwells'. Walk down to reach the stile and footbridge. Cross then follow left edge of field, then uncultivated strip. Track starts ahead, but take stile on right to follow field edge next to

it, to gate with 2 waymarkers. Faint track leads along top of following field. At end turn down into hedged-earth track which leads out past Whitcombe Farm to rejoin road.
6 Turn left to junction below Corton Denham Beacon. Turn left to slant uphill for 0.25 mile (400m). The track on the right leads to open hilltop and summit trig point.
7 Head along the steep hill rim to stile with dog slot. Continue along top of slope (Corton Denham below). Pass modern 'tumulus' (small, covered reservoir). Above, 5 large beeches slant to the waymarked gate. A green path slants down again, until a gate leading to tarred lane; follow this to reach the road below and The Queen's Arms.

The Wheelwrights Arms

Somerset

The Inn

Just a short drive from Bath and a stone's throw from the banks of the Kennet and Avon Canal, The Wheelwrights Arms sits in the sleepy village of Monkton Combe surrounded by picturesque hills and valleys. Built in 1750 as a house and a workshop by William Harold, a local carpenter, the two buildings were converted into a pub by the Harold family in 1871. Over a century later, the carpentry workshops were transformed into bed-and-breakfast accommodation, but visitors today will find that David Munn has taken The Wheelwrights Arms to a completely different level of luxury since he acquired the place in 2006.

Modern flourishes enhance exposed stone walls, framed paintings and antique furniture, while the old workshops have been carefully restored, creating seven luxury ensuite bedrooms, all with flat-screen TVs, radios, room service and wi-fi internet access. The rooms are light and airy, contemporary and stylish. Individually designed, they are complemented by stunning bathrooms featuring white tongue-and-groove panelling, wooden floorboards, free-standing baths, fluffy white towels and Provencal toiletries.

The Essentials

Time at the Bar!
11am-11pm
Food: 12-3pm, 6-10pm

What's the Damage?
Main courses from £10

Bitter Experience:
Butcombe, Bath

Sticky Fingers:
Children welcome, half portions

Muddy Paws:
No dogs

Zzzzz:
7 rooms, £110-£130

Anything Else?
Large garden with patio, car park

The Food

When it comes to the food, 'classic' and 'British' are the watchwords at The Wheelwrights Arms. There are plenty of good old-fashioned English dishes on the menu, which caters for lunchtime snackers as well as diners looking for something a little more substantial. Plenty of West Country produce is in evidence in the wholesome chicken and ham pie, chunky cod, salmon and haddock pie with peas and creamed leeks and a trio of Bath sausages served on mash with rich red wine and onion gravy.

A selection of sandwiches is popular at lunchtimes, and these are a welcome diversion for hungry walkers. They include a steak sandwich with onion marmalade and hand-cut chunky chips, and 'The Wheelwrights' club sandwich' (grilled chicken, bacon, local cheddar, salad, mayo and hand-cut chunky chips), perfect washed down with a pint of Bath Ales Wild Hare or Butcombe Blond, or a glass of wine from the lengthy list. The beef is hung for 30 days, so expect intense flavour from the 8oz hand-carved rib-eyes, cooked just to your liking and served with hand-cut chunky chips, field mushrooms and a delicious sauce of your choice.

What To Do

Shop

AVALON VINEYARD
More than six acres of organic vineyard, where you are free to wander at will or pre-arrange a guided tour. The range of drinks on sale extends beyond grape wines to local cider, fruit wines and mead, which is made from organic honey imported from Brazil.

The Drove, East Pennard, Shepton Mallet, Somerset BA4 6UA
01749 860393
www.pennardorganicwines.co.uk

BATH
There are so many delightful shops in this beautiful city it is impossible to know which to recommend. The best plan is to start near the abbey, where there are yards, lanes and walks with art galleries and specialist jewellery shops; for designer fashion visit Milsom Street or Shire's Yard. Antique galleries and shops pop up everywhere: a good concentration is around The Paragon in Upper Town. Just a short hop from Pulteney Bridge are dozens of craft shops, workshops and galleries on and around Broad Street and Walcot Street. Half the fun is in finding your own favourite.

Bath & NE Somerset
0906 711 2000
www.VisitBath.co.uk

FARRINGTON'S FARM SHOP
An award-winning shop stocking a wide range of largely locally produced, organic products; from meat and game through bakery and preserves to creamery products.

Home Farm, Main Street, Farrington Gurney, Bristol BS39 6UB
01761 451698
www.farringtonsfarmshop.com

Visit

CLAVERTON PUMPING STATION
A remarkable feat of engineering, designed by the engineer John Rennie to help ensure that his Kennet and Avon Canal didn't run dry. A massive waterwheel, powered by the River Avon, can pump 100,000 gallons of river water per hour up to the canal 'pound' (level), nearly 50ft above, to top-up water lost by boats descending the flight of locks to the Avon in Bath.

Ferry Lane, Claverton, Bath,
Bath & NE Somerset
01225 483001
www.claverton.org

DYRHAM PARK
Secluded in a vast, wooded estate and deer park, and familiar from the film *The Remains of the Day*, Dyrham Park is an archetypal Cotswold country mansion. Built 300 years ago for the politician William Blathwayt, it has remained virtually unchanged since his day, with grand Delftware, textiles and paintings.

Dyrham, Gloucestershire SN14 8ER
01179 372501
www.nationaltrust.org.uk/dyrhampark

HOLBURNE MUSEUM
In the centre of Bath, this museum is testament to the collecting skills, wealth and eye of Sir William Holburne. The charming house on Great Pulteney Street overflows with fine arts: from miniature masterpieces to Gainsborough paintings; works in silver, glass and porcelain; Renaissance bronzes and art by Turner and Stubbs.

Great Pulteney Street, Bath,
Bath & NE Somerset BA2 4DB
01225 466669
www.bath.ac.uk/holburne

Activity

CANOE HIRE
Take to the water in a Canadian-style open canoe, charting a course along the tranquil Kennet and Avon Canal, passing through picturesque villages and remote countryside, heading west towards Bath or east towards distant Devizes. The canoes are easily handled by one or two people, and can be man-handled around locks.

The Lock Inn, 48 Frome Road,
Bradford-on-Avon, Wiltshire BA15 1LE
01225 868068
www.thelockinn.co.uk

CAVING & CLIMBING
Formed from million-year-old Ice Age river beds, the Cheddar Gorge caves offer some challenging and exciting activities to those prepared to take the risks. Choose from tackling tight squeezes and hidden glories on a caving expedition in the cathedral-like caverns, or perhaps abseiling into Cheddar Gorge, Britain's largest. And maybe rock-climbing back out, if it takes your fancy. All of the options are tailored to suit beginners and will fill a morning or afternoon.

Rocksport, Cheddar, Somerset BS27 3QF
01934 742343
www.cheddarcaves.co.uk

MENDIP GLIDING CLUB
A trial lesson in a modern glider, launched by ground winch or aerotow, can get you up to 2,000ft (610m) above the Mendips, floating over Cheddar Gorge and the Mendip edge. There is no more glorious way to appreciate the countryside.

New Road, Priddy, Wells, Somerset BA5 3BX
01749 870312
www.mendipglidingclub.uklinux.net

The Walk - Brunel's Great Tunnel

A high and hilly walk around Box Hill.

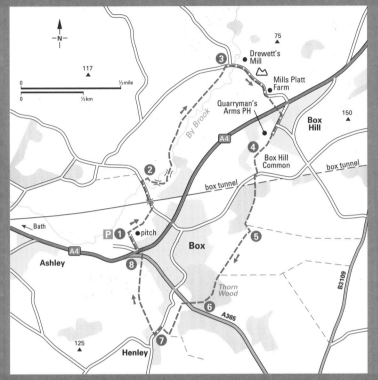

Walk Details

LENGTH: 3.25 miles (5.3km)

TIME: 1hr 45min

ASCENT: 508ft (155m)

PATHS: Field and woodland paths, bridle paths, metalled lanes, 15 stiles

SUGGESTED MAP: aqua3 OS Explorer 156 Chippenham & Bradford-on-Avon

GRID REFERENCE: ST 823686

PARKING: Village car park near Selwyn Hall

INFORMATION: This walk is over the county border in Wiltshire

❶ Facing the recreation ground, walk to the lefthand side of football pitch; join the track in the corner, close to railway line. At lane, turn left, pass beneath the railway, cross the bridge and take arrowed footpath, to right, before 2nd bridge.

❷ Walk by the river, cross the footbridge and turn left. Cross the next footbridge and continue to the stile. Walk through the water-meadows close to the river, go through the squeeze stile and maintain direction. Shortly, bear left to the squeeze stile in the field corner. Follow the righthand edge of field to the stile and the lane.

❸ Turn right, then right again at the junction. Cross the river, pass Drewett's Mill and ascend the lane.

Past Mills Platt Farm, take the arrowed footpath ahead and climb over the stile. Continue uphill to the stile; cross the A4. Ascend the steps to the lane and proceed straight on up Barnetts Hill. Keep right at the fork, then turn right again; pass by the Quarryman's Arms.

❹ Keep left at fork; continue beside Box Hill Common to junction. Take path ahead into woodland. Almost immediately, fork left and follow path close to woodland edge. As it curves right into beech wood, bear left and follow path through gap in wall, then right at junction of paths.

❺ Follow the bridlepath to the fork. Keep left, then turn right at the T-junction and take path left to stile. Cross further stile and descend into

Thorn Wood, following the stepped path to the stile at the bottom.

❻ Continue through scrub to stile; turn right by fence to wall stile. Bear right to further stile, then left uphill to stile and A365. Cross and follow drive ahead. Where it curves left by the stables, keep ahead along the arrowed path to the house. Bear right up the garden steps to drive and continue uphill to T-junction.

❼ Turn left; on entering Henley, take path right, across stile. Follow field edge to stile; descend to allotment and stile. Continue to stile and gate.

❽ Follow the drive ahead, bear left at garage; take path right, into Box. Cross the main road and continue to the A4. Turn right, then left down access road back to Selwyn Hall.

The Wheatsheaf

Somerset

The Inn

Run by Adele and Ian Barton and expertly managed by their children, it's hardly surprising that The Wheatsheaf feels like such a family-run affair. Located in idyllic countryside just 15 minutes from Bath, this impressive 16th-century pub has been stripped back to its original stone walls and flagstone floors, but enhanced by more contemporary furnishings. Inside, it's all solid oak tables, comfortable sofas and Lloyd Loom chairs but, when the weather allows, the tables dotted around the stunning terraced gardens are highly sought-after. Set on two levels, the grassed garden has the most tranquil views of the nearby hills and it's little wonder that the pub is so favoured by walkers and local shooting parties.

Walk down the stone steps from the garden and you'll find a detached stone building housing three lovely bedrooms, all with state-of-the-art shower rooms. The bedrooms are contemporary with the same calm colours as the dining room and chunky teak furniture. In each, there are crisp linen sheets, White Company products, a 30-channel plasma TV screen and amusing paintings of local cows.

The Wheatsheaf, Combe Hay, Bath, Somerset BA2 7EG

The Food

Since opening in 2006, The Wheatsheaf has gained a formidable reputation for its food. The kitchen sources local produce, all of it in its rightful season. Although there's a lunchtime bar menu featuring walker-friendly Montgomery cheddar cheese and chutney sandwiches, steak baguettes and the pub's famous ploughman's, just as many foodies are attracted by a la carte dishes such as Scottish king scallops with boudin noir and sweet potato, fillet of turbot with chive creamed potato and salsify, or fillet of Buccleuch Estate beef with horseradish creamed potato and onion bhaji.

Of course, no visit to The Wheatsheaf would be complete without trying desserts such as the seductive dark chocolate fondant with Tonka bean ice cream, or ploughing through one of the two cheeseboards on offer – one English and the other entirely French. Although Butcombe beers and local Cheddar Valley cider are on tap, the Euro-centric wine list may feature too many vinous distractions. The pub's regular summer barbecues are an added attraction, with lobster and langoustines making an extravagant change from the normal burgers and steaks.

The Essentials

Time at the Bar!
12-3pm, 6-11pm (closed Mon)
Food: 12-2.30pm, 6-9.30pm
(10pm Sat)

What's the Damage?
Main courses from £16.50

Bitter Experience:
Butcombe and IPA

Sticky Fingers:
Children welcome

Muddy Paws:
Dogs welcome in the bar

Zzzzz:
3 rooms, £95-£120

Anything Else?
Terrace, garden, car park

What To Do

Shop

NB GALLERY

A specialist gallery concentrating on British arts and crafts using only natural materials, including glass, textiles and a wide range of jewellery. All items are displayed among a regularly changing series of exhibitions that could include abstract paintings and a stream of new work from on-site craftspeople and artists. See tapestry artist and gallery owner Kimberley Jackson weaving tapestries in her workshop.

4 Church Walk, Trowbridge,
Wiltshire BA14 8DX
01225 719119
www.NBgallery.co.uk

CHEDDAR GORGE CHEESE COMPANY

Watch the traditional cheddar-making at the dairy before buying some in the on-site shop, which also sells a range of biscuits and chutneys to serve with the cheese.

The Cliffs, Cheddar Gorge,
Somerset BS27 3QA
01934 742810
www.cheddargorgecheese.co.uk

JON THORNER FARM SHOP

Foodies will love the huge range of mostly locally sourced foodstuffs available here, including more than 50 cheeses; Mendip beef, pork and lamb; smoked goods; game from local estates and a selection of exotic specialist meats. For over 30 years Jon Thorner has worked closely with West Country farmers and food producers to ensure only top-quality produce is sold in his Pylle and Street farm shops.

Pylle, Shepton Mallet, Somerset BA4 6TA
01749 830138
www.jonthorners.co.uk

Visit

MUSEUM OF COSTUME

This fascinating museum is housed in The Assembly Rooms, designed by John Wood the Younger in 1771, and is one of Bath's finest public buildings, recalling the Georgian city in its opulent, carefree heyday. The museum houses one of the largest and most prestigious collections (more than 30,000 objects) of fashionable dress for men, women and children since the time of Elizabeth I with a serious nod to modern fashion history. The regularly changing special exhibitions entice fashion design students from all over the country.

Bennett Street, Bath,
Bath & NE Somerset BA1 2QH
01225 477785
www.museumofcostume.co.uk

TYNTESFIELD

A stunning 19th-century country house and estate situated on a ridge overlooking the beautiful Yeo Valley and run by the National Trust. It was built in 1864 for a wealthy merchant, William Gibbs, and is memorable for its extraordinary Gothic-revival architecture, most notably the spectacular array of towers, turrets and chimneys that adorns the building. Its true worth is slowly being revealed as restoration progresses. Inside the house are collections of Victorian decorative arts and furnishings as well as artefacts giving detailed insight into below-stairs life in High-Victorian England. Outside you will find a complete walled kitchen garden as well as parkland estate.

Wraxall, North Somerset BS48 1NT
0870 458 4500
www.nationaltrust.org.uk/tyntesfield

Activity

CYCLING

Hire a bicycle and tackle the more challenging roads, byways and tracks of the Mendip Hills or the complex web of lanes threading the low-lying Somerset Levels. Either way, you'll discover the countryside and villages around Cheddar and north Somerset.

Cheddar Cycle Store, Valley Line Industrial
Park, Wedmore Road, Cheddar,
Somerset BS27 3EE
01934 741300
www.cheddarcyclestore.co.uk

SOMERSET WILDLIFE TRUST

The Trust has dozens of reserves throughout Somerset and arranges frequent events, varying from hands-on conservation to animal watches, walks and talks. One of the largest is Ubley Warren, a former lead-mining area with many relics of this old industry, plus specialist plants and grand views. The area is accessed from Blackmoor Nature Reserve, Charterhouse.

01823 652400
www.somersetwildlife.org

SPA TREATMENT

Britain's only natural thermal spa (the water is a constant 45°C) is adjacent to the Roman foundations. Here you can enjoy modern spa-based treatments in the spirit of the Roman days. Do as the Celts and Romans did and enjoy various therapies and pamper yourself in style in the steam rooms and baths, including the magnificently refurbished Georgian bath.

The Hetling Pump Room, Hot Bath Street,
Bath, Bath & NE Somerset BA1 1SJ
01225 335678
www.thermaebathspa.com

The Walk - Cotswolds Meet Mendips at Wellow

A green valley walk, tracing a legacy of abandoned industry and failed technology.

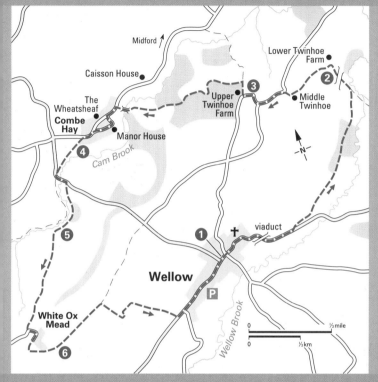

Walk Details

LENGTH: 6.5 miles (10.4km)

TIME: 3hrs 30min

ASCENT: 984ft (300m)

PATHS: Byways, stream sides and some field paths, 12 stiles

SUGGESTED MAP: aqua3 OS Explorer 142 Shepton Mallet

GRID REFERENCE: ST 739583

PARKING: Street parking in village centre, or large car park below Peasedown road

❶ Head past the church and walk under the viaduct. Immediately after Wellow Trekking, the track starts just above the road. Where it becomes unclear, cross to the hedge opposite; continue above it. The new track runs through the wood, then down to the valley floor. Where the bridleway sign points right, turn left to pass under the railway bridge.

❷ Just before Lower Twinhoe Farm, turn left onto the signposted track. At the hilltop, the track fades into thistly ground. Bear right, before Middle Twinhoe, to small gate. Turn right along farm's driveway to lane. Turn left, then right around farm buildings and left towards Upper Twinhoe. Just before the farm, a signed track descends to the right.

❸ After 130yds (118m) turn left through the double gate and along the field top. The path slants down through woodland towards Combe Hay. From the woodland edge follow the lower edge of the field to the stone bridge into Combe Hay village. Follow the main road left, to pass the Manor House.

❹ After the last house of Combe Hay, find gap in wall on left. Bear right, down to Cam Brook; follow to road bridge. Cross and continue with stream down to right through field and wood. Follow the stream across another field to the stile, then along foot of short field to gateway.

❺ Don't go through the gateway, but turn up the field edge to reach the stile on the right. Slant up left across the next field to the nettled way between thorns. At the top bear right on the rutted track to the lane. Turn uphill to White Ox Mead; follow the lane to the stile. Slant up to another stile; turn up the tarred track to where it divides near to the shed without any walls.

❻ Keep ahead on the rutted track along the hill crest. Ignore the waymarked stile to pass under some electric cables. Here a small metal gate on the right leads to the hoof-printed path down beside the fence. At the foot of the field turn left, then turn left again (uphill), and head round the corner to the gate. Turn left across the field top and walk down the edge to the street leading back into Wellow village centre.

The Shave Cross Inn

Dorset

The Inn

Situated in a remote and peaceful spot in the beautiful Marshwood Vale, this picture-postcard, 14th-century thatched cob-and-flint inn was once a resting place for pilgrims and monastic visitors on their way to the shrine of St Witta at Whitchurch Canonicorum. They frequently had their tonsures trimmed as a mark of respect while staying, hence the unusual name. A worn stone floor, vast inglenook fireplaces, head-cracking low beams and rustic furnishings in the timeless bar testify to the inn's age. There's a gorgeous flower-filled suntrap garden in which to sup pints of local Branoc ale.

Marshwood-born Roy Warburton returned to his roots from Tobago in 2003 to restore the fortunes of this cracking country pub, and 2007 saw the addition of seven individually designed bedrooms in a newly built Dorset flint stone building. Named after local hills, they sport beautiful stone floors, heavy oak beams, luxuriously draped four-poster or comfortable sleigh beds, plasma screens and swish ensuite bathrooms. For stunning views across the Vale, book Lamberts Castle or the Pilsdon Pen Honeymoon Suite.

The Essentials

Time at the Bar!
11am-3pm, 6-11pm (11am-11pm Jul
& Aug). Closed Mon except Bank Hols
Food: 12-3pm, 6-9.30pm (7-8pm Sun
in Jul & Aug)

What's the Damage?
Two-course set menu from £24.95;
three-course from £28

Bitter Experience:
Branscombe Vale Brannoc

Sticky Fingers:
Children welcome; small portions
available

Muddy Paws:
Dogs welcome in the bar

Zzzzz:
7 rooms, £160-£190; single £90

Anything Else?
Garden, car park, skittle alley

The Food

With Roy came a Caribbean chef, who really spiced up the menu with a mix of Caribbean-, Cajun- and Thai-influenced dishes, noteworthy in an area of the country renowned for traditional pub food. Look to the imaginative two- or three-course set menu for such exotic offerings as crab spring rolls with sweet chilli and garlic, salad of jerk chicken, plantain and crisy bacon with aioli, and seared local scallops with banana relish and basil oil for starters.

The selection of imaginative main dishes may take in roasted Creole duck breast with black cherry compote, hot spicy Cuban bouillabaisse, and juicy Dorset fillet steak served with a delicious rum brandy and Caribbean peppercorn sauce.

Traditional tastes are well catered for at lunchtime, with the bar menu listing freshly battered haddock and chips, rump steak, and decent ploughman's lunches (very local Denhay cheddar), and fresh crab sandwiches. Other than plantain, spices and exotic fish, all produce is sourced from Dorset and Somerset. For pudding, try one of Roy's tropical ice creams or tuck into home-made chocolate truffle torte, or round off with a selection of Dorset cheeses.

What To Do

Shop

BROADWINDSOR CRAFT & DESIGN CENTRE

Old farm buildings have been renovated to house a centre with a wide variety of regional products for sale: hand-made ironwork by Lyme Bay Forge Blacksmiths, musical instruments, jewellery, gardening gear, traditional toys. There's also a cafe offering wholesome home-made meals and Dorset cream teas.

Broadwindsor, Beaminster, Dorset DT8 3PX

01308 868362

www.broadwindsor-crafts.co.uk

LEAKERS BAKERY

Using locally milled flour, award-winning baker Aidan Chapman produces a range of delicious breads including organic, yeast and wheat-free varieties, and also good old-fashioned cakes and pies.

29 East Street, Bridport, Dorset DT6 3JX

01308 423296

PIERREPOINT ART GALLERY

You'll find contemporary, abstract and traditional work in this handsome Georgian gallery, full of light and space.

76 South Street, Bridport, Dorset DT6 3NN

01308 421638

www.pierrepointgallery.co.uk

WASHINGPOOL FARM SHOP

Located in lovely countryside near the coast, Washingpool Farm Shop sells locally grown and sourced fruit and vegetables, artisan bread, farmhouse cheeses, home-reared meat and fresh fish, jams, chutneys and preserves.

Dottery Road, North Allington, Bridport, Dorset DT6 5HP

01308 459549

www.washingpool.co.uk

Visit

FORDE ABBEY

This former Cistercian monastery has astonishingly opulent state rooms. The award-winning 30-acre grounds include a charming kitchen garden, a Magnolia grandiflora, an Ionic temple and huge redwoods.

Chard, Somerset TA20 4LU

01460 220231

www.fordeabbey.co.uk

MANGERTON MILL

This 17th-century working water mill in a tranquil valley on the River Manger gives a real insight into ancient rural Dorset life. There's a good tea room, selling crafts – you can also do some trout fishing here.

Mangerton, Bridport, Dorset

01308 485224

MAPPERTON HOUSE & GARDENS

This magnificent manor house built with glowing sandstone has views across a lovely Italianate garden. Inside, the panelled drawing room has a rococo fireplace and Tudor-decorated ceiling. The gardens, on brick terraces dotted with topiary, yew and box, include an orangery and 17th-century fish ponds. There's also a fine cafe for lunch.

Beaminster, Dorset DT8 3NR

01308 862645

www.mapperton.com

PALMERS BREWERY

Suppliers of ale to Dorset pubs since 1794, some of the buildings in this beautiful brewery are thatched. Take the tour, and enjoy a glass or two of Dorset Gold or Tally Ho!

The Old Brewery, West Bay Road, Bridport, Dorset DT6 4JA

01308 422396

www.palmersbrewery.com

Activity

LLAMA TREKKING

Discover the glorious Dorset countryside in the company of llamas, who make delightful (if not very talkative) travelling companions. Best of all, they are prepared to take the load and carry your bags and picnic lunch.

UK Llamas, New House Farm, Mosterton, Beaminster, Dorset DT8 3HE

01308 868674

www.ukllamas.co.uk

THRILLS ON THE HILLS

There are all sorts of high-octane activities on offer at Henley Hillbillies. How about having a go at quad biking, clay pigeon shooting, off-road rallying in a custom-built Mini Maverick, and hovercrafting – floating 15cm (6in) above the ground at 40mph over 15 acres in the Dorset hills.

Henley Hillbillies

Old Henley Farm, Buckland Newton, Dorchester, Dorset DT2 7BL

01300 345293

www.henleyhillbillies.co.uk

ZORBING

If you're a real adrenalin junkie, and the idea of hurtling down the Dorset hills at 30mph inside a gigantic inflatable sphere is your idea of fun, zorbing could be the sport for you. It's 100 per cent safe – you can choose to be harnessed inside the sphere or slosh about in water, which, if the water is really cold, is a sure-fire cure for a hangover. Apparently.

Zorb South UK

Pine Lodge Farm, Bockhampton, Dorchester, Dorset DT2 8QL

01929 426595

www.zorbsouth.co.uk

The Walk - A Golden Cap in Trust

Climb a fine top, owned by one of the country's most popular charities.

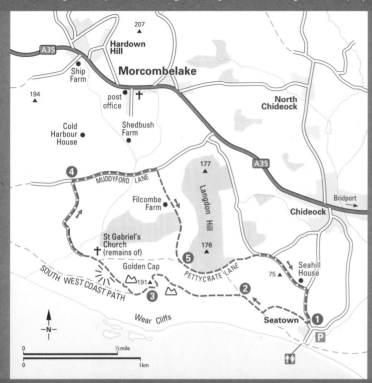

Walk Details

LENGTH: 4 miles (6.4km)

TIME: 2hrs 30min

ASCENT: 1,007ft (307m)

PATHS: Field tracks, country lanes, steep zig-zag gravel path, 7 stiles

SUGGESTED MAP: aqua3 OS Explorer 116 Lyme Regis & Bridport

GRID REFERENCE: SY 420917

PARKING: Car park (charge) above gravel beach in Seatown; beware, can flood in stormy weather

❶ Walk back up through Seatown. Cross the stile on the left, on to the footpath ('Coast Path Diversion'). Cross the stile at the end, bear left to cross the stile and the footbridge into woodland. Cross the pair of stiles at the other side; bear right up the hill ('Golden Cap').

❷ Where the track forks, keep left. Go through the trees and over a stile. Bear left, straight across the open hillside, with the National Trust's Golden Cap ahead of you. Pass through the line of trees and walk up the fence. Go up some steps, cross the stile and continue ahead. At fingerpost go left through gate; follow path of shallow steps up through bracken, heather, bilberry and bramble to top of Golden Cap.

❸ Pass the trig point and turn right along the top. Pass stone memorial to Earl of Antrim. At the marker stone turn right and follow the zig-zag path downhill (great views along bay to Charmouth and Lyme Regis). Go through the gate and bear right over the field towards ruined St Gabriel's Church. In the bottom corner turn down through the gate, passing ruins on the right; go through the 2nd gate. Go down the track, passing cottages on the left, and bear right up the road ('Morcombelake'). Follow up between the high banks and hedges. Continue through the gateway.

❹ At the road junction, turn right down Muddyford Lane ('Langdon Hill'). Pass the gate of Shedbush Farm and continue straight up the hill. Turn right up the concreted lane towards Filcombe Farm. Follow the blue markers through the farmyard, bearing left through 2 gates. Walk up the track, go through 2 more gates and bear left over the top of the green saddle between Langdon Hill and Golden Cap.

❺ Go left through the gate in the corner and down the gravel lane (Pettycrate Lane) beside the woods ('Seatown'). Ignore the footpath to the right. At the junction of tracks keep right, downhill, with the patchwork of fields on the hillside ahead. Pass Seahill House on the left and turn right, on to the road. Continue down the road into Seatown village to return to the car.

The European Inn

Dorset

TWO beautiful bedrooms now available

The Inn

Drive six miles north of Dorchester through the beautiful Piddle Valley into the heart of Dorset's rolling downland landscape and you'll come across the European Inn in the sleepy, wonderfully named village of Piddletrenthide. Mark and Emily Hammick, who bought the pub in early 2007, have breathed new life into the creamy yellow building, refurbishing throughout and adding two stunning bedrooms. Chunky church candles and fresh flowers top rustic old pine tables in the single, tiled and beamed bar. You'll find Mark and Emily's charming watercolours lining the walls, a crackling log fire in the grate and top-notch ales on handpump.

Personal paintings, objets d'art and elegant touches extend upstairs to the Red and Green bedrooms – both have been kitted out with style and taste. Expect plasma screens, fresh flowers from the garden, a decanter of sherry, and fresh coffee and home-made shortbread. The Green Room's vast tiled bathroom boasts a walk-in shower, a huge roll-top bath and local, hand-made toiletries – perfect after a day walking the Dorset Downs.

The Food

The ethos at the pub is to provide good, fresh pub food using as many ingredients sourced locally and as seasonally as possible. Short, changing menus show imagination and champion local suppliers, notably the meat, which comes from Mark's parents' farm at nearby Lower Wraxall and Genesis Farmers in Buckland Newton. This translates to loin of Wraxall lamb with confit shoulder and garlic and rosemary juices, and roast Genesis pork belly with black pudding mash and cider juices. Seasonal fruit and vegetables are from local allotments and gardens.

Alternative main courses may take in beer-battered cod and chips, pea, broad bean and mint risotto, and slow-braised Halstock Dexter beef with horseradish mash and red wine juices. Kick off a good meal with seared Portland scallops with cauliflower puree, or venison and pigeon terrine with home-made plum chutney, and round off with Mappowder gooseberry crumble with strawberry ice cream, or a plate of local cheeses. Choice wines include some classic Riojas and a house white Sherborne Castle.

The Essentials

Time at the Bar!
11.30am-3pm, 6-11pm (Closed Mon)
Food: 12-2pm, 7-9pm
(No food Sun evening)

What's the Damage?
Main courses from £8

Bitter Experience:
Palmers Copper Ale, Otter Ale, guest beer

Sticky Fingers:
Children welcome; smaller portions

Muddy Paws:
Dogs allowed in bar and bedrooms (£5)

Zzzzz:
2 rooms, £80; single £55

Anything Else?
Garden, car park, wi-fi access

What To Do

Shop

ALWESTON POST OFFICE

Much more than just a post office, this is an amazing Aladdin's cave for the real foodie, selling local cakes and produce – no wonder it's one of Hugh Fearnley-Whittingstall's favourite spots.

Alweston, Sherborne, Dorset DT9 5HS
01963 23400

GOLD HILL ORGANIC FARM

'Anything you can grow in this country, we'll try to grow' is Sara and Andrew Cross's maxim – their selection of fruit and veg is impressive, and the farm is entirely organic, including the beef. You can also stock up on jams and chutneys, dairy products, bread and pasta.

Child Okeford, Blandford Forum,
Dorset DT11 8HB
01258 861413
www.goldhillorganicfarm.co.uk

HAMBLEDON GALLERY

This small but classy department store sells clothes by Orla Kiely, Avoca, Fenn Wright Manson and Betty Jackson, to name but a few. Also good for bedding, china, glass, toys and accessories. 'Worth a detour', says *Harpers & Queen*.

40–44 Salisbury Street, Blandford Forum,
Dorset DT11 7PR
01258 452880

SABINS FINE FOOD

This generously stocked shop carries a range of over 50 cheeses, many produced locally, such as Dorset blue vinney. You can also buy ham, pâté, home-made bread, Borough Hill cider and Childhay Manor ice creams.

5 Hound Street, Sherborne, Dorset DT9 3AB
01935 816037

Visit

ABBOTSBURY

There's a full day's worth of things to see and do in the beautiful village of Abbotsbury, all with spectacular views across Chesil Bank to the island of Portland.

ATHELHAMPTON HOUSE

One of the finest 15th-century manor houses in the country, Athelhampton is surrounded by amazing Grade I listed architectural gardens, with fountains, topiary, and a 15th-century dovecote. The River Piddle runs through the landscaped grounds.

Athelhampton, Dorchester, Dorset DT2 7LG
www.athelhampton.co.uk

MAPPERTON HOUSE & GARDENS

Terraced gardens surround this delightful largely Elizabethan manor house, with stable blocks, a dovecote and All Saints Church. There's a walled croquet lawn, orangery, an ornate pavilion overlooking a stunning Italianate garden with topiary, grottos and ponds. Mapperton was voted 'the Nation's Finest Manor House' by *Country Life* in 2006.

Beaminster, Dorset DT8 3NR
01308 862645
www.mapperton.com

MAX GATE

Thomas Hardy designed and built Max Gate, and lived in it for 43 years – it is where he wrote *Tess of the d'Urbervilles*, *Jude the Obscure* and *The Mayor of Casterbridge*.

Max Gate
Alington Avenue, Dorchester,
Dorset DT1 2AA
01305 262538
www.nationaltrust.org.uk

Activity

GOLF

Weymouth Golf Club has a beautiful parkland course with stunning views over the coast and countryside, and a 'challenging' 18 holes.

Weymouth Golf Club
Links Road, Weymouth, Dorset DT4 0PF
0844 980 9909
www.weymouthgolfclub.co.uk

HORSE RIDING IN BLACKMORE VALE

Enjoy woodland bridleways and the gently rolling clay pastures of Thomas Hardy's 'Wessex' country on horseback. This is traditionally dairying country, hence the patchwork-quilt fields and hedgerows bordered by the high arc of chalk hills. Described by Hardy in *Under the Greenwood Tree* and *Far from the Madding Crowd*, this is quintessential rural England.

Pound Cottage Riding Centre
Luccumbe Farm, Milton Abbas, Blandford
Forum, Dorset DT11 0BD
01258 880057

TROUT FISHING

Spend a day in peaceful contemplation – there are five natural lakes fed by spring water to choose from, well stocked with brown and rainbow trout. You can hire tackle here, so there's no need to bring your rod.

Flowers Farm Trout Lake
Hillfield, Dorchester, Dorset DT2 7BA
01300 341351

The Walk - Giant Steps at Cerne Abbas

A valley walk from Minterne Magna to see a famous chalk hill carving.

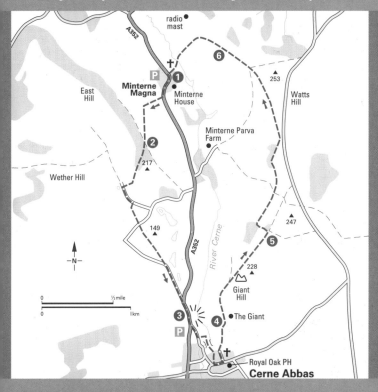

Walk Details

LENGTH: 5.5 miles (8.8km)

TIME: 2hrs 30min

ASCENT: 591ft (180m)

PATHS: Country paths and tracks, minor road, main road, 2 stiles

SUGGESTED MAP: aqua3 OS Explorer 117 Cerne Abbas & Bere Regis

GRID REFERENCE: ST 659043

PARKING: Car park (free) opposite church in Minterne Magna

❶ Turn right and walk up the road through the village. Where it curls left, turn right through the gate on to the bridleway and go up the hill. At the top, go through the gate and bear left. Follow the blue marker diagonally up to the right. Go through the gate, walk on past the trees, then bend up, round the field towards the trees.

❷ Go through the gap and take the track down diagonally left through the woods. At the bottom, turn left along the road. After the bend take footpath right, across field. After trees veer left, towards white gate. Cross road, pass right of gate, and continue down field. Pass another white gate then continue ahead on road. At end bear right on to A352.

❸ Cross to car park for best view of Giant hill carving. Take road down to village; turn left signposted 'Pottery'. Turn right by stream ('Village Centre'). Continue over slab bridge and pass old mill. Bear left, to high street. Turn left, and then left again in front of Royal Oak, to church. Walk up Old Pitch Market to Abbey. Turn right into churchyard and bear left. Go through the gate signposted 'Giant's Hill'; bear left.

❹ Cross the stile, then turn right up the steps. Follow the path to the left, round the contour of the hill, below the fence. As the path divides, keep right, up the hill, towards the top. Bear left along the ridge, cross the stile by the fingerpost and head diagonally right, towards the barn.

❺ At the barn turn left and go down through the gate. Turn right and follow the bridleway along the hillside, which offers great views towards Minterne Parva. Keep ahead at the junction of the tracks, then dip down through the gateway above the woods. Keep walking straight on; go through the gate near the road. Turn left along the grassy track. At the gateway, turn left on to the gravel lane.

❻ Directly above Minterne House, turn left through the gate and bear left. Go through gate and turn left, downhill. Continue down through several gates and keep right at the fingerpost down a broad track. Cross the stream, then walk up past the church to return to the car park.

The Stapleton Arms

Dorset

The Stapleton Arms, Church Hill, Buckhorn Weston, Dorset SP8 5HS

The Inn

They revamped the Queen's Arms down near Sherborne and made a huge success of it, so Rupert and Victoria Reeves set about repeating their winning formula at this once run-down inn in Buckhorn Weston. Naturally, the result is stunning and they have managed to breathe new life into the place. Chic, modern decor has been introduced in the slate-floored bar area, yet the pub remains a true local, one where drinkers and diners mix happily. Expect big scrubbed tables, an eclectic mix of chairs, contemporary colours and squashy leather sofas, which invite you to relax with the papers and a pint of Butcombe Bitter. The adjoining dining room has huge mirrors on deep blue-painted walls.

A peaceful night's sleep is guaranteed in one of the four quirky, classy bedrooms. Individually designed, they mix contemporary and antique furnishings, plus all have plasma TVs, DVD players, internet access, cotton sheets on big wooden beds, and huge tiled bathrooms with storm showers and posh smellies. Breakfast on Dorset bacon, free-range eggs, home-made bread and jams, then walk it off by striding across open fields.

The Food

Food is simple, modern and innovative, and the daily changing menus are prepared using quality local and seasonal produce, most from within 25 miles of the pub. Fish is delivered daily from the Dorset coast; salads and vegetables are grown on Roswells Farm near Ilminster; and meats are sourced from Dorset farms. A hand-made pork pie at the bar or a lunchtime sandwich of rare roast beef with horseradish sauce, or even a fisherman's platter – a feast for two – suits peckish drinkers. But for something more substantial, look to the main dishes: whole plaice with lime and caper butter or tagliatelle with wild mushrooms, chorizo, peas and parmesan are typical mouthwatering choices.

The evening menu extends to guinea fowl, partridge and mushroom terrine with spicy tomato chutney, followed by hake with chive mash and tomato hollandaise or duck with marmalade and pepper sauce. For pudding, try the warm plum tarte tatin with stem-ginger ice cream or the intriguing 'four spoons of chocolate'. Wash it all down with tip-top ales, real cider, Luscombe organic juices or some interesting wines.

The Essentials

Time at the Bar!
11am-3pm, 6-11pm; Sat 12-11pm;
Sun 12-10.30pm
Food: 12-3pm, 6-10pm

What's the Damage?
Main courses from £8.50

Bitter Experience:
Timothy Taylor Landlord, Butcombe

Sticky Fingers:
Children welcome; children's menu

Muddy Paws:
Dogs welcome

Zzzzz:
4 rooms, £80-£120

Anything Else?
Patio, terrace, car park

What To Do

Shop

ONE CRAFT GALLERY

This Grade II listed building, previously a saddlers, is co-operatively run and looks onto the market place with its market cross and 15th-century 'shamble'. It is home to items crafted by local artists, many of them internationally renowned. Ceramics, jewellery, millinery, knitwear, paintings and prints are among some of the arty delights.

1 High Street, Shepton Mallet, Somerset BA4 5AA
01749 343777
www.1craft.co.uk

PARKERS MENU

Parkers is a family-run catering business established in 1902 and now run by Jane, a great-granddaughter of the original owners. Their Taste of the West award-winning take-home meals are hand-made in small batches from locally sourced, seasonal ingredients – try the fish pie (made from a secret family recipe), raspberry pavlova, Dorset apple cake, shepherd's pie and goats' cheese tarts. While you're here, don't miss the walk down Gold Hill, the steep cobbled street made famous by the Hovis boy in the 1974 bread adverts.

2 Swan Yard, Shaftesbury, Dorset DT9 3AX
01935 814527
www.parkersmenu.co.uk

FERNSTROM & FARRELL DELI

This friendly deli and grocery is filled with breads, cakes and masses of other locally sourced, home-made goodies.

2 High Street, Wincanton, Somerset BA9 9JP
04963 31549

Visit

FLEET AIR ARM MUSEUM

All the iconic planes are under one roof here: World War I Sopwith Camels and Fokkers; the World War II Fairey Swordfish. The Leading Edge exhibition demonstrates how advances in design and technology allowed the British Aircraft industry to lead the world, and includes the second Concorde prototype, Hawkers and De Havillands. There's a Restoration Hangar where you can watch the latest renovation project, a well-stocked shop where you can buy kits, books, DVDs and prints, and a cafe from which – on a clear day – you can watch next door's Royal Naval Air Station planes going through their paces.

Ilchester, Somerset BA22 8HT
01935 840565
www.fleetairarm.com

LYTES CAREY MANOR

Set deep in rural Somerset, this manor house with its Tudor great hall and 14th-century chapel was the home of medieval herbalist Henry Lyte. Originally the garden was laid out in a series of 'rooms' with topiary, mixed borders and a herb garden where the plants that Lyte cultivated are still grown.

Charlton Mackrell, Somerton, Somerset TA11 7HU
01458 224471
www.nationaltrust.org.uk

SHAFTESBURY ABBEY MUSEUM & GARDEN

On the site of Saxon England's foremost Benedictine nunnery, founded by King Alfred in 888 AD, the abbey is a magical series of buildings lying in a peaceful walled garden. King Canute is said to have loved Shaftesbury and probably restored the Saxon buildings – Catherine of Aragon also stayed here. The museum vividly brings to life the history of the Abbey, through fascinating collections of excavated carved objects, medieval floor tiles and carved stonework. The plants you'll see would have been used by the nuns to flavour food, heal the sick and dye cloth. A medieval orchard has been planted, spanning the 15th to the 19th century.

Park Walk, Shaftesbury, Dorset SP7 8JR
01747 852910
www.shaftesburyabbey.co.uk

Activity

GLIDING

Fancy the idea of soaring soundlessly for an hour or two above the glorious Wiltshire and Dorset countryside? Try your hand at the controls, or just relax and enjoy the ride and the view.

Dorset Gliding Club
The Park, Kingston Deverill, Warminster, Wiltshire BA12 7HF
01380 859161
www.bwnd.co.uk

HORSERIDING IN BLACKMORE VALE

Enjoy the gently rolling pastures of Thomas Hardy's Wessex on horseback. This is traditionally dairy country, hence the patchwork quilt fields and the hedgerows bordered by the high arc of chalk hills. As described by Hardy in *Under the Greenwood Tree,* this is quintessential rural England.

Pound Cottage Riding Centre
Luccumbe Farm, Milton Abbas, Blandford Forum, Dorset DT11 0BD
01258 880057

The Walk - A Stroll Around Cucklington

Up hill and down dale, taking in a church with over a thousand years of history.

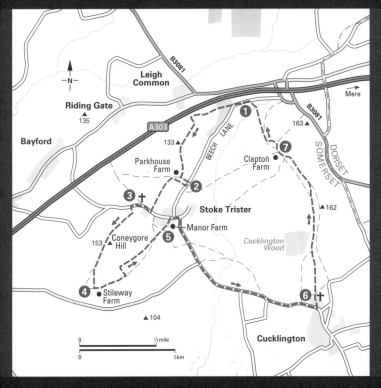

Walk Details

LENGTH: 5.5 miles (8.8km)

TIME: 2hrs 45min

ASCENT: 600ft (180m)

PATHS: Little-used field paths, which may be overgrown, 11 stiles

SUGGESTED MAP: aqua3 OS Explorer 129 Yeovil & Sherborne

GRID REFERENCE: ST 747298

PARKING: Lay-by on former main road immediately south of A303

INFORMATION: This walk is over the county border in Somerset

1 With your back to the A303, turn right on the lane to where the track runs ahead into the wood. At the far side, the fenced footpath runs alongside the main road. Turn left up the path, then right into the fenced-off path that bends left to Parkhouse Farm. After the passage to the left of the buildings, turn left again to the lane.

2 Turn back right, following the field edge back by the farm track. Go through the gate; turn left through the gate. Heading towards Stoke Trister church, follow the left edge of the field; go straight up 2nd field, turning right along lane to church.

3 Continue to the stile. Go uphill past the muddy track, but turn right alongside the hedge immediately above. Follow around Coneygore Hill, over the stile, then to 2nd; go straight down to Stileway Farm.

4 Turn left by the top of the farm buildings. Continue into the field track but immediately take the gate above; pass along the base of 2 fields, to the gate by the cattle trough. Head uphill, with the hedge to the left, to the steeper bank around Coneygore Hill. Turn right and follow the banking to the stile. Keep on to the gap between the bramble clumps; slant down right to reach the gate in the corner leading on to the green track and then to the lane near Manor Farm.

5 Turn downhill past the thatched cottage and red phone box; bear right for Cucklington. There are field paths on the left, but use the lane to cross the valley and climb to Cucklington. The gravel track on the left leads to Cucklington church.

6 Pass left of the church; cross 2 fields, passing above Cucklington Wood. In the 3rd field slant to the right to join track to Clapton Farm.

7 After the Tudor manor house the track bends right, uphill. Turn left between the farm buildings to the gate, then turn left down the wooded bank. Turn right, along the base of the bank, to the gap in the hedge. Bear left past the power pole to the field's bottom corner. Cross 2 streams; bear left to cross a 3rd and the stile beyond. Go straight up to the stile by the cattle trough and rejoin the lane you parked on.

* Bumble bee on lavender bush, Farnham, Dorset

The Museum Inn

Dorset

The Inn

Farnham is a sleepy village, enticingly lost within the rolling folds of Cranborne Chase and filled with timeless thatched cottages. At its heart is the part-thatched Museum Inn, which owes its name to the 17th-century

The Essentials

Time at the Bar!
12-3pm, 6-11pm
Food: 12-2pm (2.30pm Sat, Sun), 7-9.30pm (Sun 9pm)

What's the Damage?
Main courses from £14

Bitter Experience:
Ringwood Best, Hop Back Summer Lightning

Sticky Fingers:
Children welcome at lunchtime

Muddy Paws:
Dogs welcome

Zzzzz:
8 rooms, £95-£150

Anything Else?
Terrace, car park, conservatory

The Food

The kitchen is the domain of Clive Jory, who takes sourcing quality local produce very seriously. He uses only traditionally reared meats and free-range poultry, game from neighbouring estates and local organic vegetables. Dine informally in the bustling bar or head for the more formal Shed restaurant, which is open evenings and weekends only – booking is essential. Typical starters include chicken liver and mushroom parfait with sticky onion marmalade, smoked haddock chowder or potted brown shrimps served with rocket salad and grilled bruschetta.

To follow, there may be a hearty and satisfying Portland fish stew with saffron potatoes, simply grilled lemon sole, or well-executed modern dishes like herb-crusted rack of Dorset lamb with fondant potato, ratatouille and aubergine purée, or local estate venison with butternut squash mash and a sour cherry jus. To finish, the dark chocolate brownie served with lashings of bitter chocolate sauce and coffee ice cream is irresistible. Upmarket sandwiches like Longhorn steak, mushroom and onion are available only at lunchtime.

What To Do

Shop

ELLWOOD BOOKS
Four rooms of beautiful books, including rare and secondhand, fiction and non-fiction, local interest, history and poetry.

38 Winchester Street, Salisbury,
Wiltshire SP1 1HG

01722 322975

www.ellwoodbooks.com

HARE LANE POTTERY
Jonathan Garratt is one of Britain's foremost terracotta potters and his passion for plants informs many of the innovative shapes. Local clay is refined on site and all the work is fired exclusively with wood to give distinctive dark colours and real character. Also available: glazed tableware and garden sculpture.

Hare Lane, Cranborne, Wimborne Minster,
Dorset BH21 5QT

01725 517700

NUGGS 1268
In this beautifully restored Tudor building you will find specialist foods, culinary gifts, excellent wines, oils, vinegars and cookware.

51 Blue Boar Row, Salisbury,
Wiltshire SP1 1DA

01722 417600

WALFORD MILL CRAFT CENTRE
A converted mill in a quiet riverside setting with a Crafts Council shop and exhibition gallery, featuring the best in contemporary British design. Join a workshop and try your hand at silk weaving, stained glass and machine embroidery. Wide variety of art and craft events.

Stone Lane, Wimborne Minster,
Dorset BH21 1NL

01202 841400

www.walford-mill.co.uk

Visit

KINGSTON LACY
This elegant 17th-century country mansion was the home of the Bankes family for more than 300 years and is set in formal gardens with extensive wooded parkland. There are impressive old master paintings by Van Dyck, Titian and Brueghel, Egyptian artefacts and the famous dramatic Spanish Room with walls hung in gilded leather.

Wimborne Minster, Dorset BH21 4EA

01202 883402

www.nationaltrust.org.uk

SALISBURY CATHEDRAL
Building of the cathedral was begun in 1220 and largely completed in just 38 years, and Salisbury is unique among English medieval cathedrals for having no substantial later additions. You can also see one of only four remaining copies of the original *Magna Carta* here, as well as viewing Europe's oldest working clock dating from 1386.

Salisbury, Wiltshire

www.salisburycathedral.co.uk

STOURHEAD HOUSE & GARDENS
Built in the 1720s, this fine Palladian mansion houses a collection of Chippendale furniture, magnificent paintings and an exquisite Regency library. Surrounding the mansion is one of the finest landscape gardens in the world: winding lakeside paths lead past classical temples and follies, set against a backdrop of beautiful and exotic trees, revealing vistas that have captured the imagination of visitors for more than two centuries.

Stourton, Warminster, Wiltshire BA12 6QD

01747 841152

www.nationaltrust.org.uk

Activity

CHARTER A YACHT
Sail anywhere between the Isle of Wight and Weymouth and explore the Jurassic coast on a fully equipped 39ft Bavaria yacht, owned and skippered by sailing team Russ and Jenny Upton. Novices can build up their sailing miles for RYA courses while experienced sea dogs can be more hands-on.

One Day Yacht Charter

5 Thames St, Poole Quay, Poole,
Dorset BH15 1JN

07921 833115

www.charter-oneday.com

FLY FISHING
Catch your own dinner on a day on the lakes at Christchurch Angling Club. Two put-and-take lakes (rainbow trout) and one catch-and-release lake (brown and rainbow trout). Open all year; dry and wet fly.

Christchurch Angling Club

White Sheet Trout Fisher, Holt,
nr Wimborne, Dorset

01202 871703

WATERSKIING & WAKEBOARDING
Waterskiing for all ages and abilities with professional and friendly guidance. The training bar on the side of the boat helps beginners gain confidence. Wakeboarding is the latest extreme sport: a combination of waterskiing, snowboarding and surfing.

New Forest Water Park

Ringwood Road, Fordingbridge,
Hampshire SP6 2EY

01425 656868

www.newforestwaterpark.co.uk

The Walk - Roaming the Woods at Ashmore

A gentle amble through plantations of mixed woodland to a village highpoint.

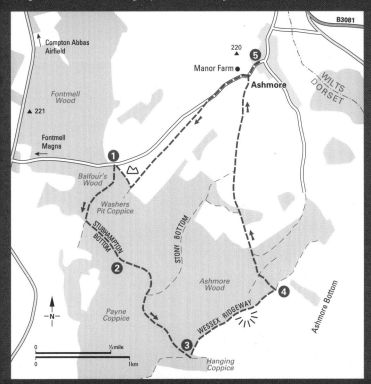

Walk Details

LENGTH: 5.75 miles (9.2km)

TIME: 3hrs

ASCENT: 427ft (130m)

PATHS: Forestry and farm tracks, woodland and field paths, 1 stile

SUGGESTED MAP: aqua3 OS Explorer 118 Shaftesbury & Cranborne Chase

GRID REFERENCE: ST 897167

PARKING: At Washers Pit entrance to Ashmore Wood

❶ With your back to the road, walk past the gate; follow the forestry road as it curves past Washers Pit Coppice on the left and Balfour's Wood on the right. After 0.5 mile (800m) ignore crossing bridleway and stay ahead on track. You're now in Stubhampton Bottom, following the winding valley through the trees.

❷ Where the main track swings up to the left, keep ahead, following the blue public bridleway marker, on the rutted track along the valley floor. The path from Stony Bottom feeds in from the left – keep straight on. Where an area of exposed hillside appears on the left, follow the blue markers on to the narrower track to the right, which runs down through woodland parallel and

below the forestry road. At Hanging Coppice, a fingerpost shows where the Wessex Ridgeway path feeds in from the right – again, keep ahead. The path soon rises to emerge again at the corner of the field.

❸ Turn left at the fence (following blue marker); walk uphill. Follow the path along the edge of forest, with good views to south-east of rolling hills and secretive valleys.

❹ After 0.75 mile (1.2km), turn left at a marked junction of tracks and walk through the woods. Cross the track and keep straight on, following the marker, to meet the track. Go straight on, following signs for Wessex Ridgeway, and passing under a beech tree. Go through the old gate. Continue up the track

for about 1 mile (1.6km), through farmland and across exposed open hilltop, with the houses of Ashmore appearing. At the end of the track turn right; walk into the village to pass by the duck pond.

❺ Retrace the route but stay on the road out of the village, passing Manor Farm (right) and heading downhill. Just before the road narrows, bear left through the gate (blue marker). Walk along the top of the field, pass the gate on the left and bear down to the right to lower of 2 gates at far side. Cross the stile and walk ahead on the broad green track. Go through the gate into the woods; immediately turn right, following the steep bridleway down the side of the hill to the car park.

The Inn

Standing smack beside one of the entrances to Longleat House, the estate-owned Bath Arms is an impressive, creeper-clad stone inn fronted by 200-year-old pollarded lime trees. Since taking it over in 2006, Christoph Brooke has worked wonders in restoring the fortunes of this grand building, employing interior designer Miv Watts to stamp her eclectic style throughout, using furnishings and fabrics imported from Rajasthan.

Big, bright paintings line the walls in the locals' bar, with its roaring log fire, bare-board floor, and local Wessex Brewery beers on tap. Next door, in the dining room, distinctive rugs and tables, unusual wall lamps, antique chandeliers, an ornate stone fireplace and a painting of Lord Bath set the scene for savouring some classic pub food.

The bedrooms are all quirky and colourful, relecting aspects of Lord Bath's style and kitted out with plasma screens, DVDs and big wooden beds, and individually decorated as befits their names: the exotic Geisha, the rather risqué Karma Sutra, or Man with its purple and lime green walls. Book a room in The Lodge for views down the long sweeping drive to the big house.

The Food

Using local suppliers is at the heart of the inn's ethos, and every effort is made to source raw ingredients from small producers within a 50-mile (80km) radius of Horningsham. The emphasis is on traditional preserving methods – smoking, curing and pickling – and using local game and rare-breed meats. Vegetables come from the inn's kitchen garden.

Don't expect fusion or Mediterranean cooking or elaborately described menus here – both are simple and very traditionally British in style and execution.

The daily lunch menu is served in the bars, restaurant, terrace and garden, and may take in pea and mint soup, lamb hotpot, crayfish salad, goats' cheese and tomato risotto, and a beef sandwich with horseradish. Kick off a memorable dinner in the dining room with seared scallops with sauce vierge, followed by chump of lamb on crushed potatoes and ratatouille, or grilled sea bass with baby spinach and squid sauce, and finish with chocolate tart or a plate of West Country cheeses.

The Essentials

Time at the Bar!
11am-11pm
Food: 12-2.30pm, 7-9.30pm

What's the Damage?
Main courses from £8.50

Bitter Experience:
Wessex Ales

Sticky Fingers:
Children welcome; children's menu

Muddy Paws:
Dogs welcome in the bar

Zzzzz:
15 rooms, £80-£130

Anything Else?
Terrace, garden, car park

What To Do

Shop

BEAU ARTS
In a fine Georgian building near the abbey, this long-established gallery displays work of major 20th-century painters, sculptors and ceramicists.
12/13 York Street, Bath, Somerset BA1 1NG
01225 464850
www.beauxartsbath.co.uk

THE WHITE COMPANY
For everything white for the house, from luxurious lifestyle accessories to pure linen and knitwear.
15 Northgate Street, Bath,
Somerset BA1 5AS
01225 445284
www.thewhitecompany.com

OIL & VINEGAR
A culinary treasure trove with hand-made pasta, oil and balsamic vinegars from Italy, virgin olive oils from Spain, and spicy sauces and chutneys from around the world.
8 Abbey Church Yard, Bath,
Somerset BA1 1LY
01225 338655

JOHN ANTHONY
Cutting-edge fashion store selling top designer clothes, including Armani and Paul Smith.
26-28 High Street, Bath, Somerset BA1 1RG
01225 424066
www.john-anthony.com

SHANNON
Sue Shannon has gathered unusual Scandinavian furniture and home accessories in her shop – choose from Wenger, Jacobsen and Aalto in her eponymous shop.
Shannon, 68 Walcot Street, Bath,
Somerset BA1 5BD
01225 424222
www.shannon-uk.com

Visit

LACOCK ABBEY
Built in 1232 and converted into a country house around 1540. The Photographic Museum commemorates the pioneering work of William Fox Talbot, a former resident. The woodland garden is stunning in the spring and there's an intimate Victorian rose garden with a summerhouse. The abbey stars in several Harry Potter films.
Lacock, Chippenham, Wiltshire SN15 2LG
01249 730459
www.nationaltrust.org

STOURHEAD HOUSE & GARDENS
Stourhead is one of the finest landscape gardens in the world. Lakeside paths lead past classical temples and follies, set against a backdrop of exotic trees. Mr Darcy's famous lake scene was shot here at the Temple of Apollo, in the BBC's adaptation of *Pride and Prejudice*. Climb King Alfred's Tower, a fine 164ft (50m) folly, and from the top you can scan three counties. Sitting majestically above the garden is Stourhead House, a grand Palladian mansion filled with Chippendale furniture, Georgian paintings and an exquisite Regency library.
Stourton, Warminster, Wiltshire BA12 6QD
01747 841152
www.nationaltrust.org

STOURTON GARDENS
Stroll along the many grassy paths that lead through the varied and colourful shrubs which include scented azaleas, camellias and over 250 varieties of hydrangeas, and don't miss the ferny secret garden. Buy unusual plants in the shop.
Warminster, Wiltshire BA12 6QF
01747 840417

Activity

EAST SOMERSET RAILWAY
The Strawberry Line running through the serene Mendip Hills has one of the steepest gradients on any preserved line: the steam engine has to work hard, though you don't. Just sit back and enjoy the countryside: why not have Sunday lunch on the magnificent Mendip Belle, and experience elegant travel from a bygone age?
Cranmore Railway Station, Cranmore,
Shepton Mallet, Somerset BA4 4QP
01749 880417
www.eastsomersetrailway.com

LONGLEAT SAFARI PARK
Stroll down the drive from the Bath Arms and within minutes you could be on safari. Get up close and personal with the lions, rhinos, giraffes and monkeys in a purpose-built 4x4, or take a boat trip to Gorilla Island, where Nico and Samba have their own mini-stately home and satellite telly! A family of Californian sea lions bobs about in the lake, accompanying you on your voyage. Worth seeing, too, is the butterfly garden, with hundreds of exotic species, some that are fully as big as your hand.
Longleat, Warminster, Wiltshire BA12 7NW
01985 844400
www.longleat.co.uk

The Walk - Woodland and Wildlife at Longleat

Glorious woodland and parkland walking at a famous country estate.

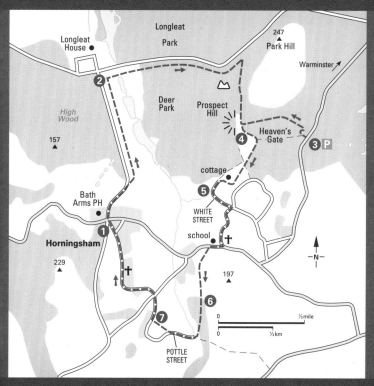

Walk Details

LENGTH: 5.25 miles (8.4km)

TIME: 2hrs 30min (longer if visiting attractions)

ASCENT: 508ft (155m)

PATHS: Field, woodland and parkland paths, roads, 4 stiles

SUGGESTED MAP: aqua3 OS Explorer 143 Warminster & Trowbridge

GRID REFERENCE: ST 810417

PARKING: The Bath Arms car park or Heaven's Gate car park, Longleat estate

① From The Bath Arms go straight across at the crossroads, walk down the estate drive and pass through the gatehouse arch into Longleat Park. With the house ahead, walk beside the metalled drive with lakes and weirs to the right. At T-junction in front of house, keep ahead to visit the house and follow the path left to reach the other tourist attractions.

② For main route, turn right and walk beside the drive, heading uphill through the Deer Park. Begin to climb steeply, then take metalled drive right beyond the white barrier. Ascend Prospect Hill and reach Heaven's Gate viewpoint. Retrace your steps back to the car park.

③ Cross the road and follow the path into the trees. Disregard the straight track left, bear right, then left along a wide worn path through mixed woodland to double gates and reach viewpoint at Heaven's Gate.

④ Facing Longleat, go through the gate in the lefthand corner. Shortly, at a crossing of paths, turn right, then keep right at fork and head downhill through woodland to metalled drive by thatched cottage. Turn right, keeping ahead where drive bears left; shortly follow path left, heading downhill close to woodland edge to pass between the garage and cottage to the lane.

⑤ Turn left on White Street to the crossroads; turn right downhill. Ascend past the church to the T-junction; turn right. Turn left opposite the school; follow the bridlepath up the track and between sheds to a gate. Bear left with track, pass through 2 gates; bear slightly right to stile on woodland edge.

⑥ Follow the path through the copse then bear off right diagonally downhill to stile and gate. Turn left along the field edge to reach the track. Turn right, go through the gate beside thatched cottage and follow the metalled lane (Pottle Street). In 200yds (183m), cross the stile on the right and cross the field to the stile and rejoin the lane.

⑦ Turn right and follow quiet lane to crossroads. Proceed straight across and follow the road through Horningsham village, passing the thatched chapel, to crossroads opposite The Bath Arms.

The Swan

Wiltshire

The Inn

Judge Jeffreys once held court in this historic 16th-century pub with rooms, but, rest assured, new owners Stephen and Penny Ross offer a far friendlier welcome. The first thing you notice about this Grade II listed building is the stunning, flagstoned hall, which runs the entire length of the ground floor. The Swan is right in the centre of Bradford-on-Avon; it was renovated in 2006 and the bedrooms have been given a fresh new look.

Each room has been individually designed and the style of decor chosen seems to effortlessly mix contemporary chic with original features. Colour schemes tend to be cream, mushroom or mulberry, with many of the walls featuring striking framed black-and-white photographs or gilt-edged mirrors. High ceilings, exposed beams and original fireplaces are a constant reminder of the building's history, but these are offset by modern touches such as power showers, deep baths and plasma screens. Egyptian cotton sheets cover the comfortable beds, and muslin drapes make for a stylish and airy alternative to the usual net curtains.

The Swan, 1 Church Street, Bradford-on-Avon, Wiltshire BA15 1LN

The Essentials

Time at the Bar!
10am-11pm
Food: 12-2.30pm (3pm Sun),
6.30-9.30pm

What's the Damage?
Main courses from £8.50

Bitter Experience:
Old Tripp, Old Speckled Hen

Sticky Fingers:
Children welcome, small portions
available

Muddy Paws:
Dogs welcome on outside terrace

Zzzzz:
12 rooms, £95-£140

Anything Else?
Terrace, car park

The Food

With their wooden floors, leather sofas and ox-blood walls, the two lounges at the front have a clubby feel to them and are perfect for an aperitif before moving into the dining room with its enormous fireplace and fresh flowers on bare tables. Although former chef Stephen Ross has long retired from the professional kitchen, the menus bear all the hallmarks of his accessible British food with its French bistro accent. Local suppliers are proudly listed on the menu and they include Hobbs House Bakery and Eades of Bath.

Start, perhaps, with courgette and tarragon soup, or Looe Bay spider crab and artichoke salad. Lighter meals include a ploughman's with Keene's cheddar and walnut bread; if you want something more substantial, look out for braised shin of local beef with horseradish and root vegetables, or Old Spot pork and apricot pudding with Somerset cider. Make room for classic comfort puds of the sticky toffee and crumble variety. To drink, there's real ale or a carefully chosen wine list that includes 12 by the glass.

What To Do

Shop

BAY TREE GALLERY

Vibrant exhibition galleries showing the works of a wide range of contemporary artists working in sculpture, pottery, jewellery, painting, photography, printing and other crafts. There is a ceramics workshop attached to the gallery.

48 St Margaret's Street, Bradford-on-Avon, Wiltshire BA15 1DE
01225 864918
www.baytreegallery.co.uk

BRISTOL

Explore the winding streets and lanes of the older part of the city and you'll find designer shops and galleries, antiques, boutiques and myriad specialist shops. The areas near to the harbour, along Whiteladies Road, the Old Corn Exchange, St Nicholas Markets and the chic streets of Clifton, at the edge of the extensive Clifton Downs, are all good places to browse for more unusual items. Look out for pieces of Bristol Blue Glass, or perhaps even visit the craft works.

0906 711 2191
www.visitbristol.co.uk

STAINED GLASS

A working stained glass studio complemented by an exhibition gallery highlighting its uses – from leaded glass to Tiffany-style pieces, sculpture to furnishings.

Alan Sparks Stained Glass Studio & Gallery
Pound Lane, Bradford-on-Avon, Wiltshire BA15 1LF
01225 868146
www.stainedglassonline.co.uk

Bristol Blue Glass
14 The Arcade, Broadmead, Bristol BS1 3SA
0117 922 6833
www.bristol-glass.co.uk

Visit

THE AMERICAN MUSEUM

This excellent museum houses a collection of American decorative and folk art dating back to the very first days of European colonisation of the eastern seaboard, plus some Native American art. The collections are enhanced by period settings in a maze of rooms and galleries. To complete the all-American effect, the grounds are planted with varieties of North American trees and shrubs.

Claverton Manor, Bath, Somerset BA2 7BD
01225 460503
www.americanmuseum.org

BOWOOD HOUSE

An early Georgian country house, designed in part by Robert Adam, and the family home of the Marquis of Lansdowne. His predecessor was a Viceroy of India, hence the collections of sub-continental costumes, sculptures and artefacts. Plus watercolours and jewellery, the famous Lansdowne Marbles collection and Georgian costume.

Derry Hill, Calne, Wiltshire SN11 0LZ
01249 812102
www.bowood.org

ROMAN BATHS & PUMP HOUSE

Britain's most spectacular Roman remains in the historic centre of Bath. Interpretive displays leave no stone unturned in explaining the importance of the hot springs to the Romans and the significance of the Temple of Sulis Minerva. Take the waters at the Pump House next door and visit the restaurant for a very civilised lunch.

Pump Rooms, Bath, Somerset BA1 1LZ
01225 477785
www.romanbaths.co.uk

Activity

BALLOONING

Enjoy a balloon flight in early morning or mid-evening, drifting over the Avon Valley towards the Cotswolds or wherever the wind decides to take you.

Bath Balloons, 8 Lambridge, London Road, Bath, Somerset BA1 6BJ
01225 466888
www.bathballoons.co.uk

CYCLING

Enjoy the network of gentle cycle rides along the tow path of the Kennet and Avon Canal into Bath or eastwards along the tranquil valley of the Avon. Lanes link in to some of the area's glorious country manors. Alternatively, join the Colliers Way near Dundas Aqueduct, riding this old railway through dimpled countryside where the classic *Titfield Thunderbolt* was filmed.

The Lock Inn, 48 Frome Road, Bradford-on-Avon, Wiltshire BA15 1LE
01225 868068
www.thelockinn.co.uk

NARROWBOAT TRIP

Hire a short, self-drive traditional narrowboat in the city of Bath and cruise one of England's most beautiful canals for a full or half-day. Potter along the spectacular section near Bradford-on-Avon and wrestle with the intricacies of operating locks and stopping for a pub lunch, or you could take a hamper and moor wherever you fancy for a relaxing picnic. Boats are also available for hire at Hilperton, near Trowbridge.

Bath Narrow Boats, Sydney Wharf, Bathwick Hill, Bath, Somerset BA2 4EL
01225 447276
www.bath-narrowboats.co.uk

The Walk - A Miniature Bath at Bradford-on-Avon

Combine a visit to this enchanting riverside town with a relaxing canal-side stroll.

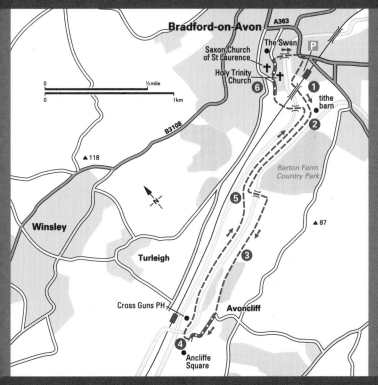

Walk Details

LENGTH: 3.5 miles (5.7km)

TIME: 1hr 45min

ASCENT: 164ft (50m)

PATHS: Tow path, field and woodland paths, metalled lanes

SUGGESTED MAP: aqua3 OS Explorers 142 Shepton Mallet;156 Chippenham & Bradford-on-Avon

GRID REFERENCE: ST 824606 (on Explorer 156)

PARKING: Bradford-on-Avon station car park (charge)

❶ Walk to the end of the car park, away from the station, and follow the path to the left beneath the railway and beside the River Avon. Enter Barton Farm Country Park and keep to the path across the grassy area to the information board. Here you can visit craft shops housed in former medieval farm buildings and marvel at the great beams and rafters of Bradford-on-Avon's magnificent tithe barn, the 2nd largest in Britain. With the packhorse bridge to the right, keep ahead to the right of tithe barn to the Kennet and Avon Canal.

❷ Turn right along the tow path. Cross the bridge over the canal in 0.5 mile (800m) and follow the path right to the footbridge and stile.

Proceed along the righthand field edge to the further stile, then bear diagonally left uphill away from the canal to the kissing gate.

❸ Follow the path through the edge of the woodland. Keep to the path as it bears left uphill through the trees to reach the metalled lane. Turn right and walk steeply downhill to Avoncliff and the canal.

❹ Don't cross the aqueduct at this point, instead pass by the Mad Hatter Tea Rooms, descend the steps on your right and pass beneath the canal. Keep right by Cross Guns and join the tow path towards Bradford-on-Avon. Continue for 0.75 mile (1.2km) to reach the bridge you passed on your outward route.

❺ Bear off left downhill along the metalled track and follow it beside the River Avon back into Barton Farm Country Park. Now cross the packhorse bridge and the railway line to reach Barton Orchard.

❻ Follow the alleyway to Church Street and continue ahead to pass Holy Trinity Church and the Saxon Church of St Laurence, the jewel in Bradford-on-Avon's crown and not to be missed. Founded by St Aldhelm, Abbot of Malmesbury in 700 AD, this building dates back to the 10th century. Now cross over the footbridge and walk straight through St Margaret's car park to reach the road. Turn right, then right again back into the station car park where the walk began.

The Castle Inn

Wiltshire

The Essentials

Time at the Bar!
9.30am-11pm
Food: 11.30am-3pm, 6-9.15pm

What's the Damage?
Main courses from £7.50

Bitter Experience:
Butcombe Bitter, Shepherd
Neame Spitfire

Sticky Fingers:
Children welcome; half portions

Muddy Paws:
No dogs

Zzzzz:
11 rooms, £100-£165

Anything Else?
Courtyard garden

The Inn

With no street lights, no TV aerials, roads lined with ancient buildings (every one of them listed), Castle Combe is certainly 'chocolate box' to look at, but there's a lot more to unwrap. The Castle Inn, for example, dates from the 12th century and is an appealing mix of exposed stone, beams, heritage-style colours, mullioned windows, open fires, and squishy sofas. Open for tea and coffee from 9.30am, with Butcombe Bitter and Shepherd Neame Spitfire on tap in the long, low bar, and cream teas served in the afternoons, this is a civilised place with broad appeal.

The inn has much to recommend it, not least the light, contemporary garden room, which gives onto a pleasant courtyard, as well as the dining room proper, a small, intimate space with candles on simply laid polished wood tables. Eleven individual ensuite bedrooms blend the old and new with considerable style, taking in timbered walls, beams, antique furniture, French beds, scatter cushions, rich colours and smart modern bathrooms, while views from most windows are of the ancient village and beyond.

The Food

The kitchen offers a wide range of dishes, from traditional English to modern eclectic (with Mediterranean and Asian touches) to match the different dining areas – restaurant, garden room, bar or courtyard. Old-fashioned pub staples, such as steak and kidney pie, baked ham, egg and chips, or farmhouse sausage and mash, are served in the bar, contrasting with the inventive modern ideas found on the restaurant menu – starters such as mackerel fillet with ginger and herb crust, or marinated chicken in lime and apple brandy, served with Puy lentils.

The results on the plate more than live up to expectations – first-class, often local ingredients and plenty of technical skill are all apparent. Main courses might bring chargrilled rib-eye steak with pepper and shallot sauce, lamb shank served with red wine sauce and spring onion mash, or fillet of sea bass with stir-fried vegetables and hoisin sauce.

Treacle tart and clotted cream or spiced, poached pear, red wine and vanilla ice cream are typical puddings.

What To Do

Shop

BATH

The stunning Georgian city of Bath offers endless retail opportunities – every whim can be catered for. Visit Gallery Nine for contemporary jewellery, paintings, ceramics and sculpture. The Inspired Maker sells an eclectic and stylish mix of 20th-century furniture, contemporary crafts and accessories, and there are stylish clothes shops around every corner.

Gallery Nine
9b Margarets Buildings, Bath BA1 1LP
01225 319197
www.gallerynine.co.uk

The Inspired Maker
4 Bladud Buildings, Bath BA1 5LS
01225 460055
www.theinspiredmaker.co.uk

HOBBS HOUSE BAKERY

Three generations of the Wells family are hard at work in this award-winning bakery. Choose from a huge variety of breads, including a fantastic sourdough. In the Nailsworth shop and cafe, an old wood-fired oven is used.

4 George Street, Nailsworth,
Gloucestershire GL6 0AG
01453 839396
39 High Street, Chipping Sodbury,
Bristol BS37 6BA
01454 317525
www.hobbshousebakery.co.uk

SHIPTON MILL

There are around 40 varieties of stoneground flour to be bought at this beautifully restored mill in picturesque Long Newton.

Long Newton, Tetbury,
Gloucestershire GL8 8RP
01666 505050
www.shipton-mill.com

Visit

CORSHAM COURT

A magnificent privately owned country house, Corsham has an exceptional art collection, including Van Dycks and family portraits by Joshua Reynolds, furniture by Chippendale and Adams. There are beautiful formal gardens, where you'll find a Bath House designed by Capability Brown and remodelled by Nash.

Corsham, Wiltshire SN13 0BZ
01249 701610
www.corsham-court.co.uk

DYRHAM PARK

Dyrham is a stunning baroque country house in 274 acres of elegant parkland and gardens. It's a wonderful showcase for a unique collection of Dutch delftware. See, too, the Victorian domestic quarters, plus tenant's hall and delft-tiled dairy. There's a good shop and tea room.

Dyrham, Gloucestershire SN14 8ER
01179 372501
www.nationaltrust.org.uk

JACK RUSSELL GALLERY

A must for all fans of the game of cricket – England cricketer and artist Jack Russell's finest work of the sport is hung here, along with landscapes and wildlife. Chipping Sodbury itself is a pretty market town, well worth exploring.

41 High Street, Chipping Sodbury,
Gloucestershire BS37 6BA
01454 329583
www.jackrussell.co.uk

LACKHAM COUNTRY PARK

Outstanding formal gardens surround this handsome 18th-century house. Wander in the walled garden with beautifully laid-out herbs, flowers and vegetables, and don't miss the greenhouses with the famous giant Lackham lemons. There are also woodland walks, and a Rural Life museum in an ancient thatched building.

Lacock, Chippenham, Wiltshire SN15 2NY
01249 466800
www.lackhamcountrypark.co.uk

Activity

DRIVE A CLASSIC CAR

Take to the road in an E-Type Jag, Alfa Romeo Spider or Austin Healey to make your break really stylish.

Vintage Classics, Melksham,
Wiltshire SN12 6LY
01225 703377
www.vintage-classics.co.uk

HORSE RACING

Bath Racecourse is the home of flat racing, set in a glorious hilltop location 2 miles from the centre of Bath, and attracting top trainers.

Bath Racecourse, Lansdown, Bath BA1 9BU
01225 424609
www.bath-racecourse.co.uk

STEAM TRAIN RIDE

Treat yourself to Sunday lunch while you chug through the glorious Avon Valley towards Bath, and discover parts of the countryside you'd never see any other way. The Station Buffet in Bitton is known all over the county for its home-made cakes. Either way, you'll have a day steeped in old-style travel nostalgia.

Avon Valley Railway
Bitton Station, Bath Road, Bitton,
Bristol BS30 6HD
01179 325538
www.avonvalleyrailway.co.uk

The Walk - A Picture-book Village

Through the hilly and wooded By Brook Valley from Castle Combe.

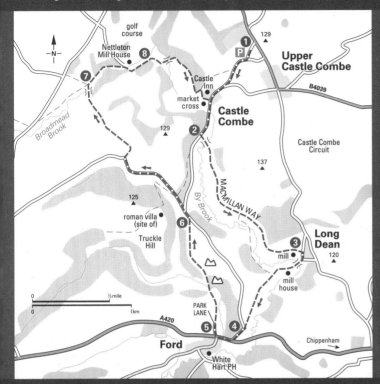

Walk Details

LENGTH: 5.75 miles (9.2km)

TIME: 2hrs 30min

ASCENT: 515ft (157m)

PATHS: Field and woodland paths and tracks, metalled lanes, 10 stiles

SUGGESTED MAP: aqua3 OS Explorer 156 Chippenham & Bradford-on-Avon

GRID REFERENCE: ST 845776

PARKING: Free car park just off B4039 at Upper Castle Combe

❶ Leave the car park via the steps and turn right. At the T-junction, turn right; follow the lane into Castle Combe. Keep left at the Market Cross, cross By Brook and continue along the road to take the path ('Long Dean'), across the 2nd bridge on the left.

❷ Cross the stile and follow the path uphill then beside the righthand fence above the valley (Macmillan Way). Beyond the open area, ascend through woodland to the stile and gate. Cross a further stile; descend into Long Dean.

❸ Pass the mill and follow the track right to cross the river bridge. At the mill house, keep right and follow the sunken bridleway uphill to the gate. Shortly enter the pasture and

follow the path around the top edge, bearing left to the stile and the lane.

❹ Turn left and descend to A420 at Ford. Turn right along the pavement and right again into Park Lane. (To visit White Hart in Ford, take the road ahead on the left, 'Colerne'.) Climb the gravel track and take the footpath left through squeeze stile.

❺ Keep right through pasture and continue through trees to water-meadow in valley bottom. Turn left, cross stream and ascend grassy slope ahead, bearing left beyond trees towards waymarker post. Follow footpath along top of field to stile and gate, then walk through woodland to the gate and road.

❻ Turn left, then immediately left again ('North Wraxall'). Keep to

the road for 0.25 mile (400m) and take the arrowed bridleway right. Follow the track then, just before the gate, keep right downhill on the sunken path to the footbridge over Broadmead Brook.

❼ Shortly, climb the stile on right and follow the footpath close to the river. Cross the stile and soon pass beside Nettleton Mill House, bearing right to the hidden gate. Walk beside the stream and cross the stile to the golf course.

❽ Turn right along the track, cross the bridge. Turn right. At the gate, follow the path left below the golf course. Follow wall to stile on right. Descend the steps to drive and keep ahead to Castle Combe. Turn left at Market Cross and retrace steps.

Spread Eagle Inn
Wiltshire

Spread Eagle Inn, Stourton, Warminster, Wiltshire BA12 6QE

The Essentials

Time at the Bar!
11am-11pm
Food: 12.30-2.30pm daily,
7-9pm Mon-Sat
(Sun dinner residents only)

What's the Damage?
Main courses from £9.95

Bitter Experience:
Wessex Kilmington Best, Butcombe

Sticky Fingers:
Children welcome, small portions
available

Muddy Paws:
No dogs

Zzzzz:
5 rooms, £110

Anything Else?
Garden, car park

The Inn

In this one-road village it's hard to miss the Spread Eagle – although being close to the entrance to Stourhead House and Garden is helpful (and convenient for the many visitors to this National Trust property). The inn is now in the hands of Stephen Ross, who comes with impeccable credentials as hotelier and restaurateur. Refurbishment has certainly brought out the best in this handsome building with stone floors, painted beams and big windows looking out onto a shady courtyard. The civilised bar is a generous, comfortable room, hung with 19th-century prints and horse brasses, and warmed by a large, blazing log burner in winter.

The best of the five traditional bedrooms are large rooms with window seats and verdant views; others are more compact but equally immaculate, painted in soft colours and offering crisp white linen, plump duvets and pillows on very comfortable beds. In addition, expect flat-screen TVs and the odd sloping floor – this is an 18th-century building after all. Admission to Stourhead (in season) is included in the room price, a very pleasant added extra.

The Food

The cooking here is first class, the kitchen offering a menu that is neither too long nor over-ambitious, with food that is simple, straightforward and reliant on prime seasonal and local produce. Lunch in the bar, in particular, emphasises local ingredients. Typical offerings are pressed coarse country pâté served alongside fruit chutney, pickled walnuts and toast; farm-shop ham, free-range egg and chips; ploughman's of West Country cheeses; and something more elaborate like slow-roasted Barbary duck leg teamed with smoked bacon and butterbean and sausage stew.

Dinner in the restaurant is a more formal affair: in winter a log fire blazes and candles cast a glow on the rich red walls, while in summer the evening light streams through big windows. Here, a meal could start with smoked haddock and prawn fishcakes with remoulade sauce, go on to estate venison casserole with juniper, red wine, rosemary and shallot dumplings, or cod fillet with wilted red chard and tomato and shallot dressing, and finish with rum and raisin cheesecake.

01747 840587, www.spreadeagleinn.com

What To Do

Shop

DAUWALDER'S OF SALISBURY

Collectors will love browsing around Britain's largest provincial stamp shop. It also sell coins, banknotes, cigarette cards, old bonds and share certificates, and small collectibles – including die-cast cars and railways.

92/94 Fisherton Street, Salisbury, Wiltshire SP2 7QY

01722 412100

www.worldstamps.co.uk

THE GALLERY AT FISHERTON MILL

Built in 1880 as a grain mill, Fisherton Mill is now one of the south's largest independent art galleries, comprising three floors of dazzling works of art including painting, sculpture, furniture, ceramics, textiles, metalwork and contemporary craft. There is also an outdoor seasonal exhibition area, studio workshops and a cafe.

108 Fisherton Street, Salisbury, Wiltshire SP2 2QY

01722 415121

www.fishertonmill.co.uk

Visit

LONGLEAT HOUSE & SAFARI PARK

Set within 900 acres of Capability Brown landscaped parkland, Longleat House is one of the best examples of high Elizabethan architecture in Britain and one of the most beautiful stately homes open to the public in the whole country. The drive through the safari park, opened in 1966, was the first of its kind outside Africa: giraffe, zebras, lions, rhino and monkeys all have right of way here.

Longleat, Warminster, Wiltshire BA12 7NW

01985 844400

www.longleat.co.uk

SHERBORNE ABBEY

Founded by St Aldhelm in 705 AD, the abbey has developed from a Saxon cathedral to the worshipping heart of a monastic community and, finally, to one of the most beautiful of England's parish churches. For many it is still the 'cathedral of Dorset', and our Benedictine heritage lives on in the daily offering of prayer and praise.

The Parish Office, 3 Abbey Close, Sherborne, Dorset DT9 3LQ

01935 812452

www.sherborneabbey.com

WILTON HOUSE

This 460-year-old building with its history, architecture, art treasures and 21 acres of gardens and parkland attracts visitors from all over the world. The south front and state rooms remain a testimony to the popularity of the Palladian style of architecture in the middle of the 17th century.

Wilton, Salisbury, Wiltshire SP2 0BJ

01722 746714

www.wiltonhouse.com

Activity

CROP CIRCLE SPOTTING

Crop circles have been appearing in the area for years. The finest have been seen in the Marlborough Downs and Pewsey Vale.

Pewsey Vale, Wiltshire

www.cropcircles.org

PAINTING CLASSES

Graham Oliver has led painting classes for 17 years in his gallery and is a regular demonstrator to art societies. His series of exercises in watercolour is ideal for beginners.

Graham Oliver Gallery, 97a Brown Street, Salisbury, Wiltshire SP1 2BA

01722 503610

www.grahamolivergallery.co.uk

HIRE A CLASSIC CAR

Grab a picnic hamper and take your pick of 1960s classics such as E-Types, Jag Mk2, Healey, MGB, Rover P5B. Based in the Nadder Valley just a few gear changes away from beautiful Cranborne Chase, you could drive to the New Forest.

Wiltshire Classics, Westfield Park, Dinton, Salisbury, Wiltshire SP3 5BT

01722 716328

www.wiltshireclassics.co.uk

HORSE RIDING

The Riding Centre at Grovely has been established for more than 50 years and offers unparalleled riding experiences, ranging from tuition, both group and private, through to participation in beautiful woodland treks and rides over rolling chalk downs with wide tracks, Roman roads and grassy droves.

Grovely Riding Centre, Water Ditchampton, Wilton, Salisbury, Wiltshire SP2 0LB

01722 742288

www.grovely.info

The Walk - Alfred's Tower at Three County Corner

An expedition through Somerset, Dorset and Wiltshire, to Stourhead and Alfred's Tower.

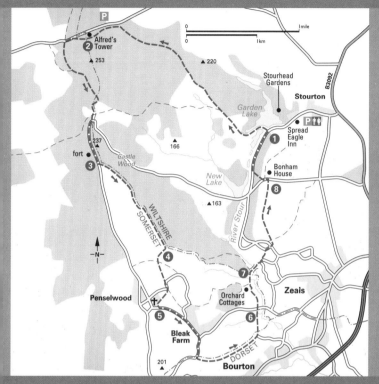

Walk Details

LENGTH: 8.5 miles (13.7km)

TIME: 4hrs

ASCENT: 950ft (290m)

PATHS: Some tracks and some small paths and field edges, 7 stiles

SUGGESTED MAP: aqua3 OS Explorer 142 Shepton Mallet

GRID REFERENCE: ST 776339

PARKING: The Spread Eagle car park, or Penselwood church; some verge parking at Bleak Farm

① From The Spread Eagle, the track bends right and heads into the wooded valley with Alfred's Tower ahead, reaching open ground at the hilltop, with road ahead. Turn left, in the grassy avenue, to Alfred's Tower.

② Join the road ahead for 220yds (201m), down to the sunken path on the left ('Penselwood'). Follow this, ignoring paths on both sides, on to track down to the major junction. Bear right to the lane, then right again, on the road ('Penselwood'), which leads over the hilltop with its hill fort. Descend until some open ground appears on the left.

③ Cross the stile; head downhill with Castle Wood left, and young trees right. Move into the wood to join the track along its edge. At the

corner of the wood, a waymarked gate on the right leads into fields.

④ Follow the left edge of 1st field to 2 gates on the left; keep ahead to the gate and a 2nd gate beyond. A track leads out to road. Turn right to sharp righthand bend, where a gate starts the field path to Penselwood church.

⑤ Go through the churchyard to the road beyond. Turn left through Bleak Farm village, then left onto the sunken track, ending at the top of the tarred lane. Turn left through the white gate ('Pen Mill Hill'). Head down to the kissing gate in the dip; follow the track past the pond to reach the road.

⑥ Cross into the path ('Coombe Street'). Pass below Orchard Cottages, then turn left over 2 stiles.

Cross the stream in the dip to the stile below the thatched cottage. The woodland path bends right to the footbridge over the River Stour.

⑦ From here to Point 8 is marked 'Stour Valley Way'. Go on to the tarred lane; turn left. Keep ahead into a hedged way to the stile. Go up and round left to another stile. The lane beyond leads to the T-junction; go across and turn left onto the bridleway. Go through the gate to follow the left edge of the field into the hedged track, to emerge opposite Bonham House.

⑧ Turn left; at the 2nd signpost bear right to the road below. Follow the road to the right, to the rustic rock arch. Take the track on the left ('Alfred's Tower') back to the inn.

The Horse & Groom

Wiltshire

The Inn

After years in the doldrums, this elegant, 16th-century Cotswold stone house finally reopened its doors in March 2007 with a new look, following a stylish spruce-up by new owners Merchant Inns. Billed as a fine dining traditional country inn, it certainly embraces the genuine 'inn' experience, as befits its history as a famous coaching inn. You can quaff pints of Archers and Old Speckled Hen at scrubbed pine tables in the buzzy, flagstoned bar, with its rustic stone walls and log fire in the original fireplace, or feast on modern British food in one of the two dining areas, where rug-strewn floors and solid oak tables lend a civilised air. Retreat to the secluded walled rear garden on warm sunny days.

The revamped upstairs rooms are decorated with earthy Farrow & Ball colours, heavy curtains, quality dark wood furnishings, huge lamps, plasma screens and free wi-fi, and gloriously soft and cool Egyptian cotton sheets on big beds. There's also spotlighting, claw-foot baths or power showers, and Damana toiletries in spacious bathrooms. Rooms at the front of house overlook the tree-sheltered front lawn.

The Horse & Groom, The Street, Charlton, Malmesbury, Wiltshire SN16 9DL

The Essentials

Time at the Bar!
12-11pm
Food: 12-2.30pm, 6.30-9pm
(9.30pm Fri & Sat); sandwich menu
2.30-6.30pm

What's the Damage?
Main courses from £9.95

Bitter Experience:
Archers Village, guest beer

Sticky Fingers:
Children welcome, smaller portions;
play area

Muddy Paws:
Dogs welcome in the bar

Zzzzz:
5 rooms, £89.95; single £79.95

Anything Else?
Garden, car park, wine tasting
dinners, cooking demonstrations

The Horse & Groom, The Street, Charlton, Malmesbury, Wiltshire SN16 9DL

The Food

Michelin-star chef Robert Clayton, who earned his gong at the Priory Hotel in Bath, develops the menus, sourcing great produce from the best local suppliers. Butcher Jesse Smith delivers his pork and stilton sausages and rib-eye steaks on the bone, which are hung for 28 days. Pork belly and bacon come from nearby Bromham, free-range chicken from a farm near Stroud, and the lamb is reared in the Cotswolds.

This translates to potted chicken liver and honey pâté with sultana and apple chutney, roast Old Spot pork belly with sage mash, braised red cabbage and apple and cider sauce, and Cotswold shoulder of lamb with honey-roasted root vegetables, mash and red wine sauce on imaginative changing menus. Classic pub dishes are not forgotten: tuck into freshly battered fish with chunky chips, pan-fried liver and bacon with mash and shallot sauce, home-made beefburger and red onion marmalade, or thick-cut sandwiches filled with farmhouse cheddar and apple chutney. Find room for sticky toffee pudding with toffee sauce or vanilla pannacotta with poached rhubarb.

What To Do

Shop

CROFT GALLERY
This small gallery is a treasure-trove of high-quality contemporary fine art, as well as paintings, ceramics and photography by local, national and international artists.
22 Devizes Road, Old Town, Swindon, Wiltshire SN1 4BH
01793 615821
www.thecroftgallery.co.uk

JESSE SMITH BUTCHERS
A small chain of shops, Jesse Smith Butchers are members of the prestigious 'Q' Guild of Butchers, selling Hereford and Buccleuch beef, Gloucestershire Old Spot pork and locally farmed lamb. The shop's a deli, too, selling cheese, olives and roast meats. The bistro behind the shop is a great place for lunch.
Blackjack Street, Cirencester, Gloucestershire GL7 2AA
01285 653387
www.castlebutchers.co.uk

MALMESBURY POTTERY
All manner of items are made here by Clive and Christine King. The showroom is an Aladdin's Cave, stocked with lighting, table items, clocks and decorative plates.
Cross Hayes, Malmesbury, Wiltshire SN16 9AU
01666 825148
www.malmesburypottery.co.uk

SWINDON FARMERS' MARKET
Well worth a visit – here you'll find award-winning Hobbs bread, freshly harvested fruit and veg, local honey, farmhouse cheeses and English grape wines.
McArthur Glen Designer Outlet, Kemble Road, Swindon, Wiltshire 01453 758060
www.fresh-n-local.co.uk

Visit

ABBEY HOUSE GARDENS
Over 10,000 different plants, and the stunning 5-acre garden includes modern sculpture and topiary.
The Market Cross, Malmesbury, Wiltshire SN16 9AS
01666 822221
www.abbeyhousegardens.co.uk

MALMESBURY
Malmesbury is one of the oldest towns in the country, and the remains of the Abbey in the centre of town are worth seeing. Noted for its historical costume collection, the Athelstan Museum also has a famous Malmesbury lace exhibition.
Athelstan Museum
Town Hall, Cross Hayes, Malmesbury, Wiltshire SN16 9BZ
01666 829258
www.athelstan-museum.org.uk

WESTONBIRT ARBORETUM
Enjoy a day out among some of the oldest, tallest and rarest trees and shrubs in the country – 18,000 of them, in 600 acres of Grade I listed landscape. Japanese maples are for sale in the well-stocked shop.
Tetbury, Gloucestershire GL8 8QS
01666 880220
www.forestry.gov.uk/westonbirt

WOODCHESTER PARK
This valley contains an enchanting lost garden – the remains of an 18th- and 19th-century landscape park with a chain of five lakes fringed by woodland. An unfinished Victorian mansion in the grounds is open on certain days of the year.
Stonehouse, Stroud, Gloucestershire GL10 3TS
01452 814213
www.nationaltrust.org.uk

Activity

DRIVE A CLASSIC CAR
Explore the county in style in an E-Type Jag, Austin Healey, MG Roadster or Jaguar MKII.
Vintage Classics
Melksham, Wiltshire SN12 6LY
01225 703377
www.vintage-classics.co.uk

GOLF
Cricklade Hotel is a magnificent Cotswold manor house with plenty of variety on the 9-hole course.
Cricklade Hotel & Golf Club
Common Hill, Cricklade, Wiltshire SN6 6HA
01793 750751
www.crickladehotel.co.uk

STEAM TRAIN RIDE
Enjoy a nostalgic trip through delightful countryside on a standard gauge steam train.
Swindon & Cricklade Railway
Blunsdon Station, Tadpole Lane, Swindon, Wiltshire SN25 2DA
01793 771615
www.swindon-cricklade-railway.org

WATERSKIING
The Cotswold Water Park is Britain's largest with 133 lakes. Watermark Leisure Club is a sheltered lake with great facilities to learn or improve your skiing technique. There's a good bar and brasserie overlooking the lake, too.
Cotswold Water Park
Keynes County Park, Shorncote, Cirencester, Gloucestershire GL17 6DF
01285 861459
www.waterpark.org
Watermark Leisure Club
Spring Lakes, 14/15 Station Road, South Cerney, Gloucestershire GL7 5TH
01285 860606
www.watermarkclub.co.uk

The Walk - The Infant Thames at Cricklade

An easy ramble across water-meadows.

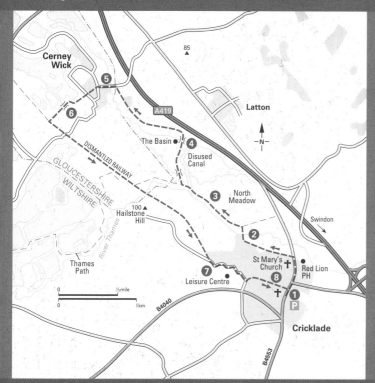

Walk Details

LENGTH: 5.5 miles (8.8km)

TIME: 2hrs 30min

ASCENT: Negligible

PATHS: Field paths and bridle paths, disused railway, town streets, 15 stiles

SUGGESTED MAP: aqua3 OS Explorer 169 Cirencester & Swindon

GRID REFERENCE: SU 100934

PARKING: Cricklade Town Hall car park (free)

❶ Turn right out of the car park, keep ahead at the roundabout and walk along the High Street. Pass St Mary's Church then turn left along North Wall before the river bridge. Shortly, bear right to the stile and join Thames Path. Cross the stile; continue along field edge to houses.
❷ Go through the kissing gate on the right and bear left across the field to the gate. Follow the fenced footpath, cross the bridge and pass through the gate immediately on the righthand side. Cross the river bridge; turn left through gate. Walk beside the infant Thames, crossing 2 stiles to enter North Meadow.
❸ Cross stile by bridge. Go through the gate immediately right and keep ahead, ignoring Thames Path left.

Follow the path beside the disused canal. Cross the footbridge and 2 stiles; at the fence, bear right to cross the footbridge close to the house ('The Basin'). Cross the stile and bear right along the drive.
❹ Cross the bridge and turn left through the gateway. Shortly, bear right to join the path along the left side of the old canal. Keep to path for 0.5 mile (800m) to road. Turn left into Cerney Wick to the T-junction.
❺ Cross the stile opposite; keep ahead through the paddock to the stile and lane. Cross the lane and climb the stile opposite, continuing ahead to a further stile. Shortly, cross the stile on the right and follow the path beside the lake. Bear right, then left, then bear off

left (follow yellow arrow) into trees where the path becomes a track.
❻ Cross the footbridge and proceed ahead along the field edge to the stile. Turn left along the old railway ('Cricklade'). Cross the Thames in 1 mile (1.6km) and keep to the path along the former trackbed to bridge.
❼ Follow the gravel path to reach the Leisure Centre. Bear left on to the road, following it right; turn left opposite the entrance to the Leisure Centre car park. Turn right, then next left and follow road to church.
❽ Walk beside the barrier and turn left in front of The Gatehouse into the churchyard. Bear left to the main gates and follow the lane to the T-junction. Turn right to return to the car park.

The Pear Tree Inn
Wiltshire

The Essentials

Time at the Bar!
11am-11pm
Food: 12-2.30pm, 6.30-9.30pm
(10pm Fri-Sat); 7-9pm Sun

What's the Damage?
Main courses from £9.95

Bitter Experience:
Wadworth 6X, Moles Tap Bitter,
Stonehenge Ales

Sticky Fingers:
Children welcome, children's menu

Muddy Paws:
Dogs welcome in the bar

Zzzzz:
8 rooms, £105

Anything Else?
Terrace, garden, car park,
conservatory

The Pear Tree Inn, Top Lane, Whitley, Melksham, Wiltshire SN12 8QX

The Inn

A former working farm dating back to 1750, the impressive mellow stone Pear Tree is set back off the aptly named Top Lane in four acres of glorious gardens, where fragrant lilacs and cottage roses border manicured lawns. Martin and Debbie Still have cleverly maintained a truly local feel in the rustic bar while at the same time seriously developing the food and accommodation side of the business. A refreshing lack of formality and pretension prevails throughout. Rug-strewn flagstone floors, worn wooden tables and a crackling log fire draw you into the bar for pints of Pigswill from Stonehenge Brewery. Most people come here to eat in the intimate dining room and bright garden room, both furnished with old farming implements and simple wooden tables.

Comfort and style sum up the eight contemporary bedrooms, split between the inn and a beautifully converted barn. All sport goose-down duvets on big beds, deep easy chairs, plasma screens, and Fired Earth tiled bathrooms with power showers over baths and posh smellies. For mullioned windows, exposed beams and rural views stay in the inn.

The Food

The heart of the business lies in the kitchen, which produces everything from fresh ingredients. The Stills are passionate about using local produce and they constantly champion organic and free-range meats and vegetables from local farms. This commitment has seen them team up with Lady Venetia Fuller to develop the Organic Farm Shop, Cafe and Bakery at nearby Atworth, where you can stock up on some quality goodies before you head home.

Daily lunch and dinner menus, the superb-value set lunch menu and a good choice of sandwiches serve both dining room and bar. Cooking is honest and the style modern and imaginative. From a typical winter dinner menu, try the likes of crispy pork belly with rocket, fennel and caper salad and baked lemon dressing, or warm squid salad with chorizo, rocket and fennel to start, followed by Stokes Marsh Farm beef fillet with dauphinois, pancetta and shallot-stuffed mushroom and red-wine butter, or sea bass with tomato and herb sauce. Leave room for pudding, perhaps rice pudding with mulled fruits and home-made jam. The short list of wines is arranged by style, with 14 by the glass.

What To Do

Shop

NESTON PARK FARM SHOP

Buy organic, humanely reared meat from the Neston Estate and local farms, plus freshly made soup, home-made cakes and pastries at this fabulous farm shop.

Bath Road, Atworth, Melksham, Wiltshire SN12 8HP
01225 700881
www.nestonparkfarmshop.com

THE GALLERY ON THE BRIDGE

There are several antique shops in Castle Combe, which is a warren of honey-stoned cottages, with typical thick Cotswold walls and stone roofs. Start at The Gallery on the Bridge, which sells fine art, local crafts and interesting collectibles.

The Street, Castle Combe, Wiltshire SN14 7HU
01249 782201

BRADFORD-ON-AVON

A stroll around the pretty Georgian town reveals Elise in The Shambles selling quality leather goods, the Earth Collection on Market Street offers a range of environmentally friendly clothing, while One Caring World on Silver Street is an Ethical Trading Centre with an organic vegetarian cafe and health food shop. For specialist cheeses, wines, meats and preserves why not call into The Cheeseboard on Silver Street, and for handcrafted Italian ceramic and glass visit Un Po di Piu on The Shambles.

Elise 01225 309303
Earth Collection 01225 868876
www.theearthcollection.com
One Caring World 01225 866590
The Cheeseboard 01225 868042
www.cheeseboardboa.co.uk
Un Po di Piu 01225 867663

Visit

BOWOOD HOUSE

Bowood is a perfectly proportioned Georgian mansion, standing in 2,000 acres of gardens and parkland landscaped by Capability Brown. In Robert Adam's orangery is a collection of paintings, busts and a sculpture gallery, which includes some of the famous Lansdowne Marbles. A magnificent collection of jewels is on display, along with Georgian costumes. In the grounds are a formal Italianate terraced garden, a Doric temple, a grotto, cascades and an arboretum.

Derry Hill, Calne, Wiltshire SN11 0LZ
01249 812102
www.bowood.org

THE COURTS GARDEN

The Courts is a delightful English country garden with many interesting and unusual plants, imaginative use of colour, topiary and ornaments. Stroll through the peaceful water gardens planted with irises and lilies – there's also an arboretum, a kitchen garden and a very pretty orchard.

Holt, Bradford-on-Avon, Wiltshire BA14 6RR
01225 782875
www.nationaltrust.org.uk

MUSEUM OF COSTUME

One of the finest collections of clothes and accessories, dating from the late 16th century to the present day – there are more than 30,000 pieces. Check out Biba, Dior, Chanel, Muir and McQueen! Lady Ottoline Morell's evening dresses, shoes and bags are stunning.

Bennett Street, Bath, Somerset BA1 2QH
01225 477173
www.museumofcostume.co.uk

Activity

NARROWBOAT TRIP

The *Barbara McLellen* is a traditional barge painted with castles and roses, and it winds along the Kennet and Avon Canal through picturesque countryside and across the monumental Avoncliff aqueduct en route to Bath. Avoncliff is a fascinating industrial hamlet, where grist and fuller mills remain from the 16th century.

The Kennet and Avon Canal Trust The Wharfe, Frome Road, Bradford-on-Avon, Wiltshire
01380 721279
www.katrust.org

STEAM TRAIN RIDE

Treat yourself to Sunday lunch while you chug through the glorious Avon Valley towards Bath, and discover parts of the countryside you would never see any other way. The Station Buffet in Bitton is good, too, and known all over the county for its tasty home-made cakes. Take tea here and you'll have everything you need to complete a day steeped in old-style travel nostalgia.

Avon Valley Railway
Bitton Station, Bath Road, Bitton, Bristol BS30 6HD
01179 325538
www.avonvalleyrailway.co.uk

The Walk - A Walk with Good Manors at Holt

A stroll from a Wiltshire industrial village to a 15th-century moated manor house.

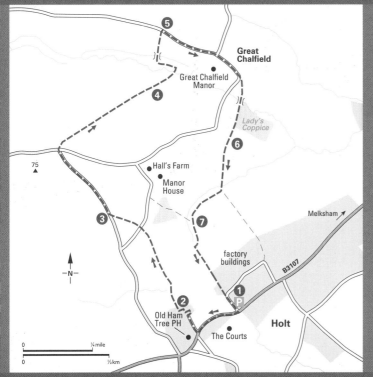

Walk Details

LENGTH: 3 miles (4.8km)

TIME: 1hr 30min

ASCENT: 147ft (45m)

PATHS: Field paths, metalled track, country lanes, 8 stiles

SUGGESTED MAP: aqua3 OS Explorer 156 Chippenham & Bradford-on-Avon

GRID REFERENCE: ST 861619

PARKING: Holt Village Hall car park

❶ Turn left out of the car park, then right along B3107 through village. Just before Old Ham Tree pub and the village green, turn right along Crown Corner. At the end of the lane take the waymarked path left along the drive. Follow the fenced path beside 'Highfields' to the stile.

❷ Keep to the right along the edge of the field, then keep ahead in the next field towards the clump of fir trees. Continue following the worn path to the right, into a further field. Keep left along the field edge to the stile in the top corner. Maintain direction to a ladder stile and cross metalled drive and stile opposite. Bear diagonally left through field to hidden stile in hedge, level with the clump of trees to the right.

❸ Turn right along the lane. At the junction, turn right towards Great Chalfield and go through the kissing gate almost immediately on the left. Take arrowed path right, diagonally across large field towards Great Chalfield Manor, visible ahead.

❹ Cross stile and bear half-right downhill to stile. Cross the stream via the stepping stones, then the stile, and bear diagonally left across the field to the gate. Cross the bridge and keep ahead beside hedge to the metalled track by the barn.

❺ Turn right, then right again when you reach the lane, passing in front of Great Chalfield Manor. At the sharp righthand bend, go through the gate ahead and bear right, then half-left across the field to cross

the footbridge over the stream. Continue straight on up the field beside the woodland to reach the gate in the field corner.

❻ Follow the lefthand field edge to the gate, then follow the path straight ahead towards the chimney on the skyline. Go through the gate, bear immediately right to the gate in the hedge and turn right along path around the field edge.

❼ Ignore the stile on the right; continue to the field corner and the raised path beside water. Go through the gate and turn left along the field edge to reach the further gate on left. Join the drive past Garlands Farm and pass between small factory buildings to the road. Turn right back to the car park.

The George and Dragon

Wiltshire

The Inn

In truth, the plain yellow, pebble-dashed façade of the George and Dragon may not set the heart racing with anticipation, as it looks like just another boozer. Things improve at the back, where there is a delightful summer garden and the higgledy-piggledy nature of the building indicates great age and character. Step inside the rustic bar, however, and you are transported back to 1645, to a world of wooden floors, simple benches and farmhouse chairs, old school tables and a log fire blazing on the hearth in the large and impressive stone fireplace. Equally unfussy is the black-and-white timbered dining room, decorated with displays of home-made chutneys, leaving the food to take rightful centre stage.

Wonky floors, wood panelling and wall timbers are prominent within the three individual bedrooms: Country, Funky and Classic. Think cool wall coverings, plasma screens, feature fireplaces, White Company goose-down duvets on big beds, iPod attachments on Logic clock-radios, and Cowshed toiletries and fluffy white bathrobes in gleaming tiled bathrooms. The Classic even has an old claw-foot bath in the bedroom.

The Essentials

Time at the Bar!
12-3pm, 7-10pm (4pm Sat & Sun)
Closed Sun eve & Mon
Food: 12-3pm (4pm Sun), 7-10pm
(6.30-10pm Sat).

What's the Damage?
Main courses from £10.50

Bitter Experience:
Butcombe, Moles

Sticky Fingers:
Children welcome; small portions

Muddy Paws:
Dogs welcome in the bar

Zzzzz:
3 rooms, £65-£85

Anything Else?
Garden, car park

The Food

Fish is the speciality here. It comes fresh from Cornwall, and the ever-changing chalkboard menu has been wowing the landlocked Wiltshire diners for years, with dishes ranging from creamy baked potted crab and smoked haddock and chive risotto to grilled sardines with lemon oil. Straightforward grills, such as whole Dover sole and skate wing with caper butter, are mixed with more enterprising ideas, like roast monkfish with green peppercorn cream, wild sea bass with pesto mash and crispy bacon, and lobster linguine with chilli tomato sauce.

If you don't fancy fish, and red meat is more to your taste, then you may find carpaccio of beef with mustard sauce or devilled kidneys for starters, and chargrilled sirloin steak with blue cheese and herb crust, or roast rack of lamb with mustard mash among the main courses. The short list of simple, traditional puddings might include hot apple and sultana crumble, and Eton mess. The set Sunday lunch (served until 4pm) is excellent value and, to drink, you'll find local Butcombe ale on tap and a raft of wines by the glass.

What To Do

Shop

BELOW STAIRS

Looking for original 19th- and 20th-century items? Head for this antique shop with five showrooms selling kitchenalia, enamel advertising signs, garden furniture, and a huge selection of lights. The Swan Inn just outside Hungerford is a good spot for lunch, serving organic food in beautiful rural surroundings.

103 High Street, Hungerford,
Berkshire RG17 0NB
01488 682317
www.belowstairs.co.uk

VINTAGE TO VOGUE

Vintage to Vogue specialises in 1850s to 1950s shoes, hats, lace, costume jewellery and formal wear. Another vintage outlet, Jack and Danny's, sells not just clothes but also musical instruments.

28 Milsom Street, Bath,
Bath & NE Somerset BA1 1DG
01225 337323
Jack & Danny's
3 London Street, Bath,
Bath & NE Somerset BA1 5BU
01225 469972
www.jackanddannys.net

Visit

NUMBER ONE ROYAL CRESCENT

As you might guess, Number One was the first house to be built in Royal Crescent, John Wood's masterpiece of Palladian design. A dining room, elegant drawing room, feminine bedroom and Georgian kitchen have been restored and furnished to create a picture of life in 18th-century Bath.

1 Royal Crescent, Bath,
Somerset BA1 2LR
01225 428126

HOLBURNE MUSEUM OF ART

One of the country's most impressive small museums, Holburne was created by local sailor William Holburne, who was widely known for his collection of silver and old masters, but also collected porcelain, glass and furniture. Exhibits include the famous Kneeling Venus Italian bronze, once owned by Louis XIV.

Great Pulteney Street, Bathwick, Bath,
Bath & NE Somerset BA2 4DB
01225 466669

AVEBURY STONE CIRCLE

A World Heritage Site, Avebury is one of the most important megalithic monuments in Europe, and it is a magical place to visit at any time of year. Wander around the stones, set at the heart of a prehistoric landscape. Some of the world's most significant archeological finds are exhibited in the Museum Galleries, where you can discover Avebury restorer and 'Marmalade Millionaire' Alexander Keiller's passion for archaeology.

Avebury, Marlborough, Wiltshire SN8 1RF
01672 539250
www.nationaltrust.org.uk

CAEN HILL LOCKS

This famous flight of locks is one of the great wonders of the canal era. Completed by John Rennie in 1810, in order to carry the Kennet and Avon Canal to a height of 237ft (72m), the flight consists of 29 locks in all, extending over 2 miles (3.2km). There's canal-side parking near Rowde, west of Devizes, and you can walk the length of the locks via the tow path.

www.waterscape.com

Activity

BALLOONING

Enjoy a balloon flight in early morning or mid-evening, drifting serenely over the Avon Valley towards the Cotswolds or wherever the wind and fancy takes you.

Bath Balloons, 8 Lambridge, London Road,
Bath, Bath & NE Somerset BA1 6BJ
01225 466888
www.bathballoons.co.uk

BOWOOD GOLF & COUNTRY CLUB

This championship course is set in the heart of the Marquis of Lansdowne's estate. Built on Capability Brown's landscaped grounds, the 18-hole course will challenge and delight you in equal measure. Visitors are welcome – you can hire everything you need for a round or two from the Pro Shop, and even take a lesson from one of the PGA professionals.

Derry Hill, Calne, Wiltshire SN11 9PQ
01249 822228
www.bowood-golf.co.uk

CYCLE THE KENNET & AVON CANAL TOW PATH

The 40-mile canal-side route runs from Bristol to Devizes, mostly along canal tow paths and, of course, you cycle (or walk) as much or as little of it as you choose. If you are starting from Bath you can hire bikes at The Bath & Dundas Canal Co, where you'll also get information about what to look out for en route – one of the first sights is the Dundas aqueduct. From here to Hilperton is one of the prettiest parts of the route.

Brass Knocker Basin, Monkton Combe,
Bath, Bath & NE Somerset BA2 7JD
01225 722292
www.bradenford.co.uk

The Walk - Exploring Bowood Park

A visit to one of Wiltshire's grandest houses from Calne town centre.

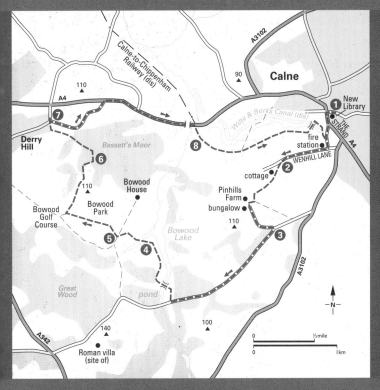

Walk Details

LENGTH: 7 miles (11.3km)

TIME: 3hrs 30min

ASCENT: 360ft (110m)

PATHS: Field, woodland and parkland paths, metalled drives, pavement beside A4, former railway line, 3 stiles

SUGGESTED MAP: aqua3 OS Explorer 156 Chippenham & Bradford-on-Avon

GRID REFERENCE: ST 998710

PARKING: Choice of car parks in Calne

❶ Locate the new library on The Strand (A4); walk south along New Road to the roundabout. Turn right along Station Road; take the footpath left opposite the fire station. Turn right at Wenhill Lane; follow it out of the built-up area.
❷ Near the cottage, follow the waymarker left and walk along the field edge. Just beyond the cottage, climb the bank and keep left along the field edge to the bridge and stile. Keep to the lefthand field edge and bear left to the stile. Follow the path right, through rough grass around Pinhills Farm to the stile opposite bungalow and turn left along drive.
❸ At the junction, turn right along the drive; continue for 1 mile (1.6km). Near the bridge, take the footpath right, through the kissing gate and walk through parkland beside the pond. Cross the bridge, go through the gate; turn right by Bowood Lake.
❹ Follow the path left to the gate and cross the causeway between lakes to the gate. Keep straight on up track; follow left, then right to cross driveway to Bowood House.
❺ Beyond gate, keep ahead along field edge, then follow path left across Bowood Park. Keep left of trees and field boundary to the gate. Turn right along the drive beside Bowood Golf Course. Where drive turns sharp right to the cottage, keep straight into woodland.
❻ Follow the path left, downhill through the clearing (often boggy) along the line of telegraph poles. Bear right with the path back into the woodland and follow it uphill beside the golf course. Turn right into the break in the trees; now go through the main gates to Bowood House into Derry Hill.
❼ Turn immediately right along Old Lane. At the A4, turn right along the pavement. Shortly, cross to the opposite pavement and continue downhill. Pass beneath footbridge and take the drive immediately right.
❽ Join the former railway line at Black Dog Halt. Turn left and follow it back towards Calne. Cross the disused canal and turn right along the tow path. Where the path forks, keep right to Station Road. Retrace your steps to the town centre.

The Compasses Inn

Wiltshire

The Inn

There's a timeless feel to this attractive 16th-century thatched inn, set in rolling Wiltshire countryside. It's quite remote, but locating it via a series of tortuously narrow lanes off the A30 is fun. Once here you won't want to leave this quintessential country pub; there's even an old cobbled path leading up to a low latch door. Duck on entering and find a charmingly unspoilt bar, which has a low-beamed ceiling, partly flagstoned floor and an interesting assortment of traditional furniture arranged in secluded alcoves. Various old-fashioned advertising posters and a collection of primitive-looking farm tools and tackle from times past cover the open-brick walls, and you can toast your toes by a blazing log fire in winter.

Step outside and climb the covered stair to reach the four cottagey bedrooms, one tucked beneath the heavy thatch with a big wooden bed and low beams – watch your head! Expect flat-screen TVs, biscuits with your coffee, and good ensuite facilities, two with showers only. The pub owns the sweet little cottage next door, which you could rent and use as a base from which to really explore this beautiful area.

The Food

You'll find the menu chalked up on boards in the bar, with additional specials written on the canopy of the wood-burning stove in the inglenook. Dishes change daily, reflecting the seasons and the availability of the local farm produce that owner Alan Stoneham is keen to support. Typically, start with smoked duck and red onion tart, a big bowl of mussels cooked in bacon, cream, garlic and white wine, or the day's soup, perhaps mushroom and rosemary. The classic main dishes take in a hearty steak and kidney pie with suet pastry, lamb shoulder slow-roasted with red wine, molasses and soy sauce, or a warm salad of scallops, crayfish and spicy chorizo.

Portions are more than generous and you won't leave dissatisfied. If you have room, do try the chocolate brownie that arrives with scoops of blackcurrant ice cream. Mini onion loaves filled with rib-eye steak and onions, salads and ham, egg and chips provide great lunchtime fare. Quaff a pint of Wadworth 6X, one of 12 wines by the glass or, if whisky is your tipple, there's a raft of malts to choose from.

The Essentials

Time at the Bar!
12-3pm, 6-11pm
Food: 12-2pm, 6.30-9pm

What's the Damage?
Main courses from £10

Bitter Experience:
The Large One, Hidden Quest

Sticky Fingers:
Children welcome; children's menu

Muddy Paws:
Dogs welcome

Zzzzz:
6 rooms, £85-£90, plus cottage from £100

Anything Else?
Courtyard, 2 gardens, car park

What To Do

Shop

CRANBORNE STORES

The Marquis of Salisbury has had a passion for rearing rare breeds of pig for many years – and now you can buy the resulting pork, along with free-range beef and lamb, in the estate stores. Own-cured bacon, home-made sausages and estate game can be taken home, too, along with local cheeses, home-baked pies and terrines. No small wonder the Cranborne Stores is one of Rick Stein's Food Heroes.

1 The Square, Cranborne, Dorset BH21 5PR
01725 517210
www.cranbornestores.co.uk

HARE LANE POTTERY

Jonathan Garratt has rapidly established himself as one of the country's leading terracotta potters/garden artists. His passion for plants informs many of his innovative designs for wall pots, planters and more unusual containers for particular plants. Local clay is fired with wood to create distinctive dark colours, and Jonathan's 'Garden punctuation' takes traditional ideas from sculpture and 'knits' these pieces into the plants and pots. There's a handsome 18th-century courtyard garden and, as you'd expect, a gallery where you can buy a unique pot or two to take home.

Hare Lane, Cranborne, Dorset
01725 517700
www.jonathangarratt.com

Visit

WILTON HOUSE

Wilton House stands magnificently in 21 acres of landscaped parkland, and is the home of the 18th Earl of Pembroke. Over 460 years old, the house was rebuilt by Inigo Jones in the Palladian style, and is one of the treasure houses of Britain – see the stunning state rooms and the world-famous collection of paintings by Van Dyck, Rubens, Reynolds and Breughel. The Tudor Kitchen, Victorian Laundry and Pembroke Palace Dolls House are well worth visiting, and outside, the Rose Garden, Palladian Bridge and the Millennium Fountain are all within easy walking distance. Make a day of it and have lunch in the restaurant, and stock up on plants in the garden centre.

Salisbury, Wiltshire SP2 0BJ
01722 746714
www.wiltonhouse.co.uk

MOMPESSON HOUSE

A perfect example of Queen Anne architecture, Mompesson is an elegant, spacious 18th-century house just outside of Salisbury city centre, with fine Georgian features, intricate plasterwork and a monumental oak staircase. There's a world-class collection of Turnbull drinking glasses, and many superior porcelain pieces. The delightful walled garden has a pergola and traditional herbaceous borders. The house doubled as the redoubtable Mrs Jennings' London residence in Emma Thompson's production and screenplay of Jane Austen's novel *Sense & Sensibility*.

The Close, Salisbury, Wiltshire SP1 2EL
01722 335659
www.nationaltrust.org.uk

Activity

GOLF

Enjoy a round of golf at Rushmore Golf Club, an 18-hole championship parkland course set within one of England's most historic estates on the Wiltshire/Dorset border.

Rushmore Park Golf Club
Tollard Royal, Salisbury, Wiltshire SP5 5QB
01725 516328
www.rushmoregolfclub.co.uk

HORSE RACING AT SALISBURY

One of the oldest race courses in England, there's been horse racing here at Salisbury since the 16th century. The historic course is set in the Wiltshire downland, with a great view of Salisbury Cathedral.

Netherhampton, Salisbury, Wiltshire SP2 8PN
01722 326461
www.salisburyracecourse.co.uk

HOT- AIR BALLOONING

What better way to explore the rolling Wiltshire Downs than from a hot-air balloon? Soar above the countryside and float among the clouds, as a miniature model world appears below you.

Aerosaurs Balloons
5 Rivers Leisure Centre, Salisbury, Wiltshire SP1 3NR
01404 823102
www.ballooning.co.uk

The Walk - Along the Unspoilt Nadder Valley

Architecture, history and varied scenery on woodland pathways.

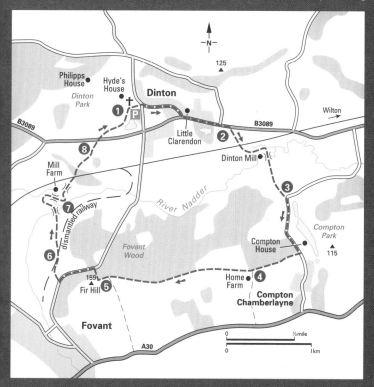

Walk Details

LENGTH: 5.25 miles (8.4km)

TIME: 3hrs

ASCENT: 360ft (110m)

PATHS: Tracks, field and woodland paths, parkland, 15 stiles

SUGGESTED MAP: aqua3 OS Explorer 130 Salisbury & Stonehenge

GRID REFERENCE: SU 009315

PARKING: Dinton Park National Trust car park

❶ Leave the car park, cross and follow the lane to the B3089. Turn left, pass Little Clarendon, and continue for 0.25 mile (400m). Take the path on the right by bus shelter.

❷ Follow track to kissing gate and cross railway line to further gate. Keep to track; bear left alongside stream to Dinton Mill. Pass left, cross the footbridge over River Nadder and follow drive to lane.

❸ Turn right and follow metalled lane into Compton Chamberlayne. Take the footpath right, opposite the entrance to Compton House. Ascend, pass the round gate and continue along the track to Home Farm and the junction of tracks.

❹ Turn right, follow the track left around buildings and remain on the track (views of regimental badges etched into chalk). Walk beside woodland; near the field corner, follow path into trees and continue close to woodland fringe. Pass the reservoir to reach the track.

❺ Turn right; walk downhill to the lane. Turn left, then, at the sharp left bend, take path right and enter field (stile left). Bear half-right to stile. Cross the track, pass through kissing gate and walk across rough grassland, then bear left to gate.

❻ Turn right along the field edge, go through the kissing gate and bear left down the righthand side of the field. At waymarker, follow the path left, downhill to the stile. Descend through the scrub, cross the footbridge, then stile, and walk

ahead to further stile. Bear left along riverbank, cross stile and continue to bridge over mill stream.

❼ Pass before Mill Farm on the path. Cross the footbridge and stile; bear diagonally right towards the railway. Cross the railwayline via stiles; bear slightly right to the stile and woodland. Walk through to the stile and keep ahead, to the rear of the barn, to the stile. Continue ahead to stile; cut across the pasture, keeping to the right of the 2nd telegraph pole to stile and road.

❽ Cross the stile opposite into Dinton Park; turn right alongside the hedge. Bear left along the path, pass the pond and head towards the church. Go through the 1st gate on the right and return to the car park.

✳ Hollyhocks in Cathedral Close, Salisbury, Wiltshire

The King's Arms

Gloucestershire

The Inn

The southern edge of the Cotswolds is all rolling countryside, with a heritage that is rich in the English passion for horses: Badminton, Gatcombe Park and Cheltenham are all nearby (as is the M4, although you'd never know it). And just the thing after a hard day in the saddle is this 17th-century coaching inn, which sits squarely on Didmarton's high street. The inn offers a traditional terracotta-tiled and beamed back bar with dark wooden tables and chairs and an impressive collection of ale pump badges. The more contemporary front bar has cool neutral colours, a cosy settle, window seats, a log fire and a collection of modern prints on the walls. It all feels very inviting.

Upstairs are three stylish doubles and a single bedroom, all with ensuite shower rooms and TV, while across the yard the coaching stable has been converted to make three self-catering cottages in the full English country style: roofs open to the ridge with exposed beams, crisp white linen and super comfy beds.

The Food

A favourite foodie haunt, the inn has won a swathe of awards for its food, cask ales and fine wines. Fresh game is a notable speciality, and the seasonal menu and blackboard specials change weekly. At lunchtime you can drop in to enjoy a hearty selection of sandwiches or classics such as Old Spot sausages, mash and onions, or calves' liver with bacon and mash; if you feel like something lighter, why not go for the likes of wild mushroom and red pepper tagliatelle.

Against a backdrop of warm red walls and high-backed padded chairs, evening meals in the restaurant are more elaborate. Garlic bruschetta, sautéed scallops and wild mushroom salad could then lead on to roast haunch of Badminton venison on butter onion mash with a red wine and juniper jus. Or for something less robust, the pan-seared sea bass fillet on a sweet tomato and prawn risotto is pure comfort eating. Don't skip desserts, they are well worth saving room for, especially the mouthwatering chocolate chip Italian meringue served with a toffee sauce.

The King's Arms, The Street, Didmarton, Badminton, Gloucestershire GL9 1DT

The Essentials

Time at the Bar!
11am-11pm, Sun 12-10.30pm
Food: 12-2.30pm, 6-9.30pm;
Sun 12-9pm

What's the Damage?
Main courses from £8.95

Bitter Experience:
Uley Bitter, Otter Ale,
Hook Norton Hooky

Sticky Fingers:
Children welcome,
smaller portions available

Muddy Paws:
Dogs welcome in the bar

Zzzzz:
4 rooms, £80-£100

Anything Else?
Terrace, garden, car park,
self-catering cottages

What To Do

Shop

CHESTERTON FARM SHOP
A farm shop specialising in supplying meat from rare breeds, including beef from Shorthorn and Dexters cattle and pork from Berkshire and Tamworth pigs. The shop also supplies locally caught game, other meats from the home farm and a variety of Cotswold farm vegetables and fruits.

Chesterton Farm, Cirencester,
Gloucestershire GL7 6JP
01258 642160
www.chestertonfarm.co.uk

TOP BANANA ANTIQUES
The heart of Tetbury old town is rich with antique shops and galleries, many collectively trading under the Top Banana marque. More than 60 dealers trade in most specialities, from clocks and furniture to fabrics, china and silver, sporting memorabilia, Victoriana and even French *objets d'art*.

1 New Church Street, Tetbury,
Gloucestershire GL8 8DS
08712 881102
www.topbananaantiques.com

Visit

BERKELEY CASTLE
This is the oldest inhabited castle in England, with treasures and fittings amassed over the centuries contributing to the sense of history – which includes the supposedly gruesome dispatch of King Edward II and a Civil War siege. Pleasantly terraced Elizabethan gardens enhance the setting within this small Severnside village.

Berkeley, Gloucestershire GL13 9BQ
01453 810332
www.berkeley-castle.com

RODMARTON MANOR
An imposing multi-gabled, Cotswold stone country house built a century ago to celebrate the Arts and Crafts movement. The furnishings and fittings are similarly influenced by those zealous artists and artisans. Formal gardens include a kitchen garden, rockery and topiary.

Cirencester, Gloucestershire GL7 6PF
01285 841253
www.rodmarton-manor.co.uk

ULEY BREWERY
One of the longest-surviving microbreweries in the Cotswolds, based in a listed, traditional tower brewery dating from the 1830s. A good range of standard, special and seasonal beers is made here using traditional methods and the best regional ingredients. Tours are by prior arrangement only; bottled beers available, draught beers on tap in the village's Old Spot pub.

31 The Street, Uley, Dursley,
Gloucestershire GL11 5TB
01453 860120
www.uleybrewery.com

WESTONBIRT NATIONAL ARBORETUM
One of the largest in Europe, where the specimen trees represent all continents except Antarctica. Spread over 600 acres, there are miles of footpaths through glades and beneath 'champion' trees, the greatest of their species; in all, more than 18,000 trees. At their best in autumn; spring colour comes from the shrubs and woodland flowers.

Tetbury, Gloucestershire GL8 8QS
01666 880220
www.forestry.gov.uk/westonbirt

Activity

COTSWOLD GLIDING CLUB
A trial flight offers novices an introduction to the sport of gliding; if you're hooked, then further lessons may be tacked on, or a full day's course arranged for more hands-on experience in this eerily silent, but strangely addictive sky-based world.

Aston Down Airfield, Cowcombe Lane,
Chalford, Stroud, Gloucestershire GL6 8HR
01285 760415
www.cotswoldgliding.co.uk

COTSWOLD WATER PARK
More than a hundred lakes between Cirencester and Cricklade, formed in disused gravel pits, are now home to a comprehensive variety of water-based activities, from the relatively sedate cycling and walking to adrenalin-rich waterskiing and sailboarding. Tuition and short experience courses are available.

www.waterpark.org

SLIMBRIDGE WETLAND CENTRE
Founded by Sir Peter Scott, Slimbridge is HQ of the Wildfowl & Wetlands Trust. This huge reserve of reedbeds, marsh and pasture beside the Severn Estuary has myriad species of resident birds and attracts scores of migrants. Particularly famous for water birds: a series of viewing points, hides and a tower allow visitors to appreciate the bird world to the full. The events and site tours that take place here range from brown hare watches to wildflower safaris.

Slimbridge, Stroud,
Gloucestershire GL2 7BT
01453 890333
www.wwt.org.uk

The Walk - On the Fringe of the Cotswolds

A pastoral ramble around the village of Sherston.

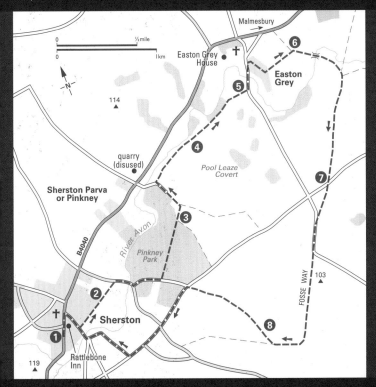

Walk Details

LENGTH: 6.5 miles (10.4km)

TIME: 3hrs

ASCENT: 131ft (40m)

PATHS: Field and parkland paths, tracks, metalled lanes, 11 stiles

SUGGESTED MAP: aqua3 OS Explorer 168 Stroud, Tetbury & Malmesbury

GRID REFERENCE: ST 853858

PARKING: Sherston High Street; plenty of roadside parking

INFORMATION: This walk is over the county border in Wiltshire

❶ On the High Street, walk towards village stores, pass Rattlebone Inn; turn right into Noble Street. Pass Grove Road; take footpath left up the steps. Cross the cul-de-sac; follow the footpath to the gate then to the rear of the houses to the gate.

❷ Bear diagonally right across the field to the gate and lane. Turn right, cross over the river and turn left ('Foxley'). At end of the woodland on the left, take the footpath left through the gate. Follow the track across Pinkney Park to the gate.

❸ Keep ahead, bearing left beside the wall to the gate. Follow the track ahead towards farm buildings; where drive curves left, turn right into farmyard. Keep right to join the path to the stile. Turn left around

the field edge to the stile; keep to lefthand field edge to stile in corner.

❹ Bear half-right across the field; follow the path along the field edge above Avon to the stile. Cross a further stile; walk beside fence (Easton Grey House left), and head downhill to the gate and lane.

❺ Turn left into Easton Grey. Cross the river bridge, turn right uphill to the footpath ahead on reaching the entrance gates on right. Cross gravelled area, go through the gate and ahead to the stile. Continue across the next field; descend to follow the track into the next field.

❻ Turn right along field edge; bear off right downhill through scrub to footbridge. Keep ahead beside ruin to gate. Cross stile and continue to

further stile and gate. Follow track downhill to stile; turn right along track (Fosse Way). Continue for 0.5 mile (800m) to road.

❼ Cross over; follow the byway to another road. Bear left and keep ahead where the lane veers left. Follow the rutted track for 0.5 mile (800m), then cross the arrowed stile on right. Head across field to gate and bear diagonally right across the large paddock to the stile.

❽ Join the track, cross racehorse gallop and go through the lefthand gate ahead. Walk through scrub to another gate; keep to track ahead to road. Turn left and continue to the crossroads. Proceed straight on to next junction; keep ahead, following the lane back into Sherston.

The Amberley Inn

Gloucestershire

The Inn

The elevated view across Minchinhampton Common (with its free-ranging cows) to the five valleys of Stroud is forever England, a setting that's perfectly matched by the country-house feel of this late Victorian baronial-style inn. High ceilings enhance the grace of the well-proportioned lounge bar and smart restaurant, and mullioned windows lend an ancient air, while lots of wood (panelling, stripped floorboards) and open fires add warmth. There is a great atmosphere here, and it's a popular place, filled with tourists and weekenders in for the food, as well as locals who usually head for the workmanlike public bar – an ideal place for downing a pint or three of well-kept Otter Ale, Old Spot or Archers.

The dozen bedrooms are split between the main house and the more secluded Garden Cottage. They are all excellent, decorated to a high standard, though quite traditionally furnished (expect muted colours and classic bedroom furniture), but good mattresses, scatter cushions, mini espresso machines and gleaming bathrooms ensure modern comforts.

The Food

This is a proper, old-fashioned country inn, and the food reflects this. It offers, on the whole, an unashamedly English bill of fare; for example Gloucestershire pork sausages and mash with a rich onion gravy, local beer-battered fish and chips with garden pea purée, or slow-braised lamb shank on mustard mash with vegetables and red wine sauce. Elsewhere there might be the more modish confit leg of duck on olive oil-crushed new potatoes with wilted rocket and spiced orange syrup, or crisp polenta cake with seared vegetables and a pesto verde to start, followed by baked fillet of salmon on crushed baby potatoes with a light casserole of chorizo sausage, Mediterranean vegetables and butter beans.

The menu is the same for dinner as at lunch (minus the very local ham, egg and chips), with a few specials on a separate sheet, and blackboards for the good choices of wine. Sunday brings traditional roasts, such as roast beef with Yorkshire pudding, or roast loin of pork with apple sauce.

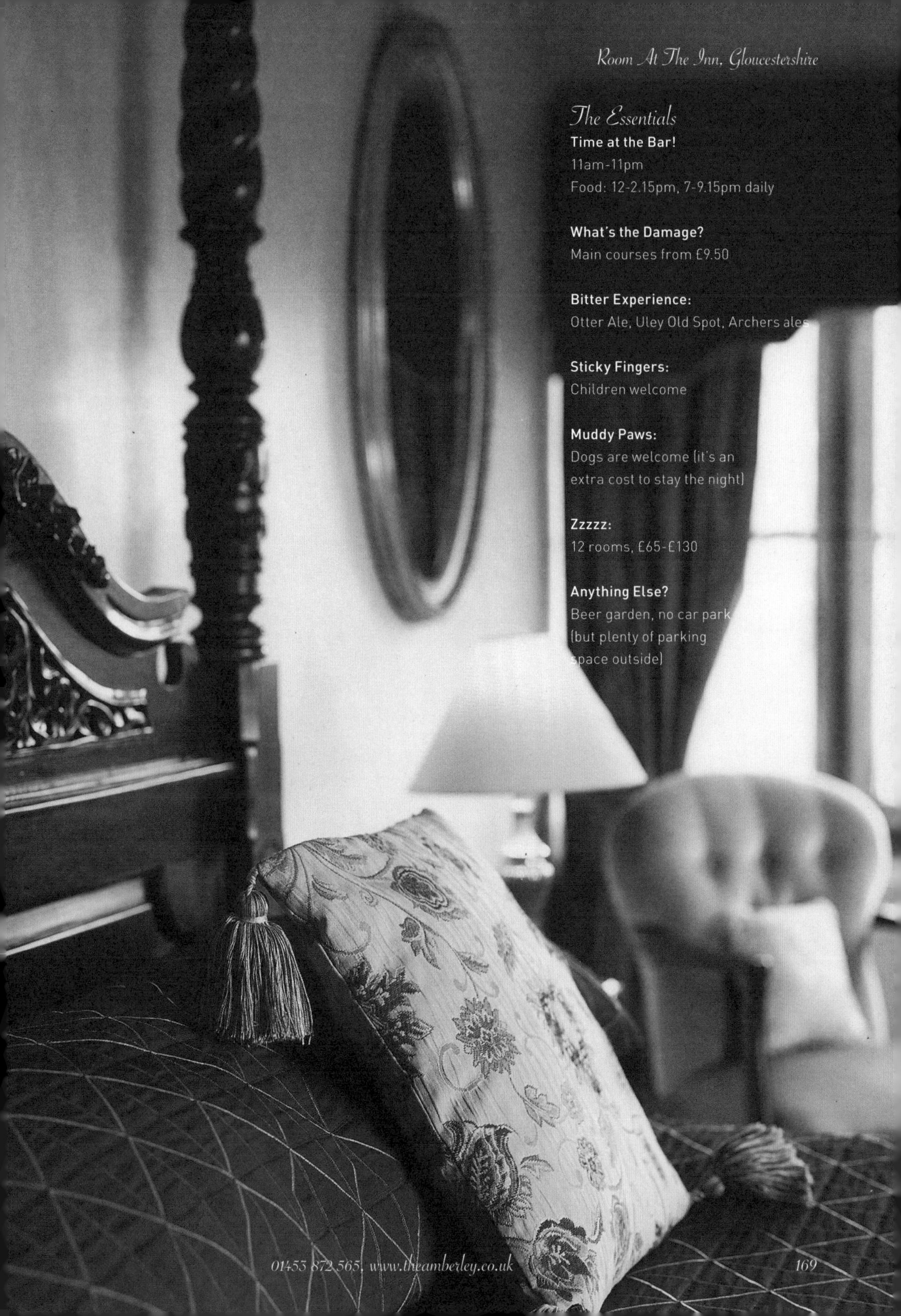

The Essentials

Time at the Bar!
11am-11pm
Food: 12-2.15pm, 7-9.15pm daily

What's the Damage?
Main courses from £9.50

Bitter Experience:
Otter Ale, Uley Old Spot, Archers ales

Sticky Fingers:
Children welcome

Muddy Paws:
Dogs are welcome (it's an extra cost to stay the night)

Zzzzz:
12 rooms, £65-£130

Anything Else?
Beer garden, no car park (but plenty of parking space outside)

01453 872 565, www.theamberley.co.uk

What To Do

Shop

GLOUCESTER ANTIQUES CENTRE

Housed in a handsome Grade II listed Victorian warehouse by the docks, this is one of the longest-established antiques centres in the country, with over 140 dealers to tempt you with their wares. Even if you are not interested in antiques it is worth visiting the Centre to try the first-floor cafe. It serves good coffee and home-made cakes, and has fantastic views over the docks.

1 Severn Road, The Docks, Gloucester, Gloucestershire GL1 2LE

01452 529716

www.gacl.co.uk

NAILSWORTH

Nailsworth is a picturesque little town known for its connection with the ancient Cotswold wool trade. These days it buzzes with 21st-century life in the form of cafes, restaurants and shops – a good place to start exploring what the town has to offer is the award-winning Williams Fish Market & Foodhall, where, among a lot of other things, you'll find pungent sausages from Toulouse; fish fresh from Cornwall and tasty bacon supplied by Richard Woodall in Cumbria. There's a very good fish restaurant over the shop, too. Hobbs Bakery is one of Rick Stein's Food Heroes, selling delicious hand-made bread.

Williams Foodhall

3 Fountain Street, Nailsworth, Gloucestershire GL6 0BL

01458 835507

www.williamskitchen.co.uk

Hobbs Bakery

4 George Street, Nailsworth, Gloucestershire GL6 0AG

01453 839396

Visit

OWLPEN MANOR

Set in a remote and picturesque wooded valley under the edge of the Cotswold hills, the magnificent Owlpen estate has 900 years of history. The Tudor Manor House is one of the most romantic buildings in the country. In the Great Hall there is a unique collection of painted textiles, Arts and Crafts furniture, fittings and family portraits; outside, the stunning formal terraced gardens with their famous ancient yew trees were once praised by Vita Sackville-West. The 15th-century listed Cider House restaurant with its cruck trusses offers gourmet meals as well as light lunches.

Uley, Gloucestershire GL11 5BZ

01453 860261

www.owlpen.com

PAINSWICK ROCOCO GARDENS

This enchanting 6-acre garden, nestling in a hidden valley, is the only complete surviving example of the flamboyant English Rococo Garden Movement. Originally laid out in the 18th century, it has magnificent views of the surrounding countryside. Stroll in the grounds and discover some extraordinary rococo buildings: The Red House, Kitchen Garden, Gothic Alcove and magical Exedra. Good lunches using produce grown in the kitchen garden are served in the Coach House Restaurant and don't leave without visiting the Present Collection shop for a range of gifts and plants to take home.

The Stables, Painswick, Gloucestershire GL6 6TH

01452 813204

www.rococogarden.co.uk

Activity

CRUISE ON THE RIVER SEVERN

All aboard the *Queen Boadicea* II, a Dunkirk 'Little Ship' built in 1936, for a memorable trip along the Gloucester & Sharpness Canal to see the countryside from a unique perspective. There's lots of wildlife to be seen, too: buzzards, kestrels and sparrowhawks, maybe even otters and mink.

Gloucester Leisure Cruises

National Waterways Museum, Llanthony Warehouse, The Docks, Gloucester, Gloucestershire GL1 2EH

01452 318200

www.nwm.org.uk

DRYSTONE WALLING

Learn a new skill in the form of the traditional craft of drystone walling. If you enrol on one of the two-day walling courses (May–Sep) across the Cotswolds you will be helping to maintain the 4,000 miles of dry-stone walls that make the area so distinctive. You can also try your hand at hedge-laying by enrolling on a two-day winter course.

01451 862034

www.cotswoldsaonb.org.uk

GLIDING

The Bristol and Gloucestershire Gliding Club is one of the oldest in the country, and what better way to explore the stunning Severn Valley than soaring high above it? Catch a thermal and discover the visual wonders of the Cotswolds from thousands of feet above them, with expert tuition on hand.

Bristol and Gloucestershire Gliding Club

Nympsfield, Stonehouse, Gloucestershire GL10 3TX

01453 860342

www.bggc.co.uk

The Walk - Weaving In The Stroud Valley

See the impact of the Industrial Revolution in the steep-sided Cotswold valleys.

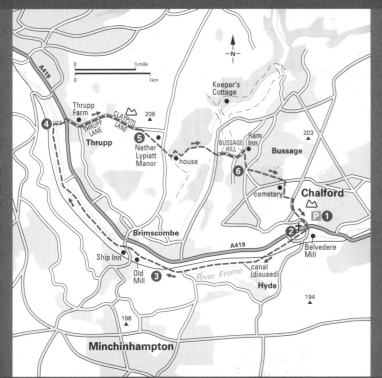

Walk Details

LENGTH: 6 miles (9.7km)

TIME: 3hrs

ASCENT: 495ft (150m)

PATHS: Fields, lanes, canal path and tracks, 3 stiles

SUGGESTED MAP: aqua3 OS Explorer 168 Stroud, Tetbury and Malmesbury

GRID REFERENCE: SO 892025

PARKING: Lay-by east of Chalford church

❶ Walk towards the church. Immediately before it, cross the road and locate the path going right, towards the canal roundhouse. Note the Belvedere Mill on the left. Follow the tow path alongside the Thames and Severn Canal (right).

❷ Cross the road. Continue along the tow path as it descends the steps. Now follow the path for about 2 miles (3.2km). It shortly disappears under the railway line via a culvert. Old mills and small factories line the route.

❸ Shortly before reaching Brimscombe, the path passes under the railway again. Soon after, it becomes the road into the industrial estate. At the road opposite the mill turn left, to reach the junction.

Cross and turn right. Immediately after the Ship Inn turn left along the road among offices and workshops. Continue along path, with factory walls to right. The canal reappears (left). Continue into country. Pass beneath 3 bridges and a footbridge.

❹ At the next bridge, with a hamlet high on left, turn right to follow the path to the road. Cross this and turn left. After a few paces turn right up a short path to meet Thrupp Lane. Turn right. At the top, turn left into Claypits Lane, turn right just before Thrupp Farm and climb steeply.

❺ After a long climb, as road levels out, you will see Nether Lypiatt Manor ahead. Turn right, beside the tree, over the stile into the field. Go half left to the far corner. Cross

a stone stile. Follow narrow path beside trees to road. Descend lane opposite. Where it appears to fork, go ahead, to descend past a house. Enter woodland and fork right near bottom. Keep the pond on the left and cross the road to climb Bussage Hill. After 100yds (91m) pass a lane on the left. At the top fork left. Opposite the Ram Inn turn right.

❻ After the telephone box and bus shelter turn left to follow the path among houses into woodland. Go ahead until you reach the road. Turn left and immediately right down the path beside the cemetery. Descend to another road. Turn right for 50yds (46m); turn left down the steep lane, leading back to Chalford. At the bottom, turn left to return to start.

The Green Dragon

Gloucestershire

The Green Dragon Inn, Cockleford, Cowley, Cheltenham, Gloucestershire GL53 9NW

The Inn

This handsome old stone pub was once a cider house and is set in some of the prettiest country in the Cotswolds, on a steep hillside approached by a dark, narrow lane. The two bars – Lower and Mouse – are stone-walled and ooze character, with chunky beams, crackling log fires in stone inglenooks, polished planks or flagstones on the floor, and soothing candlelight in the evenings. The Mouse Bar is a cosy room with furnishings hand-crafted by Robert Thompson, the famous 'Mouse Man of Kilburn', so look for the trademark mouse on the sturdy tables and chairs.

Bedrooms are named after Cheltenham Gold Cup winners and are peacefully tucked away in a modern building to the rear of the pub, with views across fields and trees. Although simply decorated with creamy yellow walls and modern pine furnishings, you can expect Egyptian cotton sheets, feather pillows, clock-radio, magazines, and power showers in fully tiled bathrooms. Splash out on the huge St George's Suite and you'll get leather sofas, a king-size bed and a vast tiled bathroom replete with free-standing bath, walk-in shower, bidet and posh Beaufort smellies.

The Essentials

Time at the Bar!
11am-11pm
Food: 12-2.30pm (3pm Sat; 3.30pm
Sun), 6-10pm (9.30pm Sun)

What's the Damage?
Main courses from £11.95

Bitter Experience:
Butcombe, Courage Directors, Hooky

Sticky Fingers:
Children welcome; children's menu

Muddy Paws:
Dogs allowed in the bar

Zzzzz:
9 rooms, £85-£140; single £65

Anything Else?
Garden, terrace, car park

The Food

Lunch and dinner menus change weekly and combine traditional pub favourites and more adventurous freshly prepared dishes, with daily specials adding interest and choice. Typically, tuck into starters of potted smoked mackerel and prawns in a light horseradish cream, smoked breast of wood pigeon with baby morel dressing, or ham hock and apple terrine with cranberry and redcurrant sauce. To follow, there may be lamb fillets on crushed new potatoes with apple and mint chutney, chargrilled sirloin steak with pepper sauce, or a daily dish like spicy fish risotto, or a hearty beef and vegetable casserole with herb dumplings.

Lunchtime extras take in chunky sandwiches in white farmhouse bread, perhaps mozzarella, sun-dried tomatoes and courgettes with pesto, and lighter options like tuna niçoise and home-made beef burger with fries and salad. Round off with banoffee pie or local Winstones honey and ginger ice cream. In summer, head for the flower-decked and heated front terrace with a pint of Butcombe and savour the view across Cowley and the River Churn.

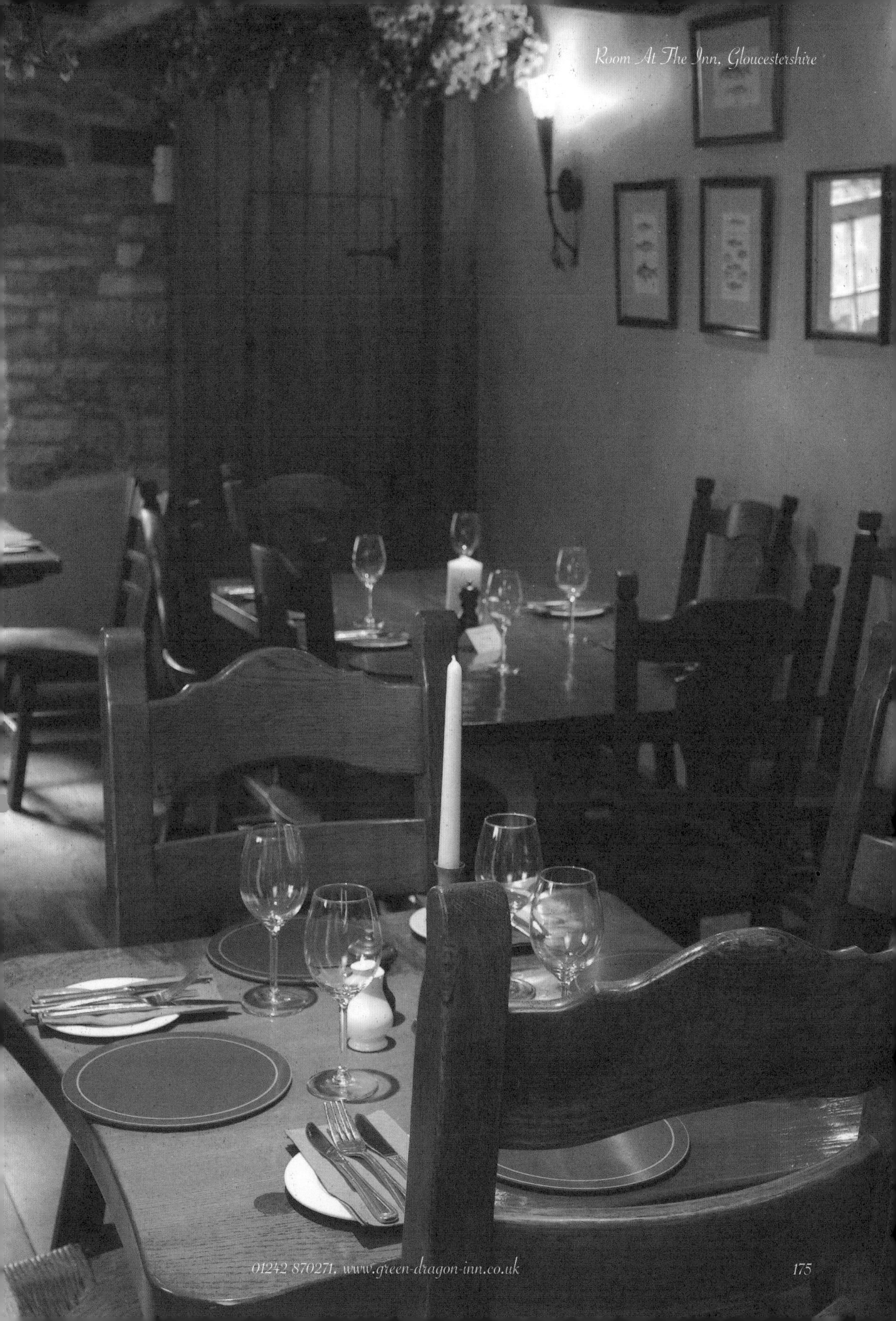

What To Do

Shop

FARMERS' MARKET
Buy locally grown, organic goodies, including delicious, artisan bread from Hobbs House Bakery, at this popular farmers' market.

Mortimore Gardens, Nailsworth, Gloucestershire
01453 833043

HAMPTONS DELI
Choose from a good selection of British cheeses, predominantly from small dairies, including the famous Stinking Bishop and local single Gloucester. There are also French-style breads from a local bakery, home-baked raised pies and interesting oils and vinegars.

1 Digbeth Street, Stow on the Wold, Gloucestershire GL54 1BN
01451 831733
www.hamptons-hampers.co.uk

THE ORGANIC FARM SHOP
This award-winning shop sells incredibly fresh, home-produced vegetables and over 100 types of herbs, free-range meat and all kinds of groceries.

Abbey Home Farm, Burford Road, Cirencester, Gloucestershire GL7 5HF
01285 640441
www.theorganicfarmshop.co.uk

WINDS OF CHANGE GALLERY
Prominently positioned in the ancient Anglo-Saxon Borough of Winchcombe, this light, airy gallery space exhibits and sells the work of established and new artists, including glass, ceramics, painting and sculpture.

8 High Street, Winchcombe, Gloucestershire GL54 5HT
01242 603281
www.windsofchange.uk.com

Visit

MISERDEN PARK GARDENS
Miserden is a magnificent 17th-century manor house (not open) in 12 acres of stunning grounds. The 300-year-old garden has naturalised bulbs, flowering trees and fine topiary and a parterre.

Stroud, Gloucestershire GL6 7JA
01285 821303

SNOWSHILL MANOR
This beautiful Cotswold stone Tudor manor house is crammed with eclectic and eccentric items from the Arts and Crafts Movement.

Snowshill, Broadway, Gloucestershire WR12 7JU
01386 852410
www.nationaltrust.org.uk

STANWAY HOUSE & FOUNTAIN
An outstanding example of a Jacobean manor house, Stanway, built in 1590, is situated in a hollow beneath a long spur of the Cotswold escarpment. The house is also famous for its spectacular 300ft (91m) fountain, the tallest in Britain.

Stanway, Cheltenham, Gloucestershire GL54 5PQ
01386 584469
www.stanwayfountain.co.uk

SUDELEY CASTLE
Winchcombe is a charming town, with warm Cotswold stone cottages, tea shops and medieval architecture, and Sudeley Castle, final home of Catherine Parr after the death of her husband Henry VIII, is one of the country's most romantic buildings.

Winchcombe, Cheltenham, Gloucestershire GL54 5JD
01242 602308
www.sudeleycastle.co.uk

Activity

GLIDING
Take to the skies for a day's lesson and get a unique perspective of the glorious Cotswolds countryside.

Cotswold Gliding Club
Aston Down Airfield, Cowcombe Lane, Chalford, Stroud, Gloucestershire GL6 8HR
01285 760415
www.cotswoldgliding.co.uk

GUILDHALL ARTS CENTRE
You'll find a world of culture under one roof here – theatre, cinema, music and exhibitions, and a very good cafe-bar.

23 Eastgate Street, Gloucester, Gloucestershire GL1 1NS
01452 505089

STEAM TRAIN RIDE
On this volunteer-run heritage line, the steam train takes you on a scenic 20-mile (32-km) round trip to Cheltenham Racecourse through lovely countryside, via the Greet Tunnel, one of the longest on a preserved track. You will enjoy superb views over the Cotswolds, Malverns and Vale of Evesham as you chug along.

Gloucestershire Warwickshire Railway
The Railway Station, Toddington, Gloucestershire GL54 5DT
01242 621405
www.gwsr.com

WATERSPORTS
Learn to windsurf, canoe, drive a speedboat or sail at this well-run park, beautifully situated in the River Avon valley.

Croft Farm Waterpark
Bredons Hardwick, Tewkesbury, Gloucestershire GL20 7EE
01684 772321
www.croftfarmleisure.co.uk

The Walk - Pathways Of The Medieval Looters

A vanished castle and secluded valleys, in Syde and tiny Caundle Green.

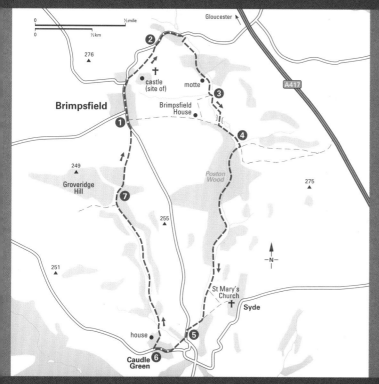

Walk Details

LENGTH: 4 miles (6.4km)

TIME: 2hrs

ASCENT: 180ft (55m)

PATHS: Fields, tracks and pavement, 9 stiles

SUGGESTED MAP: aqua3 OS Explorer 179 Gloucester, Cheltenham & Stroud

GRID REFERENCE: SO 938124

PARKING: Brimpsfield village; lay-bys on Cranham road

1 Go to the end of the road towards the village centre. Turn left. Walk through the village and, at the corner, turn right through the gate on to the track towards the church. Before the church, bear left across the meadow (site of the castle) to the stile. In the next field go half right to the corner and the road.

2 Turn right. Follow the road down to just before the cottage near the bottom. Turn right on to the drive. After a few paces, drop down to the left on to the parallel path which will bring you back on to the drive. Next, just before the cottage, turn left and go down into the woodland to follow the path with the stream on the left. Follow this for 550yds (503m), ignoring the bridge on the left, to cross 2 stiles and emerge on to the track.

3 Turn left. Follow the track as it rises to the right. After 100yds (91m) go forward over the stile into a field with Brimpsfield House to the right. Go half right to another stile, pass the gate on the right and cross another stile at the next corner. Follow the path to cross the bridge. Bear left up to the track. Follow this for 250yds (229m), until you reach the crossways.

4 Turn right to follow the footpath along the bottom of the valley. After 0.75 mile (1.2km) the track becomes grassy. Where the houses appear above you to the left you can go left up the slope to visit the church at Syde. Otherwise, remain on the valley floor and continue until you reach the gates. Take the one furthest to the right. Go ahead to pass to the left of the cottage. Follow the drive up to the road.

5 Turn left. Follow the road as it turns sharp left. At this point turn right over the stile into the field and walk up the steep bank to arrive in Caundle Green.

6 Turn right. At green, just before large house ahead, bear right to the stile. Follow the winding path down to valley bottom. Turn left, through bridle gate. Follow path along valley bottom on same line for 0.75 mile (1.2km) until you reach stile at field.

7 Once in the field, continue up the slope until you reach a gate at road. Turn left to re-enter Brimpsfield.

The Village Pub

Gloucestershire

The Inn

Unique in preserving its unusual but somewhat unimaginative name, this 'Village Pub' is certainly not your average village local. Once a row of mellow-stone roadside cottages next door to the village school, it was transformed in 2000 by Tim Haigh and Rupert Pendered and now ranks among the very best of the new breed of successful pub-restaurants-with-rooms, where innovative, modern British food combines well with a relaxed, informal atmosphere and a clutch of classy bedrooms. What's more, the guys also own Barnsley House across the road, one of the chic-est boutique hotels in England.

Warm terracotta walls, rug-strewn stone and oak floors, three open log fires and an eclectic mix of furnishings throughout a warren of beautifully refurbished rooms set the cosy, eye-pleasing scene for perusing the papers over a pint of Hooky or one of 12 wines by the glass. Style and taste extend upstairs to the seven boldly decorated bedrooms, the best being the two four-posters, kitted out in solid dark wood, and the stunning suite, replete with leather sofas, huge plasma screen, and a great bathroom with claw-foot bath, walk-in shower and Aveda smellies.

The Village Pub, Barnsley, Cirencester, Gloucestershire GL7 5EF

The Food

The cooking is ambitious and makes good use of some excellent raw ingredients – local rare breed and traceable meats from Butts Farm Shop and seasonal vegetables from Barnsley House gardens – with dishes showing immense flair and imagination. Order a pint and light bite, such as a starter of sautéed scallops with grilled fennel and curried vanilla oil, and sit at the bar, or go the whole hog and linger longer over three courses in the restaurant, with its crackling log fire.

Tuck into pigeon breast with celeriac cream, chorizo and red wine, or fish soup, and follow with halibut with shrimps, chilli and dill, pork fillet with pea purée, mint and capers, or rib-eye steak with port and peppercorn sauce and chunky chips. Leave room for a classic rice pudding with damson jam, chocolate caramel tart, or a superb plate of cheeses, perhaps Stinking Bishop and local Cerney goats' cheese. When the sun shines, make use of the honeysuckle- and rose-adorned rear, heated terrace.

The Essentials

Time at the Bar!
11am-3.30pm, 6pm-11pm
Food: 12-2.30pm (3pm Sat & Sun),
7-9.30pm (10pm Fri & Sat)

What's the Damage?
Main courses from £12.50

Bitter Experience:
Hooky Bitter, Wadworth 6X, Butcombe

Sticky Fingers:
Children welcome; small portions available

Muddy Paws:
Dogs allowed in the bar

Zzzzz:
7 rooms, £90-£150

Anything Else?
Terrace, car park; residents can visit Barnsley House Gardens

What To Do

Shop

FARMERS' MARKET
Stow is a picture-postcard town in the Cotswold hills, and at the regular farmers' market you can pick up farmhouse cheeses, local trout, wines, apple juice and cider, game and locally reared meats.

The Square, Stow on the Wold,
Gloucestershire
www.foodlinks.info/markets/stow.php

HOUSE OF CHEESE
There's a great range of British and European cheeses in this tiny, family-run shop in Tetbury, including Cornish yarg and Dorset blue vinney, and all manner of biscuits, chutneys and preserves.

13 Church Street, Tetbury,
Gloucestershire GL8 8JG
01666 502865
www.houseofcheese.co.uk

ULEY POST OFFICE
Of course, you can buy stamps here, but the Post Office in Uley also sells some of the best sausages in the land, hand-made by Stephen Curtis up the road in a former garage. You can also buy award-winning bread from the Hobbs House Bakery.

53 The Street, Uley,
Gloucestershire GL11 5SL

WONDERWALL GALLERY
At this light and airy gallery, you'll find a range of distinctive art, including paintings, ceramics, sculpture, textiles, glass and jewellery. From time to time, the gallery plays host to popular live music evenings.

7 Gosditch Street, Cirencester,
Gloucestershire GL7 2AG
01285 650555
www.thewonderwallgallery.com

Visit

BERKELEY CASTLE
The Berkeley family have lived in this castle for 850 years. The castle is famed for the murder of King Edward II – highlights include the dungeon where it took place.

Berkeley, Gloucestershire GL13 9BQ
01453 810332
www.berkeley-castle.com

CHELTENHAM ART GALLERY & MUSEUM
There are some important collections here, including fine art, jewellery and ceramics. Anyone interested in the Arts and Crafts Movement will appreciate the internationally renowned exhibits.

Clarence Street, Cheltenham,
Gloucestershire GL50 3JT
01242 262334
www.cheltenham.artgallery.museum

NEWARK PARK
This Tudor hunting lodge, later a fashionable Georgian home, perches dramatically on a 40ft (12m) cliff. The interior has an eclectic mix of period furniture and modern art, and a jumble of artefacts from across the globe.

Ozleworth, Wooton under Edge,
Gloucestershire GL12 7PZ
01453 842644
www.nationaltrust.org.uk

TRULL HOUSE GARDENS
This delightful 8 acres, designed at the start of the 20th century, is deep in rural countryside. It has terraces, lily ponds, summerhouses, a glass house, and both a walled and sunken garden.

Tetbury, Gloucestershire GL8 8SQ
01285 841255
www.trullhouse.co.uk

Activity

BALLOONING
Want a bird's-eye view of the land? Take to the skies and drift effortlessly above the rolling Cotswolds countryside with a glass of champagne for company.

Ballooning in the Cotswolds
Fallowfield, Itlay, Daglingworth,
Cirencester, Gloucestershire GL7 7HZ
01285 885848
www.ballooninginthecotswolds.co.uk

GOLF
Cotswold Hills Golf Club is a picturesque, 18-hole championship course in rolling, open countryside. Tree-lined with open fairways, it's fairly flat, despite the name.

Cotswold Hills Golf Club
Ullenwood, Gloucestershire GL53 9QT
01242 515264
www.cotswoldhills-golfclub.com

HORSE RACING
Home of National Hunt racing, Cheltenham holds some of the most prestigious events in the sporting calendar. It's a scenic course and you can arrive by train – the course has its own railway station.

Cheltenham Racecourse
Prestbury Park, Cheltenham,
Gloucestershire GL50 4SH
01242 224227
www.cheltenham.co.uk

SPEED HILL CLIMB
Pit your wits against 'The Hill'. Discover hill climbing the safe way, with a qualified instructor on this demanding but great fun course.

Bugatti Owners Club
Prescott Hill, Gotherington, Cheltenham,
Gloucestershire GL52 9RD
01242 673136
www.prescott-hillclimb.com

The Walk - Weaving Around Bibury

A walk that will unravel the charms of a weaver's village.

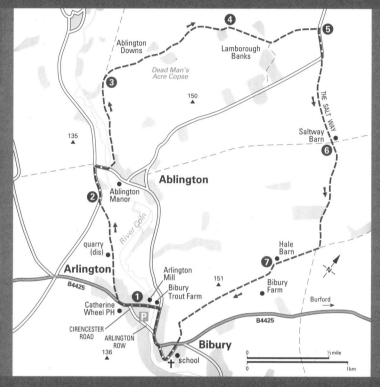

Walk Details

LENGTH: 6.25 miles (10.1km)

TIME: 2hrs 30min

ASCENT: 165ft (50m)

PATHS: Fields, tracks and lane, may be muddy in places, 6 stiles

SUGGESTED MAP: aqua3 OS Explorer OL45 The Cotswolds

GRID REFERENCE: SP 113068

PARKING: Bibury village

1 From the parking area opposite the mill, walk along Cirencester road. Immediately after the Catherine Wheel pub, turn right along the lane then keep left at the fork. Pass the cottages then go through the gates and stiles into the field. Walk on the same line across several stiles and fields until you pass to the right of house to a road.
2 Turn right. Walk down to the junction. Turn right into Ablington; cross the bridge. After a few paces, where the road goes to the right, turn left along the track with the houses on the right and the stream to the left. Continue to the gate then follow the track as it traverses open countryside, arriving at another gate after just over 0.5 mile (800m).

3 Go into the field. Turn sharp right along the valley bottom. Follow the twisting route along the bottom of the valley. At the next gate continue into the field, still following contours of valley. The route will eventually take you through gate just before barn and another immediately after.
4 Keep to the track as it bears right and gently ascends the long slope, with woodland to left. When the track goes sharp right, with gate ahead, turn left through gate on to track. Follow it all way to the road.
5 Turn right. After 250yds (229m), where the road goes right, continue ahead, to enter the track ('Salt Way'). Continue for over 0.5 mile (800m), until you reach the remains of Saltway Barn.

6 Do not walk ahead but, just after barns, turn left into the field then right along its righthand margin. Walk for just under 0.75 mile (1.2km), passing hedge and woodland and, where the track breaks to right, turn right through gate into field with wall on right.
7 Continue to pass to the left of Hale Barn. Enter the track, with the buildings of Bibury Farm away to your left. Keep on the same line through the gates where they arise. Eventually descend to drive which will lead to the road in Bibury. Cross road to walk between row of cottages. At end, near church and school, turn right. Walk along the pavement into village, passing Arlington Row and river on the left.

The Bathurst Arms

Gloucestershire

The Inn

A rambling, creeper-covered, pink-washed building beside a countrified stretch of the A435, with gardens stretching to the banks of the fast-flowing River Churn, this is an ancient inn in an enviable romantic location. Church bells ring nearby, the beautiful gardens at Cerney House are just up the lane, and the valley is surrounded by glorious Cotswold countryside.

James Walker has worked wonders at the inn, sprucing up the traditional bar, with its warm terracotta walls, flagstone and tiled floors, old scrubbed tables and wooden settles, and two fine carved stone fireplaces. He has also revamped the restaurant. The wine room-cum-lounge sports deep leather sofas, bold paintings, a crackling log fire in winter, and a truly organic wine list – pick your own labelled wine from wine boxes and shelves. Refurbishment extends upstairs to the six simply furnished bedrooms, all with painted wooden floors, comfortable beds with luxurious cotton sheets, and added touches like trendy clock-radios, and top-quality toiletries in freshly painted bath/shower rooms.

The Essentials

Time at the Bar!
12-3pm, 6-11pm
Food: 12-2pm, 6-9pm

What's the Damage?
Main courses from £9.95

Bitter Experience:
Hook Norton Hooky, Wickwar Cotswold Way, guest beer

Sticky Fingers:
Children welcome

Muddy Paws:
Dogs welcome in the bar and bedrooms

Zzzzz:
6 rooms, £75-£85; single £55-£65

Anything Else?
Terrace, car park

The Bathurst Arms, North Cerney, Cirencester, Gloucestershire GL7 8BZ

The Food

Delivered from an open-to-view kitchen in James's swish dining area, the food blends traditional pub favourites with more inventive modern British dishes. Changing menus make good use of fresh local, organic and seasonal produce, including Jesse Smith's pork sausages, served with mustard mash and red onion gravy, lamb reared in the Churn Valley, perhaps grilled and served on crushed new potatoes with wild garlic and redcurrant and rosemary sauce, and crayfish from the River Churn.

Classic dishes take in home-made beef and ale pie, the Bathurst 100% beef burger, and grilled rib-eye steak with peppercorn and brandy sauce, while for something different try roast monkfish wrapped in Parma ham with pea, broad bean and mint risotto and a cherry tomato and herb sauce. Precede with village-made Cerney goats' cheese with aubergine, courgettes, vine tomatoes, mixed cress salad and a balsamic vinaigrette, and leave room for sticky toffee and banana cheesecake. Accompany lunchtime pints of Hooky or Wickwar Cotswold Way with honey roast ham sandwiches or a ploughman's with slabs of Keens cheddar, stilton and home-made chutney.

What To Do

Shop

BLACK INK MASTERPRINTS

Black Ink sells an extensive selection of original graphics by some of the world's greatest artists. View etchings, lithographs, engravings and woodcuts by the likes of Cézanne, Chagall, Goya, Ben Nicholson and Henry Moore.

7a Talbot Court, Stow on the Wold, Gloucestershire GL54 1BQ

01451 870022

www.blackinkprints.com

BUTTS FARM SHOP

This award-winning shop is part of a family-run rare breeds farm. It sells home-cured bacon, sausages, pork, poultry, lamb and beef – all traditionally reared in a stress-free environment. One of Rick Stein's Food Heroes.

South Cerney, Gloucestershire GL7 5QE

01285 862224

www.thebuttsfarmshop.com

FARMERS' MARKET

The award-winning Gloucester Farmers' Market runs every Friday, with 30 stalls selling a wide range of fresh, locally grown products, including smoked fish, home-made cheeses, bread and pastries.

Gloucester Gate Streets Farmers' Market, The Cross & Southgate Street, Gloucester

RIVERS GALLERY

You can easily spend a day wandering round the delightful town of Nailsworth. A good place to start is this interesting gallery selling painting, sculpture, ceramics, jewellery and glass.

Market Place, Nailsworth, Stroud, Gloucestershire GL6 0BX

01453 836885

www.riversgallery.com

Visit

CERNEY HOUSE GARDENS

Hidden away in a lush Cotswold valley, this delightful romantic treasure has a Victorian walled garden, a stunning orchard and a working herb and kitchen garden – a haven of peace and tranquillity.

Cerney Lodge, North Cerney, Cirencester, Gloucestershire GL7 7BX

01285 831300

www.cerneygardens.com

CHEDWORTH ROMAN VILLA

Set in a wooded coombe, Chedworth is the remains of the largest Roman villa in the country, where you can see stunning mosaics, a bath house and a very sophisticated latrine. In the grounds, you may come across some huge Roman snails and the tiny lesser horseshoe bat, which flits in and out of a 'bat-flap' at the visitor centre.

Yanworth, Gloucestershire GL54 3LJ

01242 890256

www.nationaltrust.org.uk

KEITH HARDING'S WORLD OF MECHANICAL MUSIC

Housed in a lovely old building is this unique collection of self-playing musical instruments, music boxes and automata. There is also a fascinating workshop, a museum and a great gift shop.

The Oak House, High Street, Northleach, Gloucestershire GL54 3ET

01451 860181

www.mechanicalmusic.co.uk

LODGE PARK & SHERBORNE ESTATE

Described as a 'small property with a big history', in 4,000 acres of rolling countryside with sweeping views to the River Windrush, Lodge Park was created in 1634 by John 'Crump' Dutton, the wealthy, fast-living squire and MP with a passion for gambling and banqueting. Must-sees are the Hall, the monumental staircase leading to the Great Room, and the viewing platform on the roof with far-reaching views.

Lodge Park, Aldsworth, Cheltenham, Gloucestershire GL54 3PP

01451 844130

www.nationaltrust.org.uk

Activity

DRIVE A CLASSIC CAR

Drop the top and feel the wind in your hair – hire a convertible E-Type Jag for a day, and enjoy the elegance, style and glamour associated with open-top touring.

Classic Motoring Ltd

Smilers Cottage, Brimpsfield, Gloucestershire GL4 8LD

01452 864050

www.classicmotoring.co.uk

HORSE RIDING

Explore the magnificent countryside on horseback, hacking in the Cotswold Water Park.

South Cerney Riding School

Cerney Wick Farm, Cerney Wick, Cirencester, Gloucestershire GL7 5QH

01793 750151

WING WALKING

A truly unique way to discover the Cotswolds – on the top of a bi-plane! An unforgettable experience.

AeroSuperBatics Ltd

The Engine Shed, RFC Rendcomb Airfield, The Whiteway, Cirencester, Gloucestershire GL7 7DF

01285 831774

www.aerosuperbatics.com

The Walk - *The Cotswold Water Park*

Ramble through an evolving landscape at South Cerney.

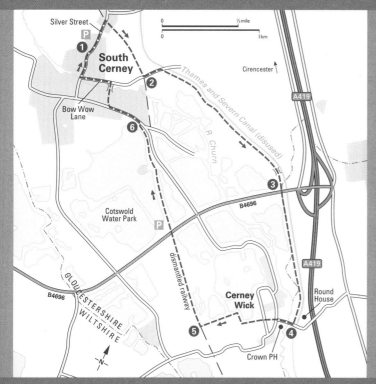

Walk Details

LENGTH: 5 miles (8km)

TIME: 2hrs

ASCENT: Negligible

PATHS: Track, tow path and lanes, 10 stiles

SUGGESTED MAP: aqua3 OS Explorer 169 Cirencester & Swindon

GRID REFERENCE: SU 048974

PARKING: Silver Street, South Cerney

❶ From Silver Street walk north out of the village. Immediately before the turning to Driffield and Cricklade, turn right over the stile on to the bank. Stay on this for 800yds (732m), to reach the brick bridge across the path. Turn right up the steps to reach the narrow road.

❷ Turn left. Walk along for 200yds (183m) until you reach footpaths to the right and left. Turn right along the farm track, following the signpost ('Cerney Wick'). Almost immediately, the remains of the Thames and Severn Canal appear to the left. When the track veers right into the farm, walk ahead over a stile to follow the path beneath the trees – the old canal tow path. At the bridge, keep ahead across

the stiles. Continue ahead until you reach the busy road.

❸ Cross with care. On the far side you have 2 choices: continue on the tow path or take the path that skirts the lakes. If you take the lakeside path, you eventually rejoin the tow path by going left at the bridge after 600yds (549m). Continue until in just under 0.5 mile (800m), you pass the canal roundhouse across the canal to the left and, soon after, reach the lane at Cerney Wick.

❹ Turn right. Walk to the junction at the end of the road, beside the Crown pub. Cross to the stile and enter the field. Walk ahead to reach the stile. Cross this aiming to left of cottage. Cross lane, go over another stile and enter field. Walk ahead and

follow path as it leads across stile on to grass by lake. Walk around the lake, going right then left. At the corner before you, cross into the field, walk ahead towards the trees and cross the stile to the track.

❺ Turn right, rejoin the old railway line and follow it all way to the road. Cross this into the car park. Go through gate on to the track. Stay on this all the way to another road and follow the path that runs to its left.

❻ Where the path ends at the beginning of South Cerney, continue along Station Road. Ignore footpath on the right but turn right at the 2nd one, which takes you across the bridge and brings you to lane ('Bow Wow'). Turn left here between the streams and return to Silver Street.

The Puesdown Inn

Gloucestershire

The Inn

Keep your revs low on the A40 approaching Cheltenham or you'll easily pass this traditional Cotswold coaching inn and miss a very hospitable place, one that draws Cheltenham race-goers, Cotswold walkers, wine buffs and jazz fans for the regular evening events. Expect acres of oak floorboards, warm, rich colours, and deep cosy sofas fronting glowing log fires throughout the rambling bar and the brasserie-style dining room. The walls are covered with an eclectic mixture of cinema, travel and advertising prints and photographs – if they like it, the owners Maggie and John Armstrong will frame it. Relax in the garden at posh teak tables in summer and take in the pleasant country views.

The three ground-floor bedrooms have separate access from the car park at the front. Stylish and supremely comfortable king-size beds await, perhaps a wooden sleigh or a cast iron bedstead, but the rooms are individually styled, whether playing with a Chinese theme or sporting Mediterranean colours, fabrics and furnishings. Bathrooms are sleek and modern, with a wet room and large showerheads to unwind beneath.

The Essentials

Time at the Bar!
10am-3.30pm, 6pm-12am
Food: 12-3.30pm, 6-10pm (closed Mon in winter)

What's the Damage?
Main courses from £14.50

Bitter Experience:
Hook Norton Hooky, Old Hooky

Sticky Fingers:
Children welcome; smaller portions

Muddy Paws:
Dogs welcome in the bar

Zzzzz:
3 rooms, £85-£95

Anything Else?
Terrace, garden, car park

The Food

John has cooked all over the world as well as alongside chefs of the standing of Brian Turner. He sums up his philosophy on the art of cooking as 'meaning it', which translates as a sincere love for food and hospitality. Fish arrives fresh from Devon and Cornwall, so why not kick off a satisfying lunch with a bowl of Fowey mussels in white wine, garlic and shallots before tucking into chargrilled red mullet with mushroom risotto and pea foam, or a traditional steak and ale pie?

Cooking steps up a gear in the evening. Begin with seared scallops with tiger prawns, black pudding and butternut squash, or warm duck confit salad. Follow with corn-fed chicken served with foie gras, leeks, fondant potato and tarragon cream, or Scottish salmon, crayfish tails, choi sum and noodles, for truly modern British cooking at its best.

If space permits, then the bread and butter pudding with marmalade ice cream fights for pole position with chocolate fondant and brandy chocolate sorbet – a virtuous 20-minute wait for this just heightens the expectation.

What To Do

Shop

BURFORD

Voted 'Antiques Shopping Street of the Year' in 2003 by the readers of *Homes & Antiques*, Burford's high street has a wide variety of craft and antique shops, clothes boutiques and art galleries. The town is also full of lovely old stone houses set on a steep hill leading down to the medieval bridge over the River Windrush.

BURFORD GARDEN COMPANY

This medal-winning company at the Chelsea Flower Show has over 30,000 hand-picked products for the home and garden. It inspires and delights both expert gardeners and keen amateurs.

Shilton Road, Burford,
Oxfordshire OX18 4PA
01993 823117
www.bgc.co.uk

SANDRA DEE LINGERIE & SWIMWEAR

The retail area of Montpellier in beautiful Regency Cheltenham has two stores guaranteed to be of interest to both male and female shoppers. With lingerie by the likes of Aubade, Lise Charmel, Prima Donna, and L'Aventure, as well as swimwear by Moontide, Louis Feraud and Nicole Olivier, a visit here could enhance your holiday.

Sandra Dee Lingerie
3 Montpellier Walk, Montpellier Street,
Cheltenham, Gloucestershire GL50 1SD
01242 238427
www.sandradee.co.uk
Sandra Dee Swimwear
10 The Courtyard, Montpellier Street,
Cheltenham, Gloucestershire GL50 1SR
01242 238426
www.sandradee.co.uk

Visit

COTSWOLD WILDLIFE PARK & GARDENS

The Park is set in 160 acres of parkland and gardens around a listed Victorian manor house. It is home to a fascinating and varied collection of mammals, birds, reptiles and invertebrates from all over the world and aspires to increase understanding of what is special about each species, and how they have evolved over time.

Burford, Oxfordshire OX18 4JP
01993 823006
www.cotswoldwildlifepark.co.uk

KELMSCOTT MANOR

A Grade I listed Tudor farmhouse adjacent to the River Thames and the home of poet, craftsman and socialist William Morris from 1871 until his death in 1896. The house contains a collection of Morris's work and that of his associates, including furniture, textiles, carpets and ceramics.

Kelmscott, Lechlade,
Gloucestershire GL7 3HJ
01367 252486
www.kelmscottmanor.co.uk

STANWAY HOUSE & FOUNTAIN

Stanway is an outstanding example of a Jacobean manor house, with fascinating furniture, a jewel-like gatehouse, church, 14th-century tithe barn, an 18th-century water garden (one of the finest in England), specimen trees and avenues. A new addition is the single jet fountain. Reaching 300ft (91m), it is the highest in Britain.

Stanway, Cheltenham,
Gloucestershire GL54 5PQ
01386 584469
www.stanwayfountain.co.uk

Activity

BALLOONING

Drift slowly with the wind over the beautiful Cotswold landscape and enjoy the unique combination of exhilaration and serenity that you will discover aboard a hot air balloon. With a glass of champagne to celebrate, this will be a flight to remember. There are launch sites at Cirencester, Stroud, Bourton-on-the-Water and Cotswold Water Park near Swindon.

Ballooning in the Cotswolds
Fallowfield, Itlay, Daglingworth,
Cirencester, Gloucestershire GL7 7HZ
01285 885848
www.ballooninginthecotswolds.co.uk

GOLF

Cleeve Hill Golf Club is a rugged heathland course with views across the Severn Vale, Malvern Hills and Brecon Beacons. The club's philosophy is open-door, and it is a friendly, inspiring and refreshing arena in which to play or learn.

Cleeve Hill Golf Club
Cleeve Hill, Cheltenham,
Gloucestershire GL52 3PW
01242 672025
www.cleevehillgolfcourse.com

WALK THE COTSWOLD WAY

Take this scenic, undulating route through quiet countryside, following the ridge through the Cotswolds via the villages of Broadway, Winchcombe, Dursley and Wotton-under-Edge. This popular trail offers beautiful rural surroundings with facilities and services always near to hand. The footpaths are well maintained, while the landscape means that the walking is within the capabilities of almost everyone.

www.nationaltrail.co.uk/cotswold

The Walk - *Around a Saxon Village*

A gentle ramble from a typical village in quintessential Gloucestershire.

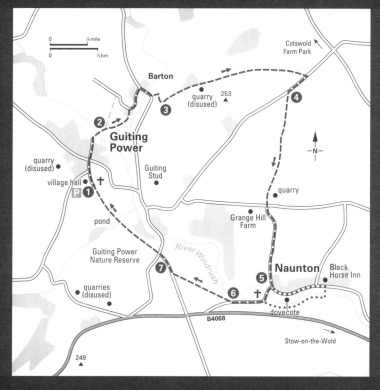

Walk Details

LENGTH: 5 miles (8km)

TIME: 2hrs

ASCENT: 295ft (90m)

PATHS: Fields, tracks and country lanes, 10 stiles

SUGGESTED MAP: aqua3 OS Explorer OL45 The Cotswolds

GRID REFERENCE: SP 094245

PARKING: Car park outside village hall (small fee)

1 From the car park, walk along the road to the village green, then cross the road to walk down the lane. At the bottom go over the stile into the field. Turn right. Walk up the bank, up to another stile. Don't cross the one ahead but clamber over the one to your right into the field.

2 Turn left. Walk straight across this field to another stile. Cross this and 2 more to pass the farmhouse in Barton village. Follow the lane down to the larger road. Turn right. Cross the bridge. Turn left up the track and, after 100yds (91m), turn right up another track.

3 After a few more paces, bear left and then walk along the track for 1 mile (1.6km), until you reach another road. Turn right and walk along the

road for 250yds (229m). Turn left on to the track.

4 Follow this track all the way to the road, past the quarry. Now cross the road and shortly enter the lane descending past the house. This lane will bring you all the way into Naunton.

5 At the junction turn right. Walk through Naunton village and cross the stone bridge by the old mill, passing the rectory to the left and the church which is concealed to the right. (To get to the Black Horse Inn, turn left at this point and walk along the street for 400yds (366m). Return by entering the drive opposite the pub, turning sharp right over a stile, and walking back along the side of the river to emerge at the road near

the church, at which point you turn left.) Continue walking up the road, out of the village.

6 After 0.25 mile (400m) turn right over the stile into the field. Turn left, walk to the stile and go into the next field. Cross this field, then enter the next one. Follow the path to the right of the trees to the gate at the road.

7 Turn right along the road. Continue to the junction at the bottom. Cross the road to enter a field and walk straight across. At the end go down the steps and pass to the right of pond. Walk across the next field then cross stile to walk to the left of the church. Before returning to the start look at the Norman doorway in Guiting church; it is a beautiful rich golden hue.

Eight Bells

Gloucestershire

The Inn

Chipping Campden is one of the loveliest small towns in the Cotswolds and the streets are lined with ancient houses, each with their own distinctive embellishments. Once you've had your fill of the antique shops, a quick detour off the high street brings you to this charming 14th-century inn. It was built to house the team of stonemasons working on the nearby church and, as the name suggests, they stored the bells here, too. A suntrap rear terrace looks onto the local almshouses and St James's church – and the bells can often be heard.

Within, flagstones and tiles give way to soft carpet; there are oak beams, large gilt mirrors and fireplaces at every turn. It has the feel of a real local – the bar is strewn with dried hops and dangling tankards waiting to be filled with Old Hooky or Butty Bach. Seven good-sized bedrooms are tucked into this ancient building and the decor blends the old and the new with considerable style. One room necessitates ducking under a huge oak beam, several overlook the terrace, and some come with super king-sized beds.

Eight Bells, Church Street, Chipping Campden, Gloucestershire GL55 6JG

The Food

There is plenty of comfortable seating, with a more formal candle-lit dining area next door to the bar (there is even a priest hole beneath the floor, currently not in use!) At lunch, pork and leek sausages with apple mash and stilton sauce, and fillet of beef stroganoff are typical, as well as brie, bacon and cranberry sandwiches and fluffy three-egg omelettes. In the evening, the choice broadens considerably, with plenty of Cotswold produce featuring on menus that have Mediterranean and Asian touches.

Expect dishes such as gammon steak with a spiced Catalan bean cassoulet or oven-baked fillet of Scottish salmon with Mediterranean vegetable risotto. Similarly, there could be monkfish tail wrapped in Parma ham with tagliatelle, vermouth cream sauce and roasted Mediterranean vegetables, followed by passion fruit cheesecake and orange sauce or English cheeses with home-made apple and cinnamon chutney and highland oatcakes. A solid wine list features all the major world wine-growing regions as well as interesting artisan wine makers. There are fruit wines to choose from, too, such as damson, plum, sloe and elderberry.

The Essentials

Time at the Bar!
12-11pm (10.30pm Sun)
Food: 12-2pm (2.30pm Fri-Sun), 6.30-9pm
(9.30pm Fri-Sat, Sun 7-9pm)

What's the Damage?
Main courses from £10

Bitter Experience:
Hook Norton Old Hooky, Goff's Jouster, Pure Gold

Sticky Fingers:
Children welcome, children's menu

Muddy Paws:
Dogs welcome on a lead in the bar

Zzzzz:
7 rooms, £55-£125

Anything Else?
Terrace, garden, no car park

What To Do

Shop

DAYLESFORD ORGANIC FARM SHOP

Quite the most luxurious farm shop you're ever likely to come across: Daylesford Organic has award-winning cheeses from the creamery, breads, pastries, cakes and biscuits from the bakery and fresh meat from their Staffordshire estate. A foodie's heaven: bring a big basket and a big appetite – you can eat here, too!

Daylesford, Kingham, Gloucestershire GL56 0YG
01608 731700
www.daylesfordorganic.com

THE ROPE STORE STUDIO GALLERY

Catering for the first-time buyer or the serious collector, this gallery has a wide range of contemporary artwork by new and established artists, designers and makers. Monthly exhibitions of paintings are shown alongside jewellery, glass, ceramics and sculpture and serve to put this gallery well at the forefront of the contemporary art scene in the Cotswolds.

The Shambles, Stroud, Gloucestershire GL5 1AS
01453 753799
www.ropestoregallery.co.uk

STUART HOUSE ANTIQUES

On your very doorstep is this well-established antique shop, famous for its fine collection of porcelain and Royal Doulton, Toby jugs and Staffordshire figurines. There's enough to keep the keenest collector occupied for hours.

High Street, Chipping Campden, Gloucestershire GL55 6HR
01386 840995
www.cotswoldstay.co.uk

Visit

HIDCOTE MANOR GARDENS

One of England's greatest gardens, this Arts and Crafts masterpiece features a series of outdoor 'rooms', each with its own character. Wander among ancient roses, plants and trees from around the world, all set against a stunning panorama across the Vale of Evesham.

Hidcote Bartrim, Chipping Campden, Gloucestershire GL55 6LR
01386 438333
www.nationaltrust.org.uk

ROYAL SHAKESPEARE THEATRE

This is one of the world's most iconic theatrical sites set in the beautiful Warwickshire countryside, on the banks of the River Avon. Take in one of the many performances held in the Swan and Courtyard Theatres. The birthplace of William Shakespeare is steeped in culture and history, so why not explore the Shakespeare Trail, visiting his family home in Henley Street, Mary Arden's house in nearby Wilmcote, Anne Hathaway's Cottage in Shottery, and Hall's Croft near Stratford's parish church?

Waterside, Stratford-upon-Avon, Warwickshire CV37 6BB
01789 403444
www.rsc.org.uk

WARWICK CASTLE

The ancestral home of the Earls of Warwick and the 'King Maker', this is the finest medieval castle in England dating from the days of William the Conqueror. There are attractions including displays of jousting and falconry.

City of Warwick, Warwickshire CV34 4QU
0870 442200
www.warwick-castle.co.uk

Activity

COTSWOLD COUNTRY CYCLES

Cycles – and even tandems – available for daily hire, with detailed cycling routes and maps provided so that you can enjoy the quieter backroads of the Cotswolds.

Longlands Farm Cottage, Chipping Campden, Gloucestershire GL55 6LJ
01386 438706
www.cotswoldcountrycycles.com

COTSWOLD GLIDING CLUB

What better way to appreciate the beauty of this part of England than from the air? Benefit from expert instruction in first-class two-seater gliders: trial lesson, day or week courses available.

Aston Down Airfield, Cowcombe Lane, Chalford, Gloucestershire GL6 8HR
01275 760415
www.cotswoldgliding.co.uk

POTTERY WORKSHOP

Discover the pleasure of pottery-making and learn to throw a pot and handle the potters' wheel, or try your hand at ceramic painting.

Honeybourne Pottery
3 High Street, Honeybourne, Evesham, Worcestershire WR11 7PQ
01386 832855
www.honeybournepots.co.uk

PRESCOTT SPEED HILL CLIMB

The Bugatti Owners' Club was founded in 1929 by enthusiasts. Prescott Hill Climb is the club's home, where members and spectators get a glimpse of what many believe to be motor sport at its most skilful and testing.

Prescott Hill, Gotherington, Cheltenham, Gloucestershire GL52 9RD
01242 673136
www.prescott-hillclimb.com

The Walk - *Chipping Campden, Olimpick Playground*

From a beautiful wool town to Dover's Hill, the site of centuries-old Whitsuntide festivities.

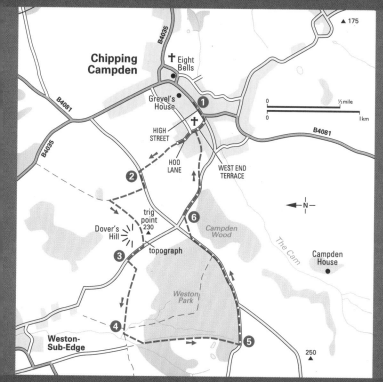

Walk Details

LENGTH: 5 miles (8km)

TIME: 2hrs

ASCENT: 280ft (85m)

PATHS: Fields, roads and tracks, 8 stiles

SUGGESTED MAP: aqua3 OS Explorer OL45 The Cotswolds

GRID REFERENCE: SP 151391

PARKING: Chipping Campden High Street or main square

❶ Turn left from the Noel Arms, continue to the Catholic church. Turn right into West End Terrace. Where this bears right, keep ahead on Hoo Lane. Follow this up to the right turn, with farm buildings on your left. Continue uphill over the stile to the path; keep going to reach the road.

❷ Turn left for few paces then right to cross to the path. Follow this along the field edge to the stile. Go over to Dover's Hill. Follow the hedge to the stile with extensive views ahead. Turn left along the escarpment edge, which drops away to your right. Pass a trig point then a topograph. Now go right, down slope, to a kissing gate on the left. Go through to road. Turn right.

❸ After 150yds (137m) turn left over the stile into the field. Cross and find the gate in the bottom righthand corner. Head straight down the next field. At the stile go into another field and, keeping to the left of the fence, continue to another stile. Head down the next field, cross the track then find the adjacent stiles in the bottom lefthand corner.

❹ Cross over the 1st stile. Walk along the bottom of the field. Keep the stream and the fence to your right and look for the stile over in the far corner. Go over, crossing the stream, then turn left, following a rising woodland path alongside the stream. Enter the field through the gate and continue to meet the track. Stay on this track, passing through

gateposts, until you reach the country lane. Turn left.

❺ After 400yds (366m) reach a busier road. Turn left for 450yds (411m). Shortly before the road curves left, drop down right on to the field path parallel with the road. About 200yds (183m) before the next corner go half-right down the field to eventually reach the road.

❻ Turn right, down the road. Shortly after the cottage on the right, go left into the field. Turn right over the stile and go half left to the corner. Pass through the kissing gate, cross the road among the houses and continue ahead to meet West End Terrace. Turn right to return to your car in the centre of Chipping Campden, where the walk began.

Horse and Groom

Gloucestershire

The Inn

Set high on a hill, this honey-coloured Cotswold stone former coaching inn is still a watering place of the highest order. The polished oak floorboards, exposed stonework, large open fireplace and walls hung with horse-related and village life prints and paraphernalia reflect brothers Tom and Will Greenstock's passion and flair for innkeeping. A more upbeat, almost continental, bar houses well-kept real ales and also Tom's short but highly varied wine list, while a grassed garden rises to the rear, providing a great area in which to soak up summer sunshine and admire the far-reaching views. A welcoming atmosphere pervades throughout and makes this a place to enjoy at a leisurely and relaxed pace.

Upstairs you will find five light and airy bedrooms with styles that range from an elegant period double to one with a more contemporary design with French doors opening onto a pretty landscaped garden; all have flat-screen TVs and DVD players. All of the rooms are ensuite with pretty bathrooms, huge soft towels and lots of cosseting toiletries.

The Food

The kitchen is Will's domain and he is determined to build on the family's well-earned reputation for delivering fine food (the boys' parents own the renowned Howard Arms at Ilmington). The menu on the large blackboard in the bar may change daily to make the most of what is fresh and available – indeed, in season, many vegetables come straight from the garden. Butternut squash soup with curry oil makes for a great winter warming start, as do Thai pork dumplings with a lemon grass dipping sauce.

Meaty mains include Dexter beef pasty with onion gravy, roast leg of Cotswold lamb with apricot stuffing, or pan-fried Gressingham duck breast on sautéed pak choi with garlic, chilli and plum sauce, while fish can come in the guise of pan-roasted skate wing with prawn, caper and preserved lemon butter. Desserts are legendary – get your order in quickly – the River Café's chocolate nemesis is a favourite, closely followed by pear, apple and blueberry flapjack crumble served with lashings of organic vanilla ice cream. James White organic juices are on offer for drivers and children, and some of the best coffee west of Naples is served here.

The Essentials

Time at the Bar!
11am-11pm (closed Sun evening)
Food: 12-2pm (2.30pm Sat-Sun), 7-9pm (9.30 Fri-Sat)

What's the Damage?
Main courses from £10

Bitter Experience:
Purity UBU, Greene King Old Speckled Hen

Sticky Fingers:
Children welcome

Muddy Paws:
Dogs in garden only

Zzzzz:
5 rooms, £70-£125

Anything Else?
Large garden, car park

What To Do

Shop

BECKFORD SILK
Skilled craftspeople design, dye and print a huge range of silks at this modern workshop outside Tewkesbury. Silk scarves, dressing gowns and ties are sold and there's access to the whole workshop.
Beckford, Tewkesbury,
Gloucestershire GL20 7AU
01386 881507
www.beckfordsilk.co.uk

DAYLESFORD ORGANIC
A selection of cheeses made in the on-site creamery; venison and lamb from the family estate; bakery products made at the shop; fresh, seasonal, locally grown vegetables and one of the best delicatessens in the Cotswolds. Crafts and countryware produced by local people are also sold here.
Daylesford, Kingham,
Gloucestershire GL56 0YG
01608 731700
www.daylesfordorganic.com

LAVENDER FARM
More than 50 acres of lavender colour the slopes of the Cotswolds above the Vale of Evesham. The flowers are steam-distilled to produce a wide range of oils, soaps and cosmetics. The farm shop also acts as a gallery for local crafts, pottery and paintings.
Hill Barn Farm, Snowshill, Broadway,
Worcestershire WR12 7JY
01386 854821
www.snowshill-lavender.co.uk

SUSAN MEGSON GALLERY
A Stow on the Wold gallery concentrating on glassware from all over the world.
Tourist Information Centre 01451 831082

Visit

SNOWSHILL MANOR
Charles Paget Wade was the ultimate eccentric collector. His eclectic tastes fill every room of this beautiful Cotswold manor house: Japanese armour, toys, clocks, antiques of every hue, domestic ephemera, musical instruments, bicycles. The manor grounds are homage to the Arts and Crafts Movement, with a series of garden 'rooms'; terraced organic gardens offer grand vistas of the Cotswolds.
Snowshill, Broadway,
Gloucestershire WR12 7JU
01386 852410
www.nationaltrust.org.uk

SUDELEY CASTLE
Once home to Catherine Parr. Connoisseur tours of some of the private parts of the castle include viewings of old masters, while exhibitions in the Long Room recall Tudor and Victorian times. The gardens include topiary, a Tudor knot garden and sculpture.
Winchcombe, Cheltenham,
Gloucestershire GL54 5JD
01242 602308
www.sudeleycastle.co.uk

TEWKESBURY ABBEY
The medieval town of Tewkesbury stands at the confluence of the rivers Severn and Avon. The former Benedictine abbey was decimated during the Dissolution; nonetheless the surviving church is larger than many cathedrals. Inside is fine medieval stained glass and some notable sculptured tombs.
Church Street, Tewkesbury,
Gloucestershire GL20 5RZ
01684 850959
www.tewkesburyabbey.org.uk

Activity

COTSWOLD COUNTRY CYCLES
Hire a mountain bike or a high-geared hybrid cycle and discover many miles of quiet lanes linking the glorious villages of the north Cotswolds and the verdant Vale of Evesham. This is the most environmentally friendly way to visit local manor houses, or perhaps the National Trust's fabulous Fleece Inn at nearby Bretforton.
Longlands Farm Cottage, Chipping Campden, Gloucestershire GL55 6LJ
01386 438706
www.cotswoldcountrycycles.com

COTSWOLD FALCONRY CENTRE
Falcons, owls, hawks, eagles and vultures can be found here: a veritable cornucopia of raptors to study and a plethora of falconry displays to enjoy. There's a strong conservation message here, too. Experience days offer training and handling skills with the chance to 'fly' a variety of the birds, including owls and even eagles.
Batsford Park, Moreton-in-Marsh,
Gloucestershire GL56 9QB
01386 701043
www.cotswold-falconry.co.uk

SALFORD TROUT LAKES
Greenhorns can learn the rudimentary skills of the graceful art of fly fishing by pre-booking some tuition at these peaceful, spring-fed lakes. Tackle hire is available; the more experienced fly angler may expect good sport from stocks of brown and rainbow trout between March and October.
Rectory Farm, Salford, Chipping Norton,
Oxfordshire OX7 5YZ
01608 643209
www.salfordtroutlakes.co.uk

The Walk - *A Taste of India at Sezincote*

Discovering the influences of India through the Cotswold home of Sir Charles Cockerell.

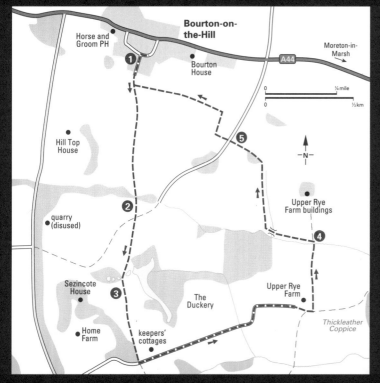

Walk Details

LENGTH: 3 miles (4.8km)

TIME: 1hr 15min

ASCENT: 85ft (25m)

PATHS: Tracks, fields and lanes, 7 stiles

SUGGESTED MAP: aqua3 OS Explorer OL45 The Cotswolds

GRID REFERENCE: SP 175324

PARKING: In the street below Bourton-on-the-Hill church, parallel with the main road

❶ Walk up the road from the telephone box with the church to your right. Turn left down a signposted track between walls. Go through the gate into the field and then continue forward to pass through 2 more gates.

❷ Cross over the stile, followed by 2 kissing gates among the trees. This is the Sezincote Estate. Its architecture and design were inspired, like many other buildings in the early 19th century, by the colourful aqua-tints that were brought to England from India by returning artists, such as William and Thomas Daniell. Built on the plan of a typical large country house, in every other respect it is thoroughly unconventional and owes a lot to Eastern influence, not least in the large copper onion dome that crowns the house and the garden buildings. Go straight ahead, following the markers and crossing the drive. Dip down to the gate among the trees, with ponds on either side. Go ahead into the field, from where Sezincote House is visible to the right.

❸ Walk into the next field and go right to the end, aiming for the top righthand corner. Pass through the gate to reach a narrow road and turn left. Walk down this road, passing keepers' cottages to your left, and through a series of gates. The road will bottom out, curve left and right and then bring you to Upper Rye Farm. Pass to right of the farmhouse, go through the gate and, immediately before the barn, turn left along the track and the road.

❹ After the 2nd cattle grid, go left over the stile. Follow the edge of the field to the footbridge. Go over it and turn right. Now follow the righthand margin of the field to reach the stile in the far corner. Cross this to follow the path through woodland until you come to stile and field, and continue on same line to another stile.

❺ Cross the track to another stile and walk on. After few paces, with Bourton-on-the-Hill plainly visible before you, turn right and follow path to next corner. Turn left and pass through 3 gates. After 3rd one, walk on for few paces and turn right through gate to return to the start.

Westcote Inn

Gloucestershire/Oxfordshire border

The Inn

Villagers Steve and Tracey Hunt and neighbour Julia Reed bought the former New Inn in 2006 and set about renovating this 300-year-old malt house bang on the Gloucestershire/Oxfordshire border. The result is impressive. The spruced-up Cotswold stone exterior conceals a traditional stone-walled bar with roaring log fires and a contemporary restaurant space sporting chunky tables, high-backed leather chairs and bold paintings and sculptures by well-known local artists. There's also a swanky champagne bar, which draws the local horse-racing set, and four swish new bedrooms. Horse-racing dominates the inn – note the framed jockey colours and Gold Cup mementoes in the bar, and surely the pub's own horse, 'Westcote', which is syndicated by enthusiasts from the village, is worth a decent bet.

Bedrooms have been kitted out with style and taste, with colourful throws and Egyptian cotton sheets on big oak beds, plasma screens and an eclectic mix of individual furnishings. You'll find free wi-fi, clock-radios with iPod connectors, fresh coffee. The smart bathrooms have fluffy bathrobes, Jo Malone toiletries and either free-standing baths or walk-in showers. Book The View for stunning views across rolling Cotswold countryside.

Westcote Inn, Nether Westcote, Oxfordshire OX7 6SD

The Essentials

Time at the Bar!
11am-11pm
Food: 12-2.30pm, 7-9.30pm

What's the Damage?
Main courses from £9.95 (bar),
£11.95 (restaurant)

Bitter Experience:
Hook Norton Hooky, Cotswold Lion

Sticky Fingers:
Children welcome; smaller portions

Muddy Paws:
Dogs allowed in the bar

Zzzzz:
4 rooms, £85-£110

Anything Else?
Garden, terrace, car park, art gallery

The Food

Chef Mathew Dare draws on the rich supply of top-notch local ingredients to create his modern British menus, including fruit and vegetables from surrounding farms, hand-made Cotswold cheeses, and Evenlode lamb reared by Alex James (former guitarist in the pop group Blur) at his farm in nearby Daylesford. In the Tack Room bar, tuck into lunchtime sandwiches (warm Cotswold brie with apple spinach and chilli jam) or the Westcote's breakfast, or start with crab and salmon fishcake with lemon mayonnaise, follow with lamb shank with rosemary jus, and finish with baked chocolate fondant. Wash it all down with a foaming pint of Hooky or a glass of Veuve Clicquot champagne.

In the spacious, split-level restaurant, savour the superb Cotswold view over a starter of scallops and pancetta with aioli dressing, then a well-presented main course, say, John Dory with watercress risotto, lobster and artichoke vinaigrette, and linger longer over iced vanilla parfait with winter fruits compote, or glazed lemon tart with raspberry sauce.

Take the opportunity to dine alfresco on the terrace when the sun shines – don't miss the lamb spit-roasts on summer weekends.

What To Do

Shop

BROADWAY

The show village of Broadway lies at the foot of the Cotswold Edge and is famous for its beauty. The long, broad high street is bordered by neat greens and flanked by charming cottages built from local golden Cotswold stone. There are small specialist shops, galleries and plenty of antique shops.

W. J. CASTLE

Located in one of the town's lovely historic buildings, Castles are members of the prestigious 'Q' Guild of Butchers, selling a wide range of carefully sourced meat and poultry, and fabulous home-made sausages! The shop doubles as a deli, so get your staples here, too.

11 High Street, Burford,
Oxfordshire OX18 4RG
01993 822113
www.castlebutchers.co.uk

CHADLINGTON VILLAGE STORE

'Chadlington Quality Foods' reads the sign. This great community shop sells local asparagus, peas, broad beans, Hook Norton beer, a good selection of French cheeses and Jersey cream from Upper Norton. It's a treasure trove of a shop bursting with good things to eat.

Chadlington, Oxfordshire OX7 3NJ
01608 676675

PICTURESQUE-ART 05

This charming village gallery is a showcase for local artists, with original paintings, prints, jewellery, pottery and hand-turned wood.

The Old Forge, Moore Road, Bourton-on-the-Water, Gloucestershire GL54 2AZ
01451 822933
www.picturesque-art.co.uk

Visit

BATSFORD ARBORETUM

In this tranquil setting is one of the largest collections of trees and shrubs in the country.

Batsford Park, Moreton-in-Marsh,
Gloucestershire GL56 9QB
01386 701441
www.batsarb.co.uk

THE LIVING GREEN CENTRE

If you're interested in 21st-century, organically run gardens, this is a must-see. Packed with ideas and glorious planting, the centre includes vegetable plots, ponds, grass roof and a walled garden.

Kevinscot, High Street, Bourton-on-the-Water, Gloucestershire GL54 2AP
01451 820942

SNOWSHILL MANOR

This graceful manor house holds Charles Paget Wade's life's work – an eclectic collection inspired by craftsmanship and design. There are musical instruments, clocks, toys and bikes, all set in an Arts and Crafts garden that Wade designed as a series of outdoor rooms.

Snowshill, Broadway,
Gloucestershire WR12 7JU
01386 852410
www.nationaltrust.org.uk

STANWAY HOUSE & FOUNTAIN

Britain's highest fountain and the world's highest gravity fountain are in the stunning parkland at Stanway, and complemented by the restored 18th-century water garden. The Jacobean house is beautiful and full of interest.

Stanway, Cheltenham,
Gloucestershire GL54 5PQ
01386 584469
www.stanwayfountain.co.uk

Activity

COURSE FISHING

At Lemington Lakes, which is set in 75 acres of rolling countryside, there are five spring-fed lakes to cater for all kinds of fishing.

Lemington Lakes, Todenham Road,
Moreton-in-Marsh,
Gloucestershire GL56 9NP
01608 650872
www.lemingtonlakes.co.uk

CYCLING

Enjoy spectacular sweeping vistas over rolling countryside and winding lanes edged with dry-stone walls and wildflower hedges on two wheels. This award-winning company based at the station will rent you a bike, and provide routes.

Country Lanes Cycle Centre
The Railway Station, Moreton-in-Marsh,
Gloucestershire GL56 0AA
01608 650065
www.countrylanes.co.uk

GLIDING

Take to the skies and enjoy a unique perspective of the Cotswolds – take the controls during a day's lesson.

Cotswold Gliding Club
Aston Down Airfield, Cowcombe Lane,
Chalford, Stroud, Gloucestershire GL6 8HR
01285 760415
www.cotswoldgliding.co.uk

OPERA

Longborough Festival Opera is a registered charity, providing high-quality operatic performances in the Cotswolds. Dress the part and take a picnic in the idyllic grounds!

Longborough Festival Opera
Moreton-in-Marsh,
Gloucestershire GL56 0QF
01451 830605
www.longboroughopera.com

Westcote Inn, Nether Westcote, Oxfordshire OX7 6SD

The Walk - A Wildlife Walk in Bourton-on-the-Water

A walk on the wilder side of a lovely village.

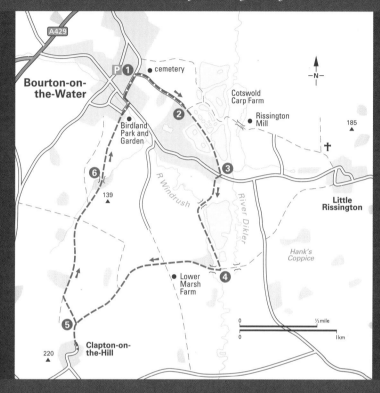

Walk Details

LENGTH: 4.75 miles (7.7km)

TIME: 2hrs

ASCENT: 230ft (70m)

PATHS: Track and field, can be muddy and wet in places, 26 stiles

SUGGESTED MAP: aqua3 OS Explorer OL45 The Cotswolds

GRID REFERENCE: SP 169208

PARKING: Pay-and-display car park on Station Road

❶ Bourton-on-the-Water can be very crowded during the summer with its river banks strewn with people picnicking and paddling – so arrive early or late to avoid the crowds. Opposite the entrance to the main pay-and-display car park in Bourton-on-the-Water locate the public footpath and continue to junction opposite cemetery. Bear right to follow lane all the way to its end. There are 2 gates ahead. Take the righthand gate, with the stile beside it, on to the grassy track.
❷ Follow the grassy track between the lakes to where it curves right. Leave the grassy track to cross the bridge and stile into the field. Go across the field, curving right, to come to a stile at the road.

❸ Cross the road, turn right and immediately left on to track. After 100yds (91m) go left over a stile into a field. Turn right. Cross a stile and return to the track, with the lake to the left. Just before gate turn right over bridge and left over stile on to path alongside River Windrush. Continue until you reach a stile at a field. Turn left, cross another stile and go left over bridge before turning right beside another lake.
❹ Where 2nd, smaller lake ends bear right to stile, followed by bridge and stile at field. Keep to right side of fields until you reach track. At house leave track and continue to stile. In next field, after 25yds (23m), turn left over stile then sharp right. Continue to stile then go half left

across the field. Continue on the same line across next field to stile. Cross this; follow the right margin of field, to climb slowly to junction of tracks. Turn left to visit Clapton-on-the-Hill, or turn right to continue.
❺ Follow the track to the field. Keep ahead then half right to pass right of the woodland. Continue to the stile, followed by 2 stiles together at the field. Go half left to the stile then follow a succession of stiles, with a stream appearing to the left.
❻ Cross bridge then go half right across field to bridge. Continue to more stiles then walk along grassy track towards houses. Cross one more stile and follow path to road. Walk ahead to cross river. Turn left, then right, to return to the start.

Index

Alfred's Tower 143
The Amberley Inn, Amberley 168–71
Ashmore 123

Badminton 164–7
Barnsley 178–81
Bath 96–7, 98–101, 102–5
The Bath Arms, Longleat 124–7
The Bathurst Arms, North Cerney
    182–5
Bedruthan Steps 35
Bibury 181
Bickley Mill, Stoneycombe 46–9
Blackdown Hills 67
Blandford Forum 120–3
Bourton on the Hill 196–9
Bourton-on-the-Water 205
Bowood Park 157
Box Hill 101
Bradford-on-Avon 128–33
Branscombe 50–1, 52–5
Bridport 106–9
Brimpsfield 177
Brunel, Isambard Kingdom 101
Bruton 89
Buckhorn Weston 114–17
By Brook Valley 137

Cadbury Castle 95
Calne 157
Castle Combe 134–7, 138–9
The Castle Inn, Castle Combe 134–7
Caundle Green 177
Cerne Abbas 113
Charlton 144–9
Cheltenham 172–7
Chipping Campden 190–1, 192–5
Cirencester 178–81, 182–5
Cockerell, Sir Charles 199
Cockleford 172–7
Coleridge, Samuel Taylor 85
Combe Hay 102–5

The Compasses Inn,
    Lower Chicksgrove 158–61
Compton Abdale 186–9
Cornwall 12–39
Corton Denham 90–5
Cotswold Water Park 185
Cotswolds 105, 167, 171
Cowley 172–7
Crewkerne 74–7
Cricklade 149
Cucklington 117

Dartington Hall Estate 49
Dartmoor 45, 68–9
Dartmoor Inn, Lydford 40–5
Devizes 154–7
Devon 40–55
Devonshire Arms, Long Sutton
    78–81
Didmarton 164–7
Ditcheat 86–9
Dorchester 110–13
Dorset 106–23
Dover's Hill 195
Driftwood Spars, Trevaunance Cove
    26–9
Dulverton 56–61

East Lambrook 81
Ebbor Gorge 85
Eight Bells, Chipping Campden
    192–5
The European Inn, Piddletrenthide
    110–13

The Farmers Inn, West Hatch 64–7
Farnham 120–3
Forde Abbey 77

The George and Dragon, Rowde
    154–7
Gloucestershire 164–205

Golden Cap 109
The Green Dragon, Cockleford 172–7
Guiting Power 189
The Gurnard's Head, Treen 16–19

Hinton-St-George 74–7
Holt 153
The Horse & Groom, Charlton 144–9
Horse and Groom,
    Bourton on the Hill 196–9

The King's Arms, Didmarton 164–7

Lamorna Cove 15
Langport 78–81
Long Sutton 78–81
Longleat 124–7
Lord Poulett Arms, Hinton-St-
    George 74–7
Lower Chicksgrove 158–61
Lydford 40–5
Lydford Gorge 68–9

Malmesbury 144–9
Manor House Inn, Ditcheat 86–9
The Masons Arms, Branscombe
    52–5
Meldon Reservoir 45
Melksham 150–3
Mendips 105
Merry Maidens 15
Mitchell 32–5
Monkton Combe 98–101
Moreton in Marsh 196–9
Mousehole 12–15
The Museum Inn, Farnham 120–3

Nadder Valley 161
Naunton 189
Nether Westcote 200–5
Newton Abbot 46–9
North Cerney 182–5

Northleach 186–9

Okehampton 40–5
The Old Coastguard Hotel,
    Mousehole 12–15

Park Head 35
The Pear Tree Inn, Whitley 150–3
Pendeen 19
Piddletrenthide 110–13
The Plume of Feathers, Mitchell
    32–5
Porthcurno Beach 20–1
Prior's Park Wood 67
The Puesdown Inn, Compton Abdale
    186–9

Queen's Arms, Corton Denham 90–5

The Rising Sun, St Mawes 36–9
The Rock Inn, Waterrow 70–3
Rowde 154–7

safety, 11
St Agnes 26–9
St Anthony Head 39
St Ives 16–19, 22–5
St Mawes 30–1, 36–9
Salisbury 158–61
Sezincote 199
Shave Cross Inn, Bridport 106–9
Shepton Mallet 86–9
Sherston 167
Somerset 56–105
South Cerney 185
Spread Eagle Inn, Stourton 140–3
The Stapleton Arms, Buckhorn
    Weston 114–17
Stoneycombe 46–9
Stourhead 143
Stourton 140–3
Stroud 168–71

Stroud Valley 171
The Swan, Bradford-on-Avon
    128–33
Syde 177

Tarr Farm Inn, Dulverton 56–61
Tarr Steps 61, 62–3
Taunton 64–7, 70–3
Thames, River 149
Thorncombe 77
Three County Corner 143
The Tinners Arms, Zennor 22–5
Tinners' Trail 19
Tisbury 158–61
Tone, River 73
Treen 16–19
Trevaunance Cove 26–9
Truro 32–5

The Village Pub, Barnsley 178–81

walking, 11
Warminster 124–7, 140–3
Waterrow 70–3
Wellow 105
Wells 82–5
West Hatch 64–7
The Westcote Inn, Nether Westcote
    200–5
The Wheatsheaf, Combe Hay 102–5
Wheelwright Arms, Monkton Combe
    98–101
Whitley 150–3
Wiltshire 124–61
Wiveliscombe 73
Wookey Hole Inn, Wells 82–5

Zennor 16–19, 22–5

Acknowledgements

The Automobile Association would like to thank the following photographers, companies and picture libraries for their assistance in the preparation of this book.

Abbreviations for the picture credits are as follows: (t) top; (b) bottom; (l) left; (r) right; (AA) AA World Travel Library.

1 The Green Dragon; 2t Amberley Inn; 2c The Horse & Groom; 2b The Manor House; 5 Tarr Farm Inn; 6t Plume of Feathers; 6c The Horse & Groom; 6b The Castle Inn; 9t Rising Sun; 9bl Tarr Farm Inn; 9br The Green Dragon; 10 The Bath Arms; 11 AA/T Mackie; 12-13 The Old Coastguard Hotel; 16-17 The Gurnard's Head; 20-21 AA/J Wood; 22-23 The Tinners Arms; 26-27 Driftwood Spars; 30-31 AA/J Wood; 32-33 The Plume of Feathers; 36-37 The Rising Sun; 40-43 Dartmoor Inn; 46-47 The Bickley Mill; 50-51 AA/N Hicks; 52-53 The Masons Arms; 56-59 The Tarr Farm Inn; 62-63 AA/N Hicks; 64-65 The Farmers Inn; 68-69 AA/H Williams; 70-71 The Rock Inn; 74-75 Lord Poulett Arms; 78-79 The Devonshire Arms; 82-83 The Wookey Hole Inn; 86-87 The Manor House Inn; 90-93 The Queen's Arms; 96-97 AA/C Jones; 98-99 The Wheelwrights Arms; 102-103 The Wheatsheaf; 106-107 The Shave Cross Inn; 110-111 The European Inn; 114-115 The Stapleton Arms; 118-119 AA/J Tims; 120-121 The Museum Inn; 124-125 The Bath Arms; 128-131 The Swan; 134-135 The Castle Inn; 138-139 AA/D Hall; 140-141 The Spread Eagle Inn; 144-147 The Horse & Groom; 150-151 The Pear Tree Inn; 154-155 The George & Dragon; 158-159 The Compasses Inn; 162-163 AA/J Tims; 164-165 The King's Arms; 168-169 The Amberley Inn; 172-175 The Green Dragon; 178-179 The Village Pub; 182 The Bathurst Arms; 183 Rob Duncalf; 186-187 The Puesdown Inn; 190-191 AA/D Hall; 192-193 Eight Bells; 196-197 The Horse and Groom; 200-203 The Westcote Inn;

Every effort has been made to trace the copyright holders, and we apologise in advance for any accidental errors. We would be happy to apply the corrections in the following edition of this publication.

In addition, David Hancock would like to thank David Ashby, Elizabeth Carter, Neil Coates, Mark Taylor and Amanda Wragg for their editorial assistance.